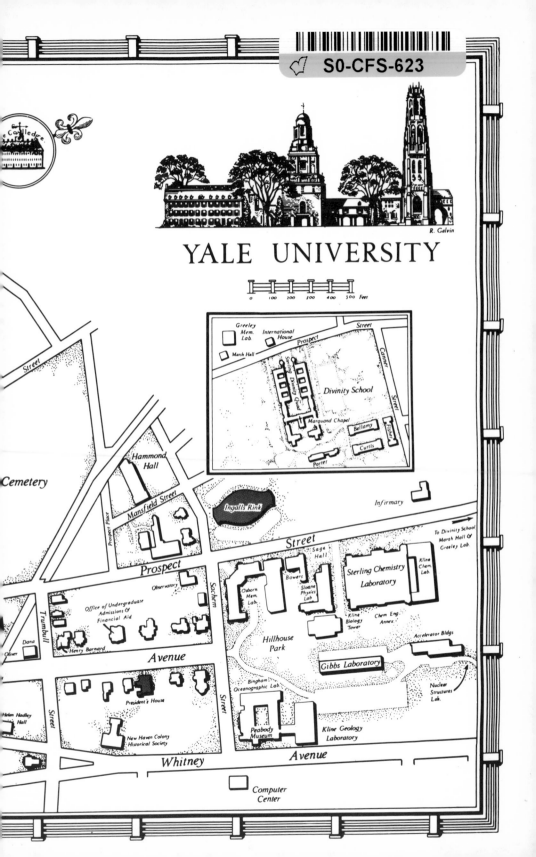

R. Galvin

YALE UNIVERSITY

0   100   200   300   400   500 Feet

Greeley Mem. Lab.
International House
Prospect Street
Marsh Hall
Canner Street
Sterling Divinity Quad
Divinity School
Marquand Chapel
Bellamy
Fisher
Curtis
Porter

Hammond Hall

Cemetery

Mansfield Street
Prospect Place

Ingalls Rink

Infirmary

Prospect Street

Sage Hall
To Divinity School
Marsh Hall &
Greeley Lab.

Bowers
Sterling Chemistry Laboratory
Kline Chem. Lab.

Observatory
Sachem Street
Osborn Mem. Lab.
Sloane Physics Lab

Office of Undergraduate Admissions & Financial Aid
Kline Biology Tower
Chem Eng. Annex

Trumbull Street
Dana
Oliver
Henry Barnard
Avenue
Hillhouse Park
Gibbs Laboratory
Accelerator Bldgs

Bingham Oceanographic Lab.
Nuclear Structures Lab.

Helen Hadley Hall
Whitney Street
President's House
Sachem Street
New Haven Colony Historical Society
Peabody Museum
Kline Geology Laboratory

Whitney Avenue

Computer Center

Mayday at Yale

MAYDAY AT YALE

A Case Study in Student Radicalism

John Taft

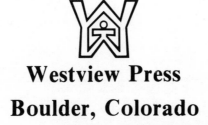

Westview Press

Boulder, Colorado

Copyright 1976 by Westview Press, Inc.

Published 1976 in the United States of America by

Westview Press, Inc.
1898 Flatiron Court
Boulder, Colorado 80301
Frederick A. Praeger, Publisher & Editorial Director

Library of Congress Cataloging in Publication Data

Taft, John, 1950-
  Mayday at Yale.

  Bibliography: p.
  Includes index.
  1. Yale University—Students. 2. Student movements—United States. I. Title.
LD6343.T33   378.1'98'097468   75-30532
ISBN 0-89158-002-6

Printed in the United States of America.

Preface

This is the first complete history of the May Day events to have been written, but I am not presenting it merely as a record of the disturbances at Yale University. My purpose in writing *Mayday at Yale* has been to point out, briefly and clearly, the basic characteristics and accomplishments of student radicalism during the late 1960s. I believe the most effective way of doing this is the case study method, rather than a general history of the student movement.

My work on this case study did not begin until January 1971, when I joined a historiography and research seminar taught by Donald Kagan, a classics professor at Yale. A large portion of the research for the book was done in Professor Kagan's seminar by a group of four Yale College juniors (P. Brook Manville, Neal Solomon, David Winn, and myself) and one sophomore (Joel Krieger). All of us were students at Yale throughout the May Day period, and although our involvement was minimal, we witnessed most of the events. In June 1971 I took over the responsibility for the project, and since then I have done additional research and written the text.

I am indebted to many people at Yale who have helped me in this undertaking. Early drafts of the manuscript were read and criticized by Roy Bryce-LaPorte, Ralph Dawson, William Farley, Martin Griffin, Gary Johnson, and George Pierson; portions of the manuscript were checked by Peter Brooks, Georges May, and David Thorburn. I particularly wish to thank Roy Bryce-LaPorte, Martin Griffin, and David Thorburn for their advice and encouragement during the early stages of my work. Other Yale people who assisted me were Jeremy Adams, Joel Fleishman, Donald Gastwirth, Edna Rostow, and Roger Sametz.

Most of this book was written in Oxford, where a surprising number of May Day leaders, including William Farley and Kurt

Schmoke, were fellow students of mine. Their presence made Oxford a convenient place to continue my research. Other people in England who lent a helping hand were Hervé Gouraige, John and Elaine O'Beirne-Ranelagh, Aleksandar Pavcović, Byron Trauger, and Angela Truell. I also wish to thank my editor, Lynne Rienner, for her patience and intelligent suggestions.

Mayday at Yale was written on a father fellowship and with the continual, astute advice of my mother. Therefore, my greatest thanks go to my parents, to whom this book is dedicated.

Oxford, 1975

Contents

Chapter

1

Introduction

The American student movement disrupted campuses and communities for more than six years. A product of the soaring birthrate after World War II and the great increase in public and private money for education in the 1960s, the movement was invigorated and sustained by black activists and the frustrations of the Vietnam war. Student radicals opened their attack in 1964 and reached a peak of activity in 1970. Thereafter, their influence rapidly declined.

Events at Yale University during the spring of 1970 comprise a lens through which the basic characteristics of the movement may be observed. At that time, the Yale community became preoccupied with the Black Panther trial taking place in the New Haven County courthouse, less than a block away from the campus. Yale radicals, assisted by national agitators and community blacks, used the trial to arouse hitherto quiescent moderates to a pitch of excitement which did not subside until after May Day. Although the disturbances in New Haven had unique aspects, all of the elements common to campus unrest were present. There were no dramatic gestures equal to building seizures, black students marching with guns, or resignations of university officials. In consequence, the basic characteristics of the student movement stand out clearly: the idealism,

1

divisiveness, and manipulative tactics of the radicals; the speedy but temporary conversion of moderate students in a highly charged atmosphere; the crucial role of young faculty members and minorities; and the conflicting views of the university's proper role in society.

Yale—the third oldest, one of the richest, and among the most esteemed universities in the United States—cannot be described as a typical American educational institution. However, its commonplace and its unusual characteristics are easily delineated. Some 10,000 students are registered in twelve separate schools, of which Yale College is one; the others include the graduate school and the various professional schools. The undergraduates (4,600 in 1970) are enrolled in Yale College and housed in twelve residential colleges, each of which is headed by a resident master. The residential colleges, built mostly in collegiate-gothic style, are close together, separated only by the public streets of New Haven. Within the colleges, by 1970 overcrowding was severe; expanding enrollments had been so sharply increased by the recent admission of undergraduate women that few single rooms were available in any college. The bachelor of arts curriculum was more flexible than ever before, and undergraduates were rarely as hard-working as students in the other Yale schools.

New Haven, in contrast, is a typical small northern city, especially with respect to its black community. In 1950 there were fewer than 10,000 blacks in the city, out of a total population of 160,000; by 1970 the total population had declined to 140,000, while the number of blacks had quadrupled. This was largely due to a migration of southern blacks during the late fifties and early sixties and the departure of many white families to the suburbs. Although federal funds from the Model Cities program were used extensively during the sixties, the blacks remained the poorest people in New Haven, and many of them complained that urban renewal served only to relocate the slums. After prolonged riots during the summer of 1967, the black community became less aggressive in asserting its discontent. Younger blacks, however, remained volatile, and all blacks retained their feelings of resentment toward the white city government and the ostensibly rich university.

2

Introduction

The university is the city's most distinctive feature. The Old Campus quadrangle and several residential colleges are north and east of the New Haven Green—the geographical core of the city. The Green, which is overlooked on the east by the courthouse and on the south by City Hall, has traditionally been the site of public demonstrations. To the west and north of Yale are the black neighborhoods, only a few blocks away from the university and the recently renewed downtown New Haven.

Sterile statistics and geography reveal little of the concept of Yale held by outsiders. If much of its mystique is ill-founded, since World War II Yale's claim to excellence has become increasingly valid. Kingman Brewster Jr. was named president in 1963—a time when Yale's future as a private institution looked particularly bright. In the mid-sixties, the competition for admission became more rigorous each year; the curriculum was expanded; recruitment efforts were redoubled; and financial aid was available for all who required it. The effects of this golden age had not vanished by the end of the decade. Economic recession and diminished financial support from Washington were imminent, but in the spring of 1970, the Yale of the sixties, like the student movement everywhere, was still in full bloom.

Chapter
2
The Rackley Case

On Wednesday, May 21, 1969, a young factory worker on a fishing trip parked his motorcycle near a bridge about twenty-five miles north of New Haven. While he was walking along the edge of the Coginchaug River, casting for trout, he saw what he described as a "set of legs" and a "body" partly submerged in the shallow water. He immediately called the police, and shortly after 5:00 p.m. the body of a black man was pulled out of the river. The man's wrists had been tied with gauze and his neck encircled by a noose fashioned from a wire coat hanger. An autopsy showed that he had been shot twice with a .45 caliber hand gun, once in the head and once in the chest; his chest, arms, and buttocks were covered with bruises, burns from cigarettes and scalding water, rope marks, and ice pick wounds. It was concluded that Alex Rackley, as he was subsequently identified by his fingerprints, had died within the preceding twelve to twenty-four hours.

Within a few hours, the New Haven police "met with a known, confidential, and reliable informant whom [they] had known for a period of 10 years" to discuss the killing. The informant, a woman "closely associated with the Black Panther movement in New Haven," identified Rackley's body from color photographs and said that she had seen him tortured by Panthers during the previous few evenings. Her story was confirmed by Frances Carter, a Black Panther who had been taken into custody earlier in the evening.

The New Haven Police Department later claimed that it had been alerted to the possibility of trouble on the evening of the murder, May 20. Apparently, they lacked sufficient information to make arrests, and although the police had the Panthers' New Haven headquarters under surveillance during the entire evening, they missed an opportunity to stop the car in which Rackley was driven out of the city.

Soon after midnight, on Thursday, May 22, a "heavily armed team comprised of uniformed and plainclothes officers" broke into two private residences in New Haven, one of which was the Panther headquarters on Orchard Street. Seven Panthers were arrested on charges of murder and conspiracy to commit murder. After the arrests—described as "the result of an investigation with 'interstate implications' that has already brought in the Federal Bureau of Investigation"—the police conducted a search of the Panther headquarters and found weapons and tape recordings of a supposed "kangaroo trial" of Rackley. Ballistics experts identified one of the weapons as the gun which had fired the fatal shots.

The seven Panthers were taken in handcuffs to the precinct stationhouse during the early morning of May 22. For the next several hours, everyone, including the prisoners' relatives and attorneys, was barred from the building. One agitated young man tried desperately to enter the stationhouse. "I want to get in," he said, "and investigate which party members have been arrested." This man, "a breath short of surrendering," identified himself as Lonnie McLucas. Detectives sent him away.

News of the murder and arrests appeared in many newspapers. The *New Haven Register's* banner headline stated: "8 Panthers Held in Murder Plot." Beneath the banner were pictures of eight black faces with one-name identifications. Included in the newspaper stories were descriptions of Rackley's mutilated body, a discussion of the evidence and items seized at the Panther headquarters, and a suggested reconstruction of the murder. According to the police, the Black Panthers had forcibly transported

Rackley to New Haven from New York during the weekend of May 17-18; they had held him at their New Haven headquarters and given him his "trial"—followed by torture—early in the week; and they had taken him out of the city and shot him early Wednesday morning.

On May 28, another Panther was arrested. On the same day, she and six of the eight Panthers originally seized, including Warren Kimbro and Ericka Huggins, were re-arrested on a Superior Court bench warrant, arraigned in the Superior Court, and held without bail. The two juveniles arrested on May 22 were detained as material witnesses, and eventually one of them testified for the prosecution. Superior Court bench warrants were issued for four other suspects who had not been found.

During the following summer, the police secured the four remaining suspects in other parts of the country. Two Panthers were arrested on June 6 in Denver, where they remained in jail fighting extradition. On the same day, FBI agents arrested Lonnie McLucas in Salt Lake City, and he spoke to them with apparent relief: "I became disillusioned with the party because of the violence . . . wanted to quit . . . afraid to quit because I had learned too much . . . I was afraid I might be killed." Describing the murder to the police, he stated that he had seen Ericka Huggins telling Bobby Seale, the national chairman of the Black Panther party, about Alex Rackley, a suspected police informer. McLucas waived his extradition rights and was brought to Connecticut immediately. Two months later, the Canadian police apprehended George Sams in Toronto, where he had fled disguised as a clergyman. Sams admitted guilt to the charge of murder and signed a statement directly implicating Bobby Seale. On August 21, Sams was turned over to United States federal agents.

Sams claimed that he and two other Panthers had arrived in New York in May 1969 to "straighten out the party on the East Coast." After picking up Alex Rackley, they had proceeded to New Haven, where they planned to hold a convocation of East Coast Panthers in order to purge members who had deviated from the party's ideology. Black Panthers later explained that this was due to a "mix-up"; Sams, they said, was not a trusted member of the party at the time.

7

Sams eventually became the prosecution's chief witness, and much of the Panthers' defense in the pretrial hearings was concerned with proving that Sams was mentally unstable and unfit to testify. An abstract of his life seems to support this contention. After spending over three years in two New York institutions as a "dangerous mental defective" and a "moron," Sams was released when tests showed his I.Q. to be seventy-five, five above the level requiring confinement. Later, in 1966, he was arrested and hospitalized after being shot in the head while attempting to rob a grocery store. People who knew him in Detroit during this time called him "Crazy George" and said that he used to carry a revolver underneath an old choir robe, which he called his *dashiki.*

Sams may also have been ideologically deviant. Introduced to the party in 1968 by Stokely Carmichael, Sams was soon expelled for stabbing a comrade in the leg and attempting to rape and murder several other Panthers. His principal function in the party had been to serve as Carmichael's bodyguard, and he was readmitted as a member on Carmichael's recommendation— despite the fact that at the time the Panthers were Marxists and disapproved of Carmichael's heretical black nationalism. The party finally broke with Carmichael in 1969, and as Carmichael's protégé, Sams was tainted. Moreover, Sams testified that after he had murdered Rackley the Panthers put him under "people's arrest" for the crime of male chauvinism.

On August 19, on the basis of Sams's statement, the FBI arrested Bobby Seale in Berkeley, California. His bail was set at $25,000 on a charge of fleeing Connecticut to avoid federal prosecution in connection with the Rackley murder. Bail was posted, but a telegraphed warrant—charging Seale with kidnapping, conspiracy to kidnap, murder, and conspiracy to murder— had already arrived from New Haven and he was immediately turned over to the San Francisco police.

New Haven Police Chief James Ahern admitted three years later that he was "astonished" when the state's attorney for New Haven County asked for an indictment of Seale: "Although the New Haven Police Department had evidence that Seale had visited the Orchard Street apartment while Rackley was there, we had no solid evidence to link him to Rackley's death or torture." This indicates that the only basis for the indictment of Seale was Sams's testimony. Ahern was personally convinced of Seale's guilt, but he apparently did not consider the evidence of Seale's presence at the Panther headquarters sufficient reason for the indictment.

On August 21, Seale was denied bail. A week later he was indicted by a grand jury in New Haven for the first degree murder of Alex Rackley and was accused of having ordered Rackley's murder the preceding May 19, when he had come to New Haven to speak at Yale in honor of Malcolm X's birthday. Seale was already under indictment in Chicago for conspiracy to incite riots during the 1968 Democratic convention, and in September he was sent there for the famous Chicago Seven trial.* His obstreperous behavior in the Chicago courtroom enraged Judge Julius Hoffman, who ordered him gagged and bound to his chair and finally sentenced him to four years' imprisonment for contempt of court. Seale was then returned to San Francisco, where he continued to fight extradition to Connecticut.

According to the Connecticut indictment, the Panthers believed Rackley was an informer who had helped the New York City police discover a bomb plot allegedly devised by the Black Panthers; therefore, Seale gave Sams and the New Haven Panthers the order to kill Rackley. Charles Garry, the chief counsel and a spokesman for the Black Panther party, offered a different interpretation: Rackley's murder had been instigated by an infiltrator who was a police agent or an agent provocateur. Garry claimed that Rackley, unlike Sams, had been a party member in "good standing" at the time of his death; the murder, concluded Garry, was part of a "frame-up" of Bobby Seale and the Black Panthers. This interpretation became the Panthers' official version of the Rackley case.

Ultimately, the New Haven Panthers were charged with murder, kidnapping, conspiracy, and binding with criminal intent. Most of them were charged as accessories, while Kimbro,

---

*Several months after Seale was returned to California, the other defendants became known as the Chicago Seven. Seale was the only black indicted for this alleged conspiracy.

9

McLucas, Seale, and Sams were charged directly with murder. All were charged with capital crimes.

In December 1969, Sams pleaded guilty to charges of second degree murder, contending that Seale had ordered him to have Rackley killed. He named Lonnie McLucas and Warren Kimbro as the Panthers who had done the shooting. On the same day, another defendant changed her plea to guilty of conspiracy to kidnap resulting in death, and she testified against several of the other Panthers. In January 1970, Warren Kimbro's brother (a police sergeant from Miami, Florida) and a New Haven police officer visited Kimbro in jail; a few days later Kimbro pleaded guilty to second degree murder. The Panther defense claimed that this confession had been unfairly elicited. Nevertheless, Kimbro described the murder for the court and admitted that, after Sams said "Now," he and McLucas fired the shots that killed Rackley. Kimbro refused to implicate Seale, insisting that he had been asleep at the time that Seale was alleged by Sams to have visited Panther headquarters and given the order to murder Rackley. Not long after his confession, Kimbro returned to the Roman Catholic faith.

Bail hearings for the imprisoned Panthers had begun in November 1969, and in December the New Haven court denied bail for all of the defendants who requested it except Frances Carter, who was subsequently released on $10,000 bond. It was said to be the first occasion in Connecticut history that bail was granted in a capital case. Two days after she was freed, Carter refused to testify under immunity and was sentenced to six months in jail for contempt of court. Meanwhile, Governor Ronald Reagan had ordered Bobby Seale's extradition from California, and on March 13, 1970, Seale was flown to Connecticut to await trial.

The Panthers had had a difficult time organizing their New Haven chapter. In January 1969, Ericka Huggins, the widow of a Panther who had been shot in California by black nationalists, had brought her husband's body back to New Haven, where both their families lived. She arranged an elaborate funeral, which proved to be the first step in her brief effort to build a Panther organization in the city. Some thirty young blacks were attracted by the program, but most members of the black community, although they approved of some of the Panthers' aims and methods, questioned the value of armed struggle as a solution to ghetto problems. A few months after Huggins's arrest, the national party sent several Panthers, including Doug Miranda, to reconstruct the decimated New Haven chapter. Perhaps because he found only lukewarm support for the Panthers in the black neighborhoods, Miranda began to put pressure on Yale, especially Yale blacks, to protest the trial. The Panthers had always believed in the efficacy of working with students. In this case, however, a series of campus rallies, discussion panels, class disruptions, and appeals for funds had little success. Miranda won active support only from those who were already strongly sympathetic: a large portion of the black students, a small number of white radicals, several religious groups, and a few faculty members. By March 1970, the New Haven Panther chapter was reorganized and active, but its campaign at Yale had bogged down.

With the arrival in Connecticut of Bobby Seale, titular head of the national Black Panther party, the eyes of Panther sympathizers throughout the country turned to New Haven. The Yale College spring recess ended two weeks later, and the Panthers and their supporters redoubled their efforts to involve Yale students. At the beginning of April, the New Haven Panther Defense Committee (NHPDC) announced plans for protest rallies to be held on behalf of the New Haven Nine—as the incarcerated Panthers were now called. The *Yale Daily News* reported on April 6 that Tom Dostou, a white radical and coordinator of the NHPDC, was predicting that as many as a million people would come to New Haven to demonstrate against the trial.

Dostou was an advocate of eschatological extremism rather than realizable doctrines. Before he emerged as a Panther enthusiast, his political orientation had been somewhat different. In early 1970 he had been the leader of a populist party in New Haven which claimed to speak for poor whites and which had as its emblem the Confederate flag. Dostou did not come from New Haven and never attended Yale, but he developed a virulent

11

grudge against many Yale dignitaries, especially President Brewster. He repeatedly threatened to burn down Yale buildings and foretold an imminent revolutionary holocaust in the United States. A long-time user of hallucinogenic drugs, he gave these up in March 1970, when he joined the NHPDC.

The NHPDC was organized in early March "to inform people of the facts concerning the trial and events connected with it." Anne Froines, the wife of one of the Chicago Seven, was a member of the NHPDC; more than a dozen other members were Yale students or dropouts. The membership was entirely white, and while the Panthers were using the group mainly as a fund-raising organization, it had become important as a link between the Panther party and the overwhelmingly white Yale University. By early April, the NHPDC was collecting eighty to one hundred dollars a day from Yale students and faculty members in support of the Panther cause; almost all of this money was immediately passed on to the Panthers.

Short of outright terrorism, the NHPDC practiced the most extreme forms of radical student politics. Tom Dostou endeavored to maintain a military barracks atmosphere at head-quarters, and violators of revolutionary discipline were punished by being forced to stand throughout the night while reading quotations from Chairman Mao Tse-tung. A woman whose husband was leading a sugarcane-cutting brigade in Cuba loaned her New Haven apartment to the NHPDC for use as its headquarters. The apartment was guarded with around-the-clock vigilance and a small arsenal of weapons.

Dostou complained, in the *Yale Daily News* article of April 6, that his committee was being harassed by the police and that its telephones were being tapped. His complaints were well-founded. Police Chief Ahern has admitted that his men were following committee members' cars and generally trying to keep a close check on the NHPDC. During the Yale spring vacation, the police had raided the NHPDC's headquarters on the pretext of searching for stolen property. Breaking in without difficulty, they confiscated the weapons, recorded the titles of books, and arrested Dostou. After paying bail, Dostou was released.

At the time, most political moderates on the Yale campus regarded these incidents with indifference. Those few who were more perceptive recognized that Yale might be held hostage for the Panther prisoners and that the trial was a potentially explosive issue on campus. Political upheavals typically occurred at prestigious universities that had previously been peaceful. In April 1970, Yale was one of the few universities of distinction that had been spared any serious political disturbances. Spring was the high season for student rebellion, and undergraduates were restless. It was an ideal setting for an emotional outburst.

The most visible signs of the Panthers' presence were the newspapers sold on sidewalks around the campus—papers which gave advice on the use of firearms and endlessly reiterated such slogans as "Off the pigs!" and "Up against the wall, whitey!" Since the previous autumn, students had been exposed to more persuasive statements by Charles Garry, who declared that there was "a national scheme by various agencies of the government to destroy and commit genocide upon members of the Black Panther party." Student credulity was reinforced by news reports of the two dozen Panthers who had died in "a series of gun battles between Panthers and police throughout the nation" which amounted to a "lethal undeclared war." The killing of two Panthers in Chicago made a particularly gruesome story. Leading newspapers and magazines, as well as such public figures as the Reverend Ralph Abernathy Jr. and Leonard Bernstein, appeared to have joined a crusade to stop the government's alleged attempt to destroy the Panthers.

———

Several of the proceedings in the Rackley case were challenged in the pretrial hearings. The defendants filed an extensive complaint protesting the conditions of pretrial detention; they specifically mentioned the censorship of defendants' mail and reading material, the prohibition of meetings among defendants, the restrictions on visitors (including lawyers), and the refusal to provide the defendants with doctors of their own choice. The Panthers' supporters also claimed that prison guards treated party members with extreme brutality—a standard protest that was difficult to prove or disprove. The other allegations

13

were never fully answered by the prosecution, but they were all frequently used procedures.

The arguable nature of some government actions supports the claim that officials chose legal options which were particularly harmful to the Panthers—perhaps in order to put the Panthers, especially Bobby Seale, behind bars at least until the end of the trial. For example, several defendants submitted a complaint that the grand jury which indicted them had been chosen by the sheriff from among his own cronies; Seale's grand jury may have been chosen in the same way. This method of selecting a grand jury, though common, is a questionable practice. The grand jury determines whether the evidence shows probable cause to bring a suspect to trial. While few lawyers would deny that there was probable cause to try most of the Panther defendants, Bobby Seale's indictment was dubious enough to support the contention that he had been imprisoned in order to disrupt the Panther party.

Other complaints made by the Panthers in the pretrial hearings are hard to justify. First, it was said that the eight Panthers originally put in jail were arrested and their headquarters were searched without warrants. This was true; however, Connecticut law permits such arrests and searches in response to "the speedy information of others" after a committed crime. The arrests occurred twelve hours after the discovery of Rackley's body and after informants had implicated the New Haven Panthers. The information was received in the evening; if the police had waited until they obtained a warrant, the delay might have seriously jeopardized any chance of securing the suspects. In fact, some of the defendants had left the Panther headquarters by the time of the arrests.

Second, there were complaints that the defendants were detained for some time without counsel. This is not unlawful, although the results of police interrogation during this period are inadmissible as evidence unless the suspect waives his right to counsel.

Third, the defendants' lack of information about the autopsy was questioned. The defendants were not permitted to examine

14

the body because it was buried in another state. However, relevant information was provided to the defendants; several Panthers identified Rackley's body; and there was never any controversy about the cause of death.

Fourth, complaints were made about the denial of bail to most of the defendants. The usual interpretation of the Eighth Amendment of the United States Constitution holds that bail need not be granted in capital cases. In Connecticut, although the prosecution must always show that "the proof is evident or the presumption great" in order to keep a suspect in prison, the granting of bail in capital cases is almost unheard of. The defense probably used the bail hearings to force the prosecution to submit its proof of guilt, thereby revealing much of its evidence before the trial.

The foregoing facts about the Rackley case—whether incriminating or helpful to the Panthers—were available to everyone, but few Yale moderates were aware of them. At the same time, there was a widespread feeling that the government was persecuting the Panthers. This combination of ignorance and prejudice enabled Panther supporters to exaggerate the alleged irregularities in the Rackley case with great effectiveness. Some of the exaggerations were so absurd that they must have been motivated by an indiscriminate hatred of the government or an unquestioning zeal for the Panther ideology.

On April 10, Lonnie McLucas, Ericka Huggins, and two other defendants pleaded not guilty to charges which included aiding and abetting murder, kidnapping resulting in death, conspiracy to murder, conspiracy to kidnap, and binding with intent to commit a crime. Four days later, an incident occurred during a courtroom session which confirmed for many their vaguely held opinions about the government's persecution of the Panthers. In the visitors' section of the courtroom, an officer told Black Panther David Hilliard to stop speaking with another Panther, Emory Douglas, about a note which Hilliard was reading. Hilliard refused to comply with the request, and the officer put his hand on Hilliard's shoulder in what one spectator described as an attempt "to reach for the note." Jean Genet, a French writer, assisted his "black comrades" in the ensuing scuffle; he later claimed that as a white spectator who had been talking aloud, he was given only verbal warnings. Hilliard and Douglas were brought before Judge Harold Mulvey, who sentenced them to six months in jail for contempt of court, ignoring Garry's objections. Mulvey set no bail and impounded the note as evidence for the contempt citation. Panther Chief of Staff Hilliard was already under indictment in California for making a threat on President Nixon's life during the San Francisco moratorium rally the previous November. Until Mulvey's action, he had been the highest ranking Panther who was not in jail or exile.

Judge Mulvey also sentenced two people for entering the courtroom shouting Black Panther slogans. At least four more were arrested outside the courthouse in connection with skirmishes with the police, the aftermath of a small demonstration. The demonstration, in which more than a hundred students from a nearby high school were involved, disbanded at noon, when many of its participants began to vandalize the downtown area. This was allegedly a reaction to the report that Hilliard and Douglas had been arrested. A Yale art and architecture school student was also arrested for taking pictures on the steps of the courthouse; he had violated a court order which forbade photographic or sound equipment in or around the courthouse during the Panther trial. After being sentenced, he was immediately released on his own recognizance.

These events—especially the contempt sentences—shocked a great many people, and political turmoil at Yale soon began in earnest. The first student-initiated and student-run meeting—the first of hundreds—took place the next day in a Yale lecture hall. The meeting, irrational and naive as it appears to have been, set a precedent for similar meetings later on.

Chapter
3
The Making of an Entente

Tom Dostou had predicted in early April that more than half a million demonstrators would come to New Haven, and he threatened a general race war if the Panthers were not free within the next five months. The first overt, pro-Panther action outside the courtroom occurred on April 10, the day McLucas and Huggins entered their pleas of not guilty. That morning a small demonstration took place on the steps of the courthouse; it ended just before the trial hearings began in order to avoid violating a court order prohibiting demonstrations within 500 feet of the building while the Panther trial was in session. After the crowd of about 200 people moved onto the New Haven Green, Doug Miranda, the area captain of the Black Panthers, thanked them for their support. In a statement reminiscent of Dostou's threat four days before, he told them: "We don't say 'Off the pigs!' any more—we say 'Death to the pigs!' because that's what they deserve."

Even at this point the university administration was paying scant attention to the trial. John Wilkinson, dean of undergraduate affairs, later stated that he knew that Yale was "going to have a difficult situation as soon as I read in the paper that

Bobby Seale had been arrested and charged with the Rackley murder." Sam Chauncey, special assistant to President Brewster, has claimed that the administration had been considering the problem since "the first announcement that the trials were going to be held in New Haven. We knew that a problem would exist between Yale and this particular situation; so we were aware from the very beginning." Brewster himself, however, has stated that he did not think the Yale administration would "have to deal with the trial until the time that Judge Mulvey slapped the contempt citations on Hilliard and the other fellow who came down to visit the trial. Up to that time I think we were aware that there was a general concern about the trial, but I don't think there was a widespread feeling that the trial was going to be almighty unfair, or a miscarriage, until the dramatic event of those two contempt citations." Brewster's impassive outlook prevailed. At the time of the courthouse demonstration on April 10, the administration was still unprepared for the students' reaction to the Panther trial.

On Saturday, April 11, Jay Ogilvy, a young philosophy professor, delivered a letter to Brewster, warning him of "hard times ahead." Ogilvy, who would become a faculty representative on the Strike Steering Committee, had talked with several friends who were members of the NHPDC. Anticipating trouble for New Haven and Yale, he "felt like Chicken Little" in his efforts to alert people to an imminent catastrophe. His letter to Brewster began: "Doubtless you are aware of the danger facing both the city of New Haven and Yale in the coming months. Although I sense little awareness among the students and faculty around me, it seems perfectly clear that current plans to bring 500,000 people to New Haven to 'stop the trial'—even if only one-tenth 'successful'—present us with the certainty of violence." Ogilvy went on to offer his assistance if the president thought he could be helpful. Brewster did not reply. It was not unusual for Brewster to ignore a letter, but his failure to acknowledge a warning of this kind conflicted with his reputation for anticipating student issues and being ready to cope with them when they arose.

Brewster's reputation was acceptable to both liberal and conservative alumni. He was an efficient, no-nonsense fifty-year-old; a lawyer, not a scholar; and collegiate, rather than academic. His boyish face, his leftist friends, and his tendency to embrace a little too quickly many new ideas were irritating to some, but perhaps these were requisite traits in a good university administrator. While Brewster appeared idealistic, his ideas had been flexible enough to permit orderly retreats from a variety of controversial positions. Most important, he had kept Yale calm for over six years. That seemed enough.

An old friend and classmate of Brewster's arrived in New Haven on Monday, April 13, the day before Judge Mulvey issued the contempt citations. William Kunstler, Yale College '41 and chief attorney for the Chicago Seven, was not in town to call on the president of Yale University. Kunstler had been agitating for the Panthers on many campuses, and he was in New Haven to speak at a Panther rally, along with Artie Seale (wife of Bobby), Big Man (managing editor of the *Black Panther* newspaper), Tom Dostou, and Doug Miranda. They all spoke that afternoon at Yale's Woolsey Hall before an audience of 1,700, most of them students. Although the meeting was intended to be a fund-raising rally, its general tone was hortative.

Miranda introduced the program, declaring that "Yale is one of the biggest pig organizations" and that it clearly "had something to do with the conspiracy" against the Panthers. Enlarging on this theme, he issued a harsh warning: "Basically, what we are going to do is create conditions in which white folks are even going to have to kill pigs or defend themselves against black folks. . . . We're going to turn Yale into a police state. . . . You have to create peace by destroying the people who don't want peace." Tom Dostou agreed: "You have to make a basic choice between me and Spiro Agnew. . . . Fifteen Yalies have dropped out of Yale to join the Panther Defense Committee so far. Fifteen of the thousand leaders of tomorrow who have become revolutionaries, who will pick up a gun and walk into Brewster's office and say, 'Get out of the city.' "

Other speakers continued the outpouring of Black Panther vituperation, and many in the audience responded with Panther slogans. Big Man asserted that, although the Panther party wanted a Marxist coalition with whites, other blacks might force

19

the Panthers to "unleash something this country can't stand, a race war. . . . There's going to be freedom for everybody or freedom for nobody. We're going to advocate killing those motherfuckers who kidnap us. We're going to advocate killing pigs who kick our doors in." The Panthers would "turn crazy niggers loose in the street, niggers who are tired and sick, and tired of being sick and tired." Artie Seale's statements were in a similar vein, urging Yalies to "pick up guns and defend us." She promised that the Panthers would be "turning off the electricity" before they allowed her husband and his fellow defendants to go to the electric chair. "It's coming to the point now where it's either/or—either you're with us or against us."

Kunstler was the most effective speaker of the group. After describing the conspiracy to destroy the Panther party, he made an attack on the American legal system. He particularly emphasized the problem of confessions (which was relevant to the guilty pleas of three New Haven Panthers) and contended that New Haven would "be treated to the spectacle of informers, the most diabolical type of witness who can be brought to the stand. There is no way to refute the informer, no way of proving that he lies. What remains is a question of credibility. The Panther party will be tried before a middle class jury which is going to want to believe that every word the informer says is true." Kunstler singled out the *New Haven Register* as the worst offender in making the selection of an unbiased jury difficult. Exhorting the audience to "put the challenge to the system," he assured them that he was "not out to destroy the system. We, and I hope you, are out to prevent a judicial system that prides itself on being the most perfect in the world, or as near perfect as you can get, that that judicial system does not engage in a lynching." Kunstler's performance evoked the loudest applause of the afternoon, perhaps because compared to his and the Panthers' usual rhetoric, his speech seemed almost moderate.

Jean Genet, the French playwright, had also been scheduled to speak at the Panther rally, but he had been delayed in San Francisco. That evening, addressing a smaller crowd in a lecture hall, Genet defended the Panthers' advocacy of violence and declared that they had nothing else to which to resort.

20

The Woolsey Hall rally made little impression on the Yale community, in spite of the large crowd and the meeting's "violent and unsettling" tenor. Most Yalies had long been accustomed to all kinds of radical and reactionary speeches by campus visitors, as well as to the proselytizing efforts of fellow students. As a rule, college moderates on every campus required a sudden, dramatic display of government power—such as the arrest of students occupying a university building—to upset them; and even with such impetus, radicals had to work hard to mobilize a substantial following. At Yale, the sentencing of Hilliard and Douglas on Tuesday stimulated the formation of an ad hoc committee of campus radicals who called a meeting in a lecture hall on Wednesday evening, April 15.

This meeting on Wednesday was the first organized and open reaction of Yale students to the Panther trial. Many came who had not been at Woolsey Hall on Monday; they had been aroused by secondhand reports of Panther agitation or by the contempt sentences of the day before. One observer described the Wednesday gathering as "terribly ugly." Another called it the meeting at which the propoganda of the radical white students was first unleashed. Certainly it was at this meeting that the most extreme proposals were made, and some leaders openly encouraged an ambience of hysteria. A crowd of over 400 filled the small lecture hall, and those at the back of the room were unable to hear speakers at the front. There was a predominance of radicals, but it was soon obvious that no one group was in control. A large portion of the people present were not Yale students; some were members of extremist political organizations who had come from other parts of Connecticut. No group seemed to know exactly what it wanted the audience to do, but nearly all thought that the Panthers should somehow be freed.

The meeting started with the reading of two demands: an immediate moratorium of classes in support of the Black Panthers on trial in New Haven; and a donation of $500,000 by the Yale Corporation to the Panther defense fund. The floor was then opened to proposals and tactical suggestions, which were written on a blackboard as they were presented. The demand for $500,000 was favored by many who felt it would be impossible for

the university to comply, which would allow students to respond
to the refusal in any way they wished. Others felt that, since the
money might be needed, it was their duty to raise it by practical
measures such as kidnapping President Brewster or demanding
the sale of the two Gutenberg bibles in Yale's Beinecke library.
Extreme statements were more blandly received as the meeting
progressed: occupy Woodbridge Hall (site of Brewster's offices);
shut off the New Haven water supply; blow up Yale; stack rifles
on the Green for any and all to use. To one suggestion—"If you
want your manhood, man, you've got to pick up a gun—no other
way"—a girl replied, "But I'm not interested in my manhood."

The most extreme suggestion came from a second-year Yale
Law School student. Arguing that only the ultimate sacrifice
would show the country how serious the students were, he
proposed that a hundred volunteers step forward and agree that
each day one of them—chosen by lot—would commit suicide
until Seale and the other eight Panthers were free. "Why die?"
asked someone in the audience. The law student responded, "To
die like a Panther, to die like a man." The chief reaction to his
proposal was laughter:

They laughed nervously, uneasily, as if to reassure each other that the
proposal was indeed crazy, the proposer demented. It was a revelation to
observe how people who were pretending to be so fanatically devoted to a
cause would have nothing to do with testing their devotion in so practical,
if extreme, a fashion. Crazy as it may have been, the proposal was made
seriously; but, given its reception, the proposer had no choice but to
leave the platform. He came back to the corridor alongside the auditorium,
where I was standing. The girl he had left near me was in tears because
of the way he had been received inside. She begged him to go back and
make the proposal again. She insisted that people could not have understood
what he meant. She assumed that the audience would not have reacted the way
they did if they had understood the seriousness and the merits of the proposal.
She persuaded the guy to reenter the auditorium. He made his proposal again. It
came out sounding the same way and it got the same reaction—although there
was anger in the laughter now that had not been there before. And ugliness
too.

More down-to-earth speakers supported the moratorium.
Kenneth Mills, an assistant professor of philosophy, a black born
in Trinidad and educated at Oxford, pointed out the drawbacks

of some of the previous proposals in elegant and elaborate phrases. Although Mills was a known Marxist and wanted an immediate moratorium, his accent and style outwardly set him apart from the other radical speakers. A member of the class of '71 spoke enthusiastically in favor of the demand on Yale's Board of Trustees: "To me it makes a whole lot of sense that the Yale Corporation donate the money because the university, contrary to what people might say, is involved in what's going on in the courtroom. The trial is a part of New Haven, and we're a part of New Haven. I think that it's a progressive thing for the university to do." Several leaders of SDS (Students for a Democratic Society) made a characteristic attempt to put the current crisis into a traditional Marxist framework, exhorting the audience "to fight the racism the Panther trial represents by fighting the racist policy Yale uses against its employees."

Tom Dostou provoked the greatest response. He spoke bluntly: "I don't think any pickets or strikes will work. The pigs are ready to kill. We've got to say that Yale will be electrocuted if Bobby Seale is brought to trial. You better go into the trial and shut down the courtroom physically." In most cases, it is difficult to know whether such extreme statements arose from the desire to impress a girl friend, from sarcasm, paranoia, a sense of theater, or from sincere political conviction. One witness reported that Dostou spent some time during the meeting conferring in the corridor with a six-man bodyguard which seemed to feed his sense of self-importance; yet his speech was effective because it was obviously serious. His statement that he would stack rifles on the New Haven Green received the most publicity during the weeks that followed and summed up his scornful attitude toward the nonviolent approach that most Yale students preferred.

The meeting came to a disorderly end after two or three hours of "discussion and proposals." The group did finally vote on the two original proposals and passed them by a large majority. It was also decided that students at the meeting should arrange smaller meetings at their residential colleges in order to discuss the issues and mobilize support for the moratorium. Many people had departed too early to vote on either of the proposals, and

23

many others left the meeting uncertain of the exact specifications of the moratorium proposal. The call for a moratorium beginning the next day—April 16—directed students either to turn the discussion in each class to the issue of the Panther trial or to boycott classes entirely. The question of whether the vote had been for a three-day or a four-day moratorium was unanswered, and whether or not the intervening weekend days were to count as a part of the moratorium was apparently left to each individual's judgment.

This was the first important student reaction to the Panther trial. It was marked by an irrational sense of urgency, which included no intimation of the many issues raised later. The committee that had announced the meeting was in great confusion, as was apparent from the chaos of the meeting itself, but it established its headquarters in Dwight Hall and began calling itself the Moratorium Committee. Subsequent meetings in the residential colleges were also hastily assembled and unproductive, but they did have the effect of spreading the word about the moratorium—however imprecisely that word was defined. News of a serious riot on Harvard Square, in which more than 300 people were injured, contributed to the developing atmosphere of crisis, both real and imaginary.

Thursday, the first day of the moratorium, was quiet. "For a large percentage of the campus . . .," stated the *Yale Daily News,* "life went on as usual. If not apathetic, many students were quiescent." The *News* noted that approximately one-half of the classes in the humanities and social sciences devoted time to discussions of the trial, most of them voting first on whether it was appropriate to do so. But there was little disruption, and supporters of the strike took no other coercive action. For many, Ogilvy's prediction of "hard times ahead" would still have seemed absurd. There was no feeling of an immediate problem to cope with until after the weekend, when plans for a projected demonstration began to receive widespread publicity. The general direction of the movement to support Bobby Seale was still undetermined. The headquarters of the Moratorium Committee were the only center for activity, and to that center all of the Panthers' supporters flocked.

24

At a press conference on Wednesday, April 15, Big Man condemned the jailing of Hilliard and Douglas. He announced plans for a May Day rally on the New Haven Green and predicted a crowd of 35,000 to 50,000. On Wednesday and Thursday, Miranda, a few other Black Panthers, and Tom Dostou spoke at meetings in Dwight Hall in order to impress upon white students the imminence of May Day and the necessity of Yale's wholehearted support of the Panthers. They obviously meant business. At one meeting the Panthers nearly jumped on a conservative student who was objecting to their coercive tactics. Warning that it would be necessary to use force to liberate Seale, Miranda spoke with fecal threats and violent innuendo: "There's gonna be shit dealt on May 1, and you gotta relate to that shit, and either you're gonna be dealin' the shit or else you're gonna be dealt the shit, and when the shit hits, you'd better be on the right side." When Yalies reacted with astonishment, Dostou made a more specific suggestion: "Oh, you're all full of shit! If you won't do that, at least go burn down Beinecke library." His audience became increasingly animated, and when the Panthers abruptly departed, the students were in disarray. It was at these meetings, rather than by his speeches before large audiences, that Miranda inspired fear and emotionalism in a small but receptive block of Yale radicals. In so doing, he obtained their unquestioning support in his effort to win over the moderates.

Miranda knew that in order to stimulate Yale radicals he should talk about violence only in a manner which made it appear romantic. After the Dwight Hall meeting, a group of black undergraduates accosted him and asked if his threats were serious. "Man, I know what I'm doing," Miranda answered; "this same shit worked at San Francisco State." "But this ain't San Francisco State," said a black student; "you can't expect these Yalies to get guns and go marching down the New Haven Green to the courthouse." Miranda outlined his plans: "Man, hell no. I don't expect those whites to do that. But they ain't done shit yet, except talk. We're trying to get a strike going here, man. Now, you can't just tell them, 'Strike!' You've got to give them something more extreme, and then you let them fall back on a strike." Miranda was equally cynical when asked about the physical danger to white students: "Man, I don't care about these whites.

25

I'm just using them to get Chairman Bobby out of jail. And I'll use them any way I have to. The party knows our place is with black people. But the times call for coalition. We're in a fight for survival, brother. And if we've got to work with whities to survive, then we'll do it. And we'll use them any way we can."

The small number of blacks who attended the first few Moratorium Committee meetings soon drifted away, making it difficult for the committee to formulate a common policy. It is not surprising that the committee, which met every day, was unable to persuade black students to join and give assistance. Blacks kept their distance because they felt that the committee was too dilettantish, too ideologically diverse, and perhaps too subject to Panther manipulation. The Black Student Alliance at Yale (BSAY) included almost all of the 250 black undergraduates and was one of the best organized political groups on campus. It seemed to the BSAY that it could obtain more satisfactory results by means of its own strike organization, which was in the making; members were also arranging their own teach-ins in colleges. Blacks at Yale were not only skeptical of the sincerity of the whites' commitment to the Panthers—they had long been uncertain about their own commitment. As it turned out, the BSAY probably was wise to stick to Yale's Afro-America House and steer clear of Dwight Hall.

The Moratorium Committee had applied for permission to use office space in Dwight Hall as a clearinghouse for strike information. They were admitted on the understanding that "there would be no guns and no drugs and that they would not be publishing or distributing literature inciting arson or violence." Unlike the Moratorium Committee, which was not at this time openly advocating violence, the New Haven Panther Defense Committee was permitted to meet only occasionally in the Dwight Hall common room. The NHPDC never asked for an office in the building—probably because the Yale administration provided office space elsewhere.

Dwight Hall was fast becoming a center for most of the radical political activity at Yale. Organized by the YMCA, Dwight Hall had always maintained ties with the "social action religious community." Any organization with any sort of cause was purportedly able to obtain office space in the building as long as its policies did not support "racism, violence, exploitation, or in any way seek forcibly to overthrow the university." This was usually interpreted to exclude any political group that could be labelled conservative.

SDS had recently received permission, by a unanimous vote of the Dwight Hall directors, to use the building for a weekend conference—to the expressed displeasure of the university administration. The relationship between Dwight Hall and the Yale administration had always been uneasy. The building belonged to Yale and was lent to the YMCA only "so long as it should be convenient to the university," but Dwight Hall frequently took in organizations whose existence was far from "convenient to the university." Although the administration sometimes grumbled, it rarely did anything. The Moratorium Committee initially appeared to be in the same undesirable category as SDS, yet from the outset there were no specific complaints from the Yale hierarchy. Ten days after the committee opened its office, the university began paying for the Dwight Hall telephones in order to encourage "communication."

The Moratorium Committee paid for its use of the Dwight Hall printing press on a day-by-day basis. Technically, any opposing political group could have done the same. None did. Conservatives had been rebuffed in the past; in this instance the radicals, who were practically monopolizing the building's facilities, were so hostile that the conservatives felt there was no point in trying.

_____

The day the moratorium began, the Yale College faculty met to decide on a proposal that failing grades need not appear on students' records. Before that order of business came up, Georges May—a small, energetic Frenchman who was the dean of Yale College—said that he would initiate a discussion of the Black Panther trial at the end of the meeting. He also announced that another faculty meeting would be called "very soon" at which the issue of the trial would be discussed and President Brewster would be present.

Faculty members spent almost two hours debating the grading proposal. After it was rejected by one vote a woman ran in,

27

shouting that she had been in the bathroom, and created a tie by voting in favor of the proposal; it was rejected decisively when the secretary of the faculty voted against it. Jay Ogilvy, incredulous that so much time was being wasted on a "trivial debate" over grading, slept through most of the meeting. He finally made an effort to point out the gravity of the situation, urging his colleagues to talk to their students in order to prevent the disastrous split which the trial was encouraging. Other faculty members submitted two resolutions for a vote: one expressed concern for the constitutional rights of the defendants; the other proposed a university watchdog committee to observe the trial. Both resolutions were rejected as violations of the university's responsibility to remain neutral.

Immediately after the meeting, Georges May said that the discussion of the trial was a move unprecedented in his tenure as dean: "Over the years I had taken the position that the faculty should not be a forum for questions outside its duties." In this respect he reflected the opinion of a majority of those present. But he added, "I was afraid under the circumstances that our silence might be taken for indifference. We are certainly not indifferent. Every member of the faculty agrees, in my view, with the following two points: (1) we are eager to do everything we can to see that justice does not miscarry; (2) the very highly charged emotional atmosphere that is rising around us should not be allowed to prevail over reason." May went on to emphasize that one reason no formal action had been taken was that less than a quarter of the faculty had been present. Much later, he noted that a more important reason for the inaction was that the item had not appeared on the agenda before the meeting convened.

The announced meeting with Brewster was exceptional, since a scheduled meeting had just taken place—although there had been a similar emergency meeting as recently as the previous November during the aftermath of an SDS seizure of a campus building. A number of concerned faculty members willingly postponed any action until the much larger meeting, which they knew would take place the next week. A few never did deeply involve themselves in the growing turmoil; however, the events of the next week caused most members of the faculty to abandon academic neutrality entirely.

The Yale administration probably was jolted into action by the Harvard Square riot and by the announced plans for a May Day rally. Brewster has said that he felt drawn into the picture at the time of the contempt sentences on April 14. Presumably, his decision to meet with the faculty a week later was a response to this. He soon made Sam Chauncey the overall coordinator of the administration's actions relating to May Day, a position which Chauncey has likened to that of a Pantheresque "chief of staff." Other administration members also played an important role in the impending struggle: Alfred Fitt, a special adviser to Brewster on legal matters who had spent several years as an advisor to the U.S. army; Cyrus Vance, former deputy secretary of defense and a trustee of the Yale Corporation; Acting Provost Alvin Kernan; and Deans May and Wilkinson.

The decision-makers now faced what they saw as a choice between welcoming the demonstrators and closing Yale's doors for a siege. Even at this early stage, they were reluctant to close the university and send the students away. The students were already in residence; it would be extremely difficult to evict them forcibly; some of them would certainly keep the residential colleges open on their own. Because the administration felt that any tactic short of welcoming the demonstrators would increase the danger of violence to an unacceptable level, the Yale hierarchy probably decided to extend an official welcome shortly after the demonstration was announced. Chauncey has said that they kept their intentions secret for psychological reasons: "We made the decision to open up, although we did not reveal our decision to most people. Psychologically, it was important to start from a fairly rigid point of view and end up fairly flexible. In that way, you get people to work with you." In this respect, Yale's policy resembled Miranda's. But Kernan, unlike Chauncey, did not think that the administration was so self-assured:

Really the deepest feeling that I take away from the May Day events is a sense of sitting here static, fixed, locked in, trying to create a series of responses to a situation which could not be defined. We never knew how many people were actually coming to town. We never knew what those people were going to be like. We didn't know how many students could remain here, how many would go home, what the attitude of those who remained would really be. We didn't know what events would take place, what was likely to happen. All you could do

29

was simply try to guess what was likely to happen, to prepare a response to the situation, and then once it started, just hope that it worked.

What is surprising about the decision is that the administration considered only two alternatives: that of welcoming the demonstrators and that of shutting them out. A university is an open place where visitors and strangers are free to come and go. An official welcome, in effect a betrayal of academic neutrality, in order to pacify a political assemblage seems less than courageous. The formal decision to "open up" Yale on May Day can only be explained as a submission to extreme fear and pressure.

On Friday, April 17, Judge Mulvey denied bail to Hilliard and Douglas. The defense had argued that bail should be granted because it might take six months for the appeal to reach the court docket. A number of sources indicate that at this point the atmosphere at Yale had become so highly charged that expectations of violence were widespread. In reality, such expectations still belonged only to a minority of students—a minority that was unsure of the precise reasons for the fear. An important turning point, in terms of making the Panther issue known to every Yale student, came on Sunday, April 19. On that day, for the first time, a university official took the initiative and attempted to give direction to the growing movement.

The Reverend William Sloane Coffin, Yale chaplain and pacifist dissenter of nationwide fame, had been meeting for some days with various members of the Yale community—including Alfred Fitt, Brewster's legal adviser—in an effort to decide how he should respond to the trial. In his April 19 sermon at Battell Chapel, Coffin said that he felt two "whirlpools" operating around Yale, "on the one hand the promotion of change through violence, and on the other, the repression of violence caused by no change." He saw the need for a more constructive third option and announced his idea—a nonviolent march on Friday, April 24, to the New Haven courthouse, where the marchers would peacefully submit to arrest for a still undetermined charge. The march, organized by a group of concerned faculty members and clergymen, would be led by himself and the dean of the Yale Divinity School.

Coffin stated that white oppressors of the Panther party should be treated as American colonials had treated George III. Relating the Panthers' difficulties to a national habit of moral inconsistency, he cited his own legal plight: "After Dr. Spock and the rest of us had been pronounced guilty [of urging draft evasion], one of the jurors publicly confessed his anguish, saying tht he found us legally wrong but morally right. I myself cannot judge or rather prejudge the defendants in this trial. The evidence is as yet inconclusive. But I am prepared as an anguished citizen to confess my conviction that it might be legally right but morally wrong for this trial to go forward."

It seemed to Coffin that the general welfare would be promoted if the jailed Panthers were set free: "To those who say, 'What if this were a Klansman on trial and his fellow Klansmen were threatening destruction?' I can only answer that, while releasing a Klansman would be increasing the power of the oppressor, the releasing of the defendants in this case would mean the sharing of power with the oppressed." Before the trial was over, Coffin predicted, the congregation would see the National Guard and martial law in New Haven, but he urged civil disobedience, not violence, claiming that the situation was "prerevolutionary" and that violence would only bring about more repression. His suggestions for action fell short of direct attack: a "fair trial" vigil on the Green; the deployment of civilian marshals; more aid from Yale to the black community. The Yale administration's first obligation, Coffin said, was to the black community, not to the Panther party, as the Panthers themselves agreed. Nor did he lack biblical support. After quoting Ephesians 2:14, he ended his sermon with a disturbing blend of two slogans—"All power to Almighty God!"

The sermon provoked some vehement reactions. During another service, a member of the congregation stood up and denounced Coffin. Five days later, the *New York Times* responded to the sermon in an angry editorial:

In an emotional sermon that stood moral principles on their head, the Rev. William Sloane Coffin Jr., chaplain of Yale, denounced the trial as "legally right but morally wrong," thus doing his best to guarantee moral confusion among his student followers. Mr. Coffin said that even if Mr. Seale were to be found guilty as charged, the entire nation stands accused of bringing him to the state of mind

31

in which the alleged crime might have been committed. This is a legally and morally wrong and dangerous concept, even when supposedly elevated to the level of theological doctrine.

President Brewster, on the other hand, later told Coffin that he approved of the sermon as a whole and particularly commended the proposal for a nonviolent march.

Coffin and Brewster were justly associated in the minds of most observers. Brewster once told a Yale classmate that Coffin was "worth three full professors," and they were good friends whose political beliefs often ran parallel. Coffin, however, was outspoken, whereas Brewster used finesse. Ten years earlier, Coffin had arranged civil rights marches in which Brewster only casually took part. When, in 1970, Coffin perceived moral evil two blocks from his own church, he was no less blunt in condemning it, even implying that violent revolution was eventually inevitable. Coffin was big-hearted and exuberant. At the same time, his moral earnestness and his reluctance to stand to the right of any radical occasionally led him into making Marxist pronouncements and superficial judgments. These tendencies, combined with his Christian pacifism, left him in a difficult political situation during the next week.

Coffin's sermon, though predictable, was important for the Panthers because it was the first open espousal of their cause by a prominent university figure. Published the next day in the *Yale Daily News,* the sermon alerted many to what was happening—and to its seriousness—while the proposed march gave others a potential outlet for their emotions. To most radicals, however, the idea of submitting to arrest without "any illusion that one is going to succeed" seemed outmoded or absurd—or both. It was a throwback to the early days of the antiwar movement and to civil rights marches, which the escalating violence of the late sixties had made unfashionable. Commenting later on the lack of enthusiasm for his march, Coffin identified an underlying adolescent psychology as the cause of it:

At that point there were a lot of people who really felt that probably I was a bad influence, that the march was against a more militant stand. I hate to be criticized. I've gotten used to being criticized from the Right, but it always hurts a bit to be criticized from the Left. What really upset me was the degree to which Yalies got sucked in on the question of "balls." I never realized to what degree cowardice was such a deep fear on the part of so many students. It's something you can easily forget, once you've been through enough yourself, like [the Korean] war in my case. I don't have to fear being a coward any more, I've been through that. But when guys come around and say, "Grab a gun and prove you've got balls," it never occurred to me that many people would be taken in. And the other thing that surprised me, though less, was the degree to which guilt could really be preyed upon. Of course, every black, no matter how obnoxious he may be, has credibility with whites, because every white naturally feels guilty. But what's important is not one's guilt, but one's responsibility, and I felt that people's guilt and people's fear of cowardice were being exploited to an extraordinary degree.

I'm not persuaded nonviolence is a thing of the past. I know that a lot of people are very impatient with it and I know there were quite a few in the "radical" group who felt this march was more of the same. No, I felt that this march wasn't going to solve an awful lot, but the original intent seemed fairly good: it would have dramatized what was going on; it would have given expression to a lot of energy. It would have been a way of expressing solidarity with those in jail and seemed to me also another way to set a tone for the nonviolent weekend which, hopefully, was to come.

Down once, Coffin rebounded a week later. By then, most Yale students were struggling to prevent violence, and Coffin's muscular pacifism came as a welcome relief.

Meanwhile, after learning that Brewster would issue a statement on Sunday evening, some fifteen faculty members and a few students arranged a meeting for Saturday morning in the faculty common room of Branford College. Many of them had come together long before the May Day events to discuss political issues; some, including J. P. Trinkaus (master of Branford College) and Kenneth Mills, had met the preceding February with a Panther representative who had explained his party's concerns and goals—perhaps in an attempt to raise funds. At the Saturday meeting, the group deputed three of its members to see Brewster and urge him to make a "strong" statement. The deputation consisted of Robert Jay Lifton (a widely known psychiatry professor), Kenneth Mills, and Robert Triffin.

Triffin, an economics professor and master of Berkeley College, had written a statement advising Brewster to appoint a committee to consider Yale's relations with the Panther trial. During the subsequent talk with Brewster, Kenneth Mills supported the appointment of the committee, but he was more

33

concerned with impressing upon Brewster the danger of the situation and the importance of not making things worse by closing down the university. Brewster agreed that Yale should remain open and that it was advisable for him to take a moral position. Although everyone at the meeting, including Brewster, appeared to agree that the appointment of a committee was an inconclusive stopgap, it was regarded as the best course available at the time, and the delegation was apparently delighted with Brewster's attitude.

Sunday afternoon, Mills attended a talk by Jean-Luc Godard, a French film director, in Battell Chapel. Most of the 300 students in the audience had come to hear Godard speak about cinematography, not about politics. However, Godard made some very censorious comments on the Panther trial and the situation of all American blacks, turning the discussion period into a consideration of his role as a "militant or revolutionary" filmmaker. At one point, Mills arose and stated that Godard's political consciousness was so far removed from that of his Yale audience that dialectical discussion was impossible: "Not until a storm breaks will people sitting here at Yale begin to understand that there is an entirely different world outside, of people who are daily oppressed."

Godard left the meeting with Mills to have dinner at Branford College, but they both returned to Battell later in the evening to attend a teach-in that had been organized by the Moratorium Committee in order to "raise the level of consciousness of the Yale community." By 8:00 p.m., 1,500 members of the Yale community had gathered in the chapel—drawn not by the lure of a particular agenda (none had been published) but by their own feelings of anxiety and curiosity. The Moratorium Committee had distributed an elaborate leaflet that described the two proposals adopted on Wednesday, as well as four new ones. Many people expected to hear a Panther talk, and most of them were counting on Doug Miranda. They were not disappointed; Miranda did appear at the last minute. One black student retrospectively observed that "Doug Miranda did a very, very good job of being at the right place at the right time. It wasn't unexpected to me that he showed up." Later, this meeting was recognized as a climax in the series of events leading to May Day.

The teach-in began with an announcement that the moratorium voted on the previous Wednesday would continue over the next two days. The first two speakers, a third-year Yale Law School student and a first-year graduate student in political science, discussed the legal questions surrounding the trial. Both of them stressed their belief that the Panther defendants could not be judged fairly because of the "political" nature of the case. The political science student was particularly well received by the crowd, and her statement that the trial had to be seen in a broader political context, "including Vietnam and domestic policies of this government," evoked a standing ovation. A macrocosmic approach to the trial was extremely popular with students; by early May, when the Indochina war became the major issue, their interest in municipal problems like the Panther trial all but vanished. On April 19, this appeal set the stage for Doug Miranda.

Miranda, who had been sitting in the chancel with Tom Dostou, stepped up to the microphone and delivered the most important statement of the entire strike—with the exception of Brewster's speech four days later. Miranda began quietly, explaining that he proposed to present "the human side of the Panther question. . . . I'm not going to tell white students to go out and kill pigs at this time because that would be idealism." The tense crowd relaxed a little as it became clear that Miranda was not going to use the threatening language usually associated with the Panthers. After giving a general description of the slum conditions that had fostered the Panthers, he went on to make a concrete suggestion: "The most minimal level you can participate on is a call for a student strike; we're saying, take your power and use it to save the institution. Take it away from people who are using it in a way it shouldn't be used. You can close Yale down and make Yale demand release. You have the power to prevent a bloodbath in New Haven." A strike could prevent "the country from using the courts as fascist tools." On Tuesday, continued Miranda, the Panthers and the Black Student Alliance at Yale would be holding a press conference to issue a national call for unity: "There's no reason why the Panther and the Bulldog can't get together!" The vivid reference to Yale's football mascot brought a cheering audience to its feet. Miranda struck again: "You cannot ponder on this point too long! That Panther and that Bulldog gonna move together!"

The rest of the meeting was an anticlimax. Several new demands made by the Moratorium Committee were aired, but it was impossible for students to become excited about them after Miranda's dramatic speech. One speaker presented a demand that Yale stop depleting the New Haven housing market and tax revenues and disclose all future plans for expansion into the community. Having important counterparts during previous strikes at Columbia and Harvard, this proposal was the most reasonable of all the demands made during the strike. Two other students discussed a demand that Yale halt all plans for the construction of a Social Science Center which was to house the Institute for Social Sciences. Explanation and discussion of the proposal, which was only tenuously related to the problems of the blacks, was so long and tedious that many in the audience left before it was over. In the midst of the discussion, an excited freshman interrupted to announce—briefly and sarcastically— the news of Brewster's formation of a committee to decide upon Yale's reaction to the trial; the announcement was received with widespread laughter. Before the meeting broke up, a black student spoke on the need for day care centers for the children of Yale employees, and an SDS member demanded that Yale allocate more money to the university's rehabilitation program for the hard-core unemployed.

Miranda had stolen the meeting. He had shown the students how they could work together in a manner supposedly useful to the Panther cause and had given direction to their confused emotions. Essentially, he had told them what they wanted to hear, toning down his more uninhibited rhetoric to link the Panther and Bulldog paw in paw. It was an appealing concept. For most, Coffin's civil disobedience proposal became obsolete the day it was announced. Yale was far more eager to follow the lead of this militant, mustachioed, young black, who was said to be only nineteen years old and had reputedly dropped out of San

Francisco State College to join the Panthers. Kenneth Mills later commented that the Panther-Bulldog speech was a virtuoso performance of public speaking which he regarded as "high spectacle" and comedy; in a general political sense the speech was purely manipulative, but "maybe all of us get caught in forms of political activity that are not ideally what we would choose." Mills himself was about to be caught in exactly that way. Immediately after Miranda's speech, he remarked to a friend that in some political situations Miranda's brand of opportunism was justifiable.

President Brewster's first public statement on the Panther trial and on Yale's official attitude toward it had been briefly noted at the Battell Chapel meeting. It turned out to be a reaffirmation of university neutrality:

Members of the University community will embrace a great variety of views and positions with respect to the pending trial of members of the Black Panther Party for the murder of Alex Rackley. The University will try to facilitate and encourage any groups which seek to assert their views and take action to further such views, as long as their action does not interfere with the rights of others. Precisely in order to be encouraging and protective of all points of view on issues, the University attempts generally to remain politically neutral. On the fundamental matter of the fact and feeling of justice in our own community, however, Yale cannot be neutral.... By the same token it would not be proper to assume that justice cannot be dispensed by the courts of this state.

Brewster also named a committee to determine the best course of action for Yale and encouraged the Yale Law School to monitor the trial. His comments on the committee were circuitous: "Because it is so difficult to do anything practically helpful, I am asking a Committee of colleagues to consider any and all suggestions that may emerge from discussions in the months ahead and to recommend what course of action seems most appropriate for Yale." Doug Miranda's inspiring strike call made the appointment of a committee seem evasive and insufficient to Yale's black faculty members, to deeply involved students, and to many others on the campus. In order to accommodate them, Brewster, like Coffin, would have to alter his approach, if not his attitude.

37

The twelve-member "Osborne Committee" included three black members, one of whom was the chairman, Ernest Osborne. Osborne, also chairman of Yale's Council on Community Affairs, was the brother-in-law of Warren Kimbro, the Panther who had already pleaded guilty to the charge of second-degree murder. At the time of his appointment, Osborne said that the committee's actions would not be limited by his relation to Kimbro, and he approached his new duty optimistically. "The committee," he noted, "deals with far more than just the Panther trial. The institution and its relationship to the community in general will be dealt with." Osborne's statement reflected the growing awareness of demands other than those concerned with the trial. Other members of the committee included Coffin, Dean Georges May, Alfred Fitt, John Hersey (a best-selling novelist who was the master of Pierson College), and Barry Lydgate, the dean of Branford College.

In a meeting at Branford College on Sunday night, right after the Battell Chapel teach-in, a number of undergraduates complained that Dean Lydgate's presence on the Osborne Committee should be a collective Branford decision, rather than a Brewster appointment which they viewed as an effort to placate a radical college. Black faculty members were no less annoyed by Brewster's appointment of three blacks, presumably to placate another dissident group. The newly formed committee came under heavy fire from all sides, and no one was willing to defend it. The heaviest criticism came from the black faculty on Monday evening.

The black faculty met in Branford College to draft a letter opposing the Osborne Committee. The letter, written collectively and sent to Brewster, declared that black faculty members felt that the committee was "an ineffectual means of dealing with an extremely pressing issue." Furthermore, "to place a black man in the role of chairman and to place two black members on a committee to study suggestions and issues over the next few months was an evasion of responsibility by the university, and, indeed, seemed to suggest that Yale might be attempting to use black faculty members as buffers to neutralize a dangerous and immediate situation." After this statement, backed by the "full support of the black faculty," the letter announced that the black members of the Osborne Committee had decided not to serve. The concluding sentence declared that "the black faculty at Yale will meet continuously over the next several days to determine exactly what demands it feels can legitimately be placed upon Yale as an institution and upon other institutions which are of necessity involved in the issues that surround the impending Black Panther trial."

Osborne himself claimed that the idea for the committee had not originated with Brewster but with the three faculty members who had visited Brewster on Sunday morning. Alfred Fitt, who was present at the Sunday meeting, later maintained that "Mills joined in urging that (what became) the Osborne Committee be appointed. The next day he publicly criticized Brewster for having appointed the committee." Mills explained it differently:

Kingman has said to people that he was whiplashed by me a couple of times during the May Day incidents. I think he felt that I had advised him to set up the Osborne Committee and then advised Osborne not to serve on it. I think this is his perspective again, which is not accurate, because what happened was that the committee suggestion came largely from Triffin. I was in Brewster's mind associated with it because I went with Triffin to see him. My main interest was really not in urging the setting up of that committee. I didn't even give any thought to the committee at all, because I didn't think that the committee would be a big thing. I really had no idea when I went to see the president what steps he would take. I certainly *did* want to urge upon him, mainly, that he not take any steps that would shut the place down.

It is likely that Mills perceived important drawbacks to the appointment of the committee when he learned of its membership and heard it discussed among students and black members of the faculty—drawbacks which had not occurred to him when he first heard Triffin's suggestion. Unfortunately, many regarded his alleged misunderstanding as deviousness.

Mills's style and appearance aggravated the hostility of those who already disliked him. He looked offbeat, standing six-feet-two-inches tall and sporting an enormous afro haircut. He wore blue jeans and bulbous sunglasses. He had a hare-lip. He seemed entirely unselfconscious, speaking and moving with deliberateness and aplomb, and his habit of taking his pauses only in the middle of sentences created the impression that he was never at a loss for words. His Caribbean-Oxford accent was smooth and singsong. Would-be detractors became absorbed in his rotund eloquence, wondering later on what had come over them. Even those who generally approved of Mills's politics often found him enigmatic, perhaps because his piebald personality clashed with every conceivable black stereotype.

As a Marxist black, Mills felt obligations to the Panthers, but he did not trust them. Nor did they trust Mills. Panthers had threatened him several times during the preceding months and had recently "borrowed" his car. In addition to his wariness toward the Panthers, Mills has pointed out that his nationality and background made his personal reaction to the idea that blacks were being "used" less strong than that of most black faculty members. Houston Baker, a junior English professor, was a sharp contrast. Chief author of the black faculty's letter to Brewster, Baker was particularly angry about the possibility that the Yale administration was compromising the black faculty. Baker, on the surface a shy, conscientious, conservatively dressed scholar, within the next few weeks became a major spokesman against the wrongs which he believed New Haven blacks were suffering at the hands of Yale.

Within Yale, the black faculty had long and fruitlessly been airing grievances about the status of the Afro-American Studies Program and the security and status of their own positions. Neither in Yale College nor in any of the professional schools were there any tenured black professors. Almost certainly, black faculty members considered the next two weeks a promising opportunity to exact a greater response from Yale than they had been able to gain during the previous two years. Roy Bryce-LaPorte, a soft-spoken Panamanian who was chairman of the Afro-American Studies Program, has indicated the growing complications of their situation:

There was a general feeling among blacks that their actions in those days would continue to have historical bearing on blacks throughout academia. Many of us realized that Yale was immobilized by panic, arrogance, and fear and also that Yale black students needed a backdrop of trusted adult support. Many members of the black faculty felt it important to see that Yale, in its efforts to save itself, did not disregard or forsake its commitment to the black community. That is not to say that there were some who wanted Yale to be embarrassed and destroyed in

40

the crisis. Most saw themselves bounded by double duty as blacks and as members of the academic community. They also realized that Yale's records, insofar as they related to the blacks on campus and in the larger community, were unsatisfactory. Earlier in the school year, the black faculty tried to encourage serious reconsideration by the university of its commitment to blacks. As for the black students, many black faculty members shared with them the uneasiness of being the target of curious observation by the country's black population. The black faculty was also aware that black students were caught up in the middle between the rhetorical pressures of the Black Panthers and their white radical supporters on the one hand and a militant but anxious New Haven black community on the other. Black students also were caught between the call for bold revolutionary action on their part and their appreciation of their association with Yale with all its promises of professional success within the system. In other words, the black faculty viewed itself as filling a multifaceted vacuum of leadership created by the crisis.

Black students were more influenced by the dignified, relatively moderate Roy Bryce-LaPorte than by the flamboyant Kenneth Mills. In fact, Bryce-LaPorte may have prevented hot heads in the BSAY from leading the others to extremes. He had always emphasized to black undergraduates that they were at Yale first to study and only secondarily to politic. Many other black faculty members had similar feelings of both pedagogic and political responsibility, which they reconciled at this time by giving lectures and holding discussions on "relevant" issues at the university and by serving on public committees in the community.

On Monday morning, April 20, the Reverend Ralph David Abernathy spoke at a New York City press conference which was chaired by David Dellinger of the Chicago Seven and covered by the national media. Abernathy told the reporters present that the same "racist justice" that drove Martin Luther King to the streets in the South in 1955 was "now driving us to the streets of the North—New York, New Haven, Chicago—signalling the beginning of the end of the Mitchell-Nixon-Agnew-Thurmond era." He denounced Judge Mulvey for having recently jailed Hilliard and Douglas for contempt, saying, "Southern style justice has come to New Haven. This is nothing more than legal lynching." The next day, David Dellinger announced that the Chicago Seven would go to New Haven to host the rally on May 1 as a first step in a nationwide effort to liberate the Panthers on trial in New Haven. Abernathy encouraged others to attend the

41

rally, but he himself did not visit New Haven during the ensuing crisis.

Such outside events as Abernathy's statements and the Harvard riot tended to have a strong effect in New Haven and at Yale. On Monday and Tuesday, several of the residential colleges voted to suspend the social activities planned for the weekend of May 1—the traditional spring frolic known as College Weekend. Eight of the twelve colleges voted to remain open during the May Day weekend and to provide housing, food, and medical supplies for the visiting demonstrators. At some of the meetings there was discussion of the various demands circulated by different political factions and the Moratorium Committee, but the topics were considered too nebulous for any definite agreements. Yale's Council of (college) Masters met on Sunday, Monday, and Tuesday to discuss these developments and to determine student attitudes. Although they signed a petition in support of "the constitutional rights of the defendants," they too were unable to reach any definite conclusions.

Against this background of uncertainty, the United Front for Panther Defense (UFPD, a new organization) and the Moratorium Committee announced plans for a mass meeting to "deal with the issues raised by the political trial of the Black Panthers in New Haven." The meeting was scheduled for Tuesday night at Yale's Ingalls Hockey Rink, the scene of other mass meetings during the anti-ROTC agitation a year before. Permission to use the rink had been given to the Moratorium Committee by Chauncey, in keeping with the administration's ostensible policy of providing auditorium space for any political group that requested it. Plans for this mass meeting had been initiated by the Moratorium Committee the week before, but when the blacks began to take a stand, the organizational initiative passed to the nonwhite UFPD. The Moratorium Committee ultimately was asked to stay out of all further planning for the meeting, which made it an entirely black-sponsored rally.

The Black Student Alliance at Yale held a meeting early Monday afternoon at which members decided that, though they were in favor of the moratorium, it would be best to defer any final decisions until after the black faculty met. When the black faculty's letter had been sent to Brewster, the steering committee of the BSAY and the United Front for Panther Defense met during the evening at Afro-America House to devise a coherent policy for arousing the whites. A Black Panther presented his plan of how the forthcoming Yale strike should be organized. This particular Panther was supposedly the party's expert on academic strikes, but his perspective—far more than Miranda's—was limited to the strike at San Francisco State College. He wanted Yale to adhere, step by step, to that model, thinking that it was merely a question of mobilizing the students to march. Several people, including Kenneth Mills, tried vainly to explain the differences between San Francisco State and Yale, not only with respect to the universities, but also with respect to the time and the politics of the areas. President Brewster would not make the same mistakes as President Hayakawa.

When the Panther tactician asked for a better suggestion, it became clear that the opinion among Yale blacks was too diverse to allow for genuine solidarity, especially in conjunction with the Panthers. In spite of their unity on certain issues—such as the trial—Yale blacks and the Panther party disagreed on the New Haven situation. Even the pragmatic Doug Miranda was hemmed in by Panther ideology, and Panther-BSAY relations began a steady deterioriation which continued through May Day. It is ironic that the superficial entente between white Yalies and the Panthers at this point began to flourish.

The Afro-America House meeting did produce positive results for the United Front for Panther Defense. The newly formed UFPD was a conglomerate of black community organizations and third world university groups such as the BSAY and the Third World Liberation Front. Core groups of the UFPD, consisting of representatives from these organizations, had been meeting for several weeks on an informal basis. At the Monday meeting, the UFPD completed its plans for a press conference the next morning and made preliminary arrangements for a national conference of black community organizations to discuss the Panther situation. The general feeling of the UFPD was that the Yale strike should be a method of raising the political consciousness of the university, as well as a method of exacting concessions from the administration.

The same evening, a well-known, right-wing sophomore claimed to have the signatures of 1,500 students who opposed what was now anticipated as a prolonged strike. Over the weekend, members of his committee had made announcements on the radio and circulated a petition in the college dining halls. The petition read: "We, the undersigned ... believe a fair trial can only be achieved if the constitutional rights of the defendants are protected; that a student strike at this time would be counter-productive." Committee members had also distributed leaflets to the student body urging that the moratorium declared on April 15 be ignored, because "the moratorium is an effort to decide cases in question not by due process of law, but by force of public opinion." The leaflets described the efforts of Panther supporters as attempts "to coerce the Yale community."

The petition and leaflets comprised one of the few conservative counterattacks of the entire period. During the previous week, a group of conservative students had invited some moderate blacks from the New Haven community to come to Yale to condemn the moratorium, but Chauncey refused to provide auditorium space, saying that it would be "too provocative." After the weekend, most conservatives, faculty as well as student, felt so overwhelmed by events that they decided that resistance was useless. The radicalization of the moderate students, engendered in small groups before the weekend, began in earnest on Sunday, April 19, and reached its apogee by the time of the Ingalls Rink rally on April 21.

On April 20, an evening meeting took place which, in a sense, produced the only legitimate student endorsement of the strike. It was little noticed on the campus, but the *New York Times* reported it in a front page headline the next day. The newly organized Yale Student Senate had scheduled an open meeting the previous week, but when less than a quorum showed up, the meeting was postponed until Sunday, April 19. That meeting, too, was cancelled, and when the senate finally convened in a lecture hall on Monday evening, just fifty-nine undergraduate senators were present, each of them duly elected from a

44

constituency of twenty Yale students. In addition to the
assembled senators, who represented less than a quarter of the
undergraduate population, the meeting was attended by
approximately a hundred other students, "visitors," and faculty
members.

The agenda for the meeting included four conservative resolutions concerning Yale's response to the Panther trial, but the
agenda was almost immediately suspended, the Senate Steering
Committee having decided to entertain motions from the floor
exclusively. In view of their desire to maintain order, this was
perhaps the senators' greatest mistake. Immediately, a motion
calling for a one day, voluntary, symbolic "strike" in support of
"justice" was presented. The motion, as such, was never voted on.
An arrogant disrespect for the rules of order on the part of the
radicals—most of whom were spectators—made a vote
impossible. There was much discussion about whether the senate
even had the right to support a strike. Heckling from the
"visitors" at the back of the room—mostly blacks and a group of
white radicals, including some SDS members—often brought the
progress of the meeting to a halt. The hecklers shouted at the
senators and called the meeting irrelevant and antiquated, saying
that it was only the college "collectives" that truly represented
student opinion. Since the chairman had a poor understanding of
parliamentary procedure, it was easy to disrupt the meeting with
deliberately meaningless proposals, although the radicals
probably would have succeeded in making the task of any
chairman impossible. When the chairman told one group of
hecklers that they were out of order, a faculty member noticed

the tense, angry face of one Black girl screaming at the chairman, "*You're* out of
order," then simply, "Bullshit, bullshit," as she moved toward the door. Then a
Black student came down to the front of the room and went up on the platform
and told the senators they were pathetic, that he had never seen anything so
pathetic in his life. He went on to announce that the blacks were holding a press
conference at 10 A.M. the next morning at which they would call for a strike,
and would introduce a little reality into the university, instead of all this
procedural bullshit.

During the havoc of the meeting, one disgusted senator
proposed that the senate dissolve itself. The motion was quickly
shouted down, although several spectators thought that it had

passed. Finally, the senators withstood the pressure from the back of the room long enough to pass a single resolution by a close vote: "The Yale Senate calls on the members of the Yale Community to attend a mass meeting tomorrow night and vote for a voluntary student strike to express our concern for justice and insuring the rights of the defendants." The meeting ended abruptly and in confusion, with the future of the senate unclear. After the adjournment, a black, bald-headed freshman went to the podium and delivered an intense and venomous speech, reviling the senators and what she felt they represented. Her words seemed to have their strongest effect on the black men at the back of the room.

Accounts of the meeting differ enormously. Some thought that it lasted only twenty minutes, while others have reported that the debate went on for two hours. One senator did not even recall voting on the final resolution. A senator in the junior class has said:

At that point—I'm not entirely sure how it arose—someone else proposed that the Student Senate abolish itself on the spot. I think it was in response to some heckling and catcalls from the back that said the Student Senate was usurping the prerogative of the local communes—I forget the exact language offhand— and that the Student Senate was unrepresentative of the Yale community, that while we were debating these things off in our little world, important things were taking place out in the streets that we weren't cognizant of. The tenor of the meeting was so emotional nothing really could get done. Someone got up and simply proposed the Student Senate disband itself. I later talked to the person and he really didn't mean that—he just wanted to liquidate the meeting as soon as possible. He was shouted down in turn, and at that point it was fairly obvious that nothing was going to get done.

Another witness has described an "atmosphere of intimidation" and of "terror," while the founder of the senate, Master Triffin, was so frightened by the events of the meeting that he asked some students to accompany him back to his house afterward. As for the decision by the Senate Steering Committee to have an open meeting, most of the senators have agreed that this was a good idea, since if the senate could not function effectively in the open, it might as well not function at all.

The hecklers successfully prevented the senate from exerting any influence on the Yale community during the next weeks. Like so many student governing bodies, the Yale Student Senate was impotent when faced with a crisis. It was indecisive and directionless, not only because of the harassment which disrupted the meeting, but because the senators were no more attuned to the exigencies of the situation than were their constitutents, who for the most part were equally indecisive and directionless. Senators reacted to a situation they only vaguely comprehended, and they reacted in the most easily available and popular way—they called for an end to all academic work. The Ingalls Rink meeting would make a strike the most popular course for many more Yalies.

Chapter
4

The Panther and the Bulldog

Tuesday's activities began in front of the New Haven courthouse with another demonstration organized by the Panthers. Although it resembled the demonstration that had taken place ten days before, resulting incidents were more serious. The participants met during the early morning on the street corner next to the courthouse, and by 9:30 thirty people had gathered on the courthouse steps with a group of Panthers, chanting and picketing as they milled about. When the small courtroom gallery was full, several New Haven policemen—whose number had increased with the size of the crowd—peaceably persuaded the demonstrators to move across the street to the Green, since the court was then in session. Two hundred people who had been denied admission to the courtroom gallery joined them, and an hour later no fewer than 300 blacks and whites were gathered on the Green behind a police line.

Before the demonstration ended, the crowd which had been turned away from the gallery struck out across the Green and circulated through the streets, disrupting traffic and barging into stores. Over twenty-five people were arrested on charges of breach of the peace and disorderly conduct. Some of them had been in the group of hecklers who had disrupted the Student Senate meeting the night before, but most were black teenagers truant from local schools, which were in turmoil over the Panther trial. The juveniles were promptly released to the custody of their parents; the rest were freed after posting bond ranging from $100 to $500.

Within the courthouse, legal proceedings continued throughout the afternoon. After meeting with Judge Mulvey behind closed doors, David Hilliard, Emory Douglas, Bobby Seale, and their lawyer, Charles Garry, delivered brief but significant speeches before the court. Garry spoke first, stating that he had originally asked Hilliard and Douglas to come to the court to "help me carry out the responsibility I assume in keeping order in the courtroom." Panther Chief of Staff David Hilliard told the judge, "It was not our intention to disrupt the court. We are trying to uphold the law and the Constitution and our rights under them, and maintain peaceful assembly in and around the courtroom. Even if we do not agree with the law, we will defend our rights under the Constitution." Hilliard concluded by apologizing for any disturbance that might have occurred at the time of his arrest for contempt. Panther Minister of Culture Emory Douglas told the court that he agreed with Hilliard's statement and said that the disturbance in court on April 14 had arisen out of a misunderstanding between himself and a plainclothes policeman who he had not realized was a court official. Douglas also concluded with an apology.

Bobby Seale made an important statement which was unheard or ignored by most of the Yale community during the next ten days. He said that his own behavior in the Chicago court had been provoked by a denial of his right to the lawyer of his choice, Charles Garry. However, in this courtroom, Garry and "the lawyers for the other defendants are here. I understand that this is necessary for a fair trial. I understand that you are trying to see that we defendants have a fair trial and to have a fair trial. We also understand the necessity for peaceful decorum in the courtroom." Making a characteristic appeal to the Constitution, he said, "It simply means that we understand that we pledge allegiance to the United States of America and to the republic of America. And I pledge allegiance to American justice. We didn't pledge allegiance to the war in Vietnam. We didn't pledge allegiance to the killing of Black Panthers or the murdering of Black Panthers in the streets." Seale denied reports that he had smuggled a paper to Hilliard but mentioned that he had given a book outline to Garry. He concluded by saying, "I respect Your Honor very much for allowing me to have a fair trial."

Judge Mulvey replied that he was pleased to hear that there would be no further disruptions by Black Panthers. "I'm not here trying a political trial," he said, "but violations of Connecticut statutes." He reduced the sentences for contempt to the time already served and ordered that Hilliard and Douglas be set free immediately. Two others, charged at the same time as Hilliard and Douglas, also were released; they, too, had apologized. Finally, Mulvey announced that he would hear motions on the trial the next day. This was expected to include a bail motion for Bobby Seale, which meant that Sams would be asked to repeat his damaging testimony.

Whether or not the students' reaction and the good offices of the Yale administration affected Judge Mulvey's decision to release Hilliard and Douglas is an important question, since it indicates the extent of the university's and the students' influence on the trial as a whole. Kingman Brewster remarked a week later that he "wouldn't begin to say whether there was any cause and effect between Judge Mulvey's suspension of the contempt sentences and the activities at Yale." Alfred Fitt, also a lawyer, was more expansive:

It was quite clear that the contempt convictions had upset a good many people— not the convictions themselves, but the severity of the sentence—and that that incident was giving impetus to the general discontent of the state of affairs. They were so severe that they reinforced the argument of those who insisted, "Bobby is on his way to the electric chair," and that the only thing to do was to dismiss all the charges against the Black Panthers, that they'd never be dealt with fairly. I think a lot of people that week were puzzling as to how they might help to bring about a reversal or an unwinding of the contempt sentences. I talked to some lawyers in town about it, and they agreed with me that it would be better if the sentences could be ameliorated in some way, and I'm sure that there were approaches made to Judge Mulvey. I didn't make any direct approach to him, but I did my best to bring about approaches which would be professionally ethical. There wasn't a university plan to try to affect the contempt sentences. Kingman knew that I was making such efforts—I don't remember talking about them with anybody else. I don't know whether my efforts made the difference, because, as I mentioned earlier, there was a common reaction. It wasn't that all virtue and indignation was confined to the university community. There was a fairly standard reaction on the part of the members of the bar in town, too. Just what sequence of events caused the judge to bring the men back to court the following week, I don't know. In the aftermath there was an expressed feeling on the part of various student groups and student leaders that their actions had been responsible for it—I think that was romanticizing it to a considerable degree.

Whatever the reason for an indirect overture to a trial judge, it is unlikely that any university official would admit that the effort had been prompted by the actions of discontented, striking students.

———————

Before the release of Hilliard and Douglas, the United Front for Panther Defense held its press conference before 300 people in the Berkeley College common room. Just after 10:00 a.m., the spokesman for the group, Ralph Dawson (a junior at Yale and moderator of the BSAY), presented the UFPD's position on five major issues: Judge Mulvey must dismiss the contempt sentences against Hilliard and Douglas; Afro-America House at Yale would be the national clearinghouse for information concerning the trial and for contributions to the Panther defense fund; the university should contribute $500,000 to the defense fund; a national conference of black community organizations to consider policies related to the Black Panthers would meet at Yale on May 9; and classes at Yale should be shut down in order to give students and faculty members an opportunity to discuss the situation "without disruption." Supplementary demands asked that Yale contribute to the Panther breakfast program for as many black children as there were black students at Yale and that health and day care centers be established for the children of Yale employees.

It is surprising that the BSAY and the UFPD supported the demand for $500,000; usually, their tactics were less theatrical than those of the striking white students. In this instance, while they were using the high figure for bargaining purposes, they may also have been responding to the promptings of the Panthers and of community blacks. Yale had promised money to the community after the 1967 riots, and many moderate blacks, believing that the promise had been broken, harbored a sense of frustration and anger against the university.

52

The proposals and demands were endorsed by nine other speakers, including Doug Miranda and three UFPD members who were important figures in the black community—Ronnie Johnson, Willie Counsel, and Fred Harris. Kenneth Mills also announced the black faculty's decision to oppose the Osborne Committee. A representative of Yale's Black Seminarians received the greatest applause of all as he called for black unity and denounced the national attack on the Black Panther party: "We interpret the universe, the nature of man, salvation, God, Jesus, and the role of the church in terms of the black liberation struggle."

On Tuesday afternoon, the Osborne Committee held its first—and last—meeting in the Corporation Room in Woodbridge Hall. Chairman Osborne formally resigned and the committee sent Brewster an almost superfluous letter of self-dissolution: "We have met and read the letter to you from the Black Faculty at Yale of April 20. We have concluded that as now constituted your committee cannot function effectively. We recommend that you consider alternative ways to fulfill your purposes. We want to be helpful. We hope that a way can be found for us to assist you."

Although Brewster had not conceived the plan for the Osborne Committee, he had been quick to embrace it. The action was too noncommittal to be described as a serious blunder, yet it was evident that the administration's first visible effort to control the university's response to the trial had failed. Brewster would now wait until the faculty meeting, where his basic strategy would be revealed. He ultimately accepted almost everything the black faculty proposed—to the satisfaction of the political left—with the implication that their proposals closely reflected his own views. Perhaps they did.

On Tuesday night, while Yale students assembled at Ingalls Rink, Brewster attended a dinner in New York. The dinner was part of a convention of newspaper executives at which Brewster and S.I. Hayakawa, president of San Francisco State College, had been asked to speak. Hayakawa condemned the "aristocratic, elitist bent" of liberal arts students and chided reporters for searching out radicals and printing long interviews, which helped set "the stage for disturbances." Praising "non-elite" students for their constructive social concern, he warned that "elitists have a profound contempt for democracy."

Brewster drew the same distinction, using other labels. He prefaced his speech with a statement about the meeting taking place at Yale, a coincidence which he termed "frightening." The students, he said, were meeting "to discuss their outrage at the circumstances of the trial of several members of the Black Panther Party in New Haven. They seek to formulate ways of demonstrating their concerns by strike or moratorium, and by proposals for more effective action by the University in behalf of social as well as legal justice." Brewster showed great sympathy for the students, in view of the fact that they were rebelling against him. He may have been preparing people for his leap leftward a few days later. He said that he recognized the risk he had taken in coming to New York instead of remaining at Yale, but he felt "the privilege of this forum may perhaps give me a chance to cure some distortions and misimpressions throughout the country about what motivates the majority of this generation of students."

The main text of Brewster's speech dealt with "the relatively silent student majority." He explained why he believed that the majority of students were "less hopeful, more dejected than they were a year ago" and cited many reasons for the students' misgivings: "The killing in Vietnam goes on without prospect of an end. . . . The poor get poorer. . . The dedication to racial equality is pushed back to the inner limits of constitutional necessity." This was "a generation quick to detect, even falsely to accuse, its elders of hypocrisy," but students did not feel any personal animosity about Nixon's election because "they did not expect much better of a hucksterized process, whoever was [elected], whichever package was sold and bought."

On the whole, Brewster's view of the student movement was pessimistic. Pointing out students' frustrations over "the disparagement of dissent and non-conformity," he said that "potentially constructive critics, skeptics, and heretics—what I would call 'considerate radicals'—are being driven into the ranks of those enraged destructionists who would tear down the system."

GENESIS OF A STRIKE

Half an hour before Brewster spoke in New York, several thousand "potentially constructive critics, skeptics, and heretics," some of them almost panic-stricken, assembled at a mass meeting called for the purpose of closing down Yale. Few had heard about the release of Douglas and Hilliard, and to many of the people attending the meeting those names were meaningless; they knew little about the Panthers and less about the trial and contempt sentences; they were going to the meeting only to find out where all the noise was coming from. Others hoped the meeting would resolve the personal confusion that had been caused by earlier speakers. A hard core hoped that the rally would point out a new direction for action, given the fact of Seale's announced respect for the court and his expectation of a fair trial. Moreover, it was unclear whether Judge Mulvey had simply corrected an error by freeing Hilliard and Douglas or had reacted to pressure. In the latter case, the possibilities for further disruption were limitless, and the most ardent proponents of the strike looked to the mass meeting for direction in this regard.

That morning, there had appeared in the *Yale Daily News* a headline that ran: "Mass Meeting Called For Tonight; Student Strike Appears Imminent." There had also been reports that a unified, student shutdown of classes would be proclaimed at the rally, in spite of the fact that no arrangements for voting had been made. No agenda had been announced, although it was said that a videotape of the morning's press conference would be shown, followed by a discussion of the strike. The Third World Liberation Front, or perhaps the BSAY, was to chair the meeting.

A crowd of over 4,500 people packed itself into the stands of the hockey rink and onto two-thirds of the playing surface. Blacks, including Yale students and faculty members, were crowded together in a block behind the speaker's platform. The "people" controlled the podium. The national media were present, but there were no microphones on the floor, and there were no visible police, campus nor municipal. While collection buckets were passed around for the Panthers, lights were tested and crowd photographs were taken. The agenda for the evening had been carefully prepared, and it would soon become apparent from the tone of the speakers that this was not a meeting; it was a strike rally in which overwhelming support was taken for granted.

Gilbert Rochon, coordinator of the UFPD and chairman of the rally, opened with a written summary of the morning's press conference at Berkeley College; the videotape was not shown. Suddenly, Bill Coffin approached the podium and told Rochon that he had an important statement to make which must involve a personal appeal. Could he have the microphone? Rochon relented and Coffin was introduced.

Coffin opened with an effusive tribute: "I can't begin to express my gratitude to the Black Student Alliance and the black faculty for exerting the leadership they have over the last few days." He then made another announcement of his planned nonviolent march, which he said would "tell the nation that some of us feel this whole trial was a dreadful mistake." There was applause from those who approved of Coffin's peaceful tactics and from those who had a general respect for him. Others remained silent, accepting a widespread rumor that the chaplain was attempting to co-opt the Panther movement. Coffin was not in tune with this meeting. His announcement of negotiations with Police Chief Ahern over the matter of arrests during the march was coolly received; even his supporters seemed struck by the contrived nature of the arrangement and the dated style of the confrontation. The announcement of the breakup of the Osborne Committee was more enthusiastically applauded than anything else Coffin had to say. When he had concluded his statement, Coffin quietly apologized to Rochon for having obtained the microphone in such a backhanded manner. Rochon responded by announcing that "the podium is back in the hands of the people"—summing up the attitude of much of the audience.

Rather than co-opting the Panthers, Coffin appeared to have himself been excluded, and the applause for Rochon's remark was far more confident than that which had greeted Coffin's appearance. Later, some of those in charge of the meeting claimed that Rochon's comment had been misunderstood as a "put down" of Coffin's pacifism; in fact, it was a tart way of rejecting Coffin's advocacy of restraint and "pointless activity" at the beginning of a meeting run by militant blacks. Although Rochon did not necessarily want violence, Coffin's march was precisely the kind of symbolic gesture that might distract Yalies from the real problems.

But now it was the people's turn—and the people turned out to be almost exclusively Panthers, community blacks, and their close associates. Ronnie Johnson, a community spokesman, quickly made what appeared to be another jab at Coffin: "We ain't going for this nonviolence. I'm not allowing them motherfuckers to kick my ass and not do anything about it. If you ain't up to ass kicking, you can at least shut this motherfucker down." A black Yale alumnus, who was employed in the university's Afro-American Studies Program, attacked Brewster and Yale as bulwarks of the status quo and said that the students should continue to apply pressure in order to bring about social change. They must prepare for May Day and must not look on the Ingalls Rink meeting as "a new Woodstock. We are here to demand of you an active commitment to a struggle black people have been waging for well over 400 years. . . . I have never been involved in a demonstration for the rights of black people that didn't turn out to be violent, because we put ourselves on the line." This was a direct underlining of the tension at the rally— the "we" of the struggling black community (revolutionary or otherwise) and the "you" of the comfortable, if suddenly radical, Yale.

Kenneth Mills came to the podium—his was a voice to which Yale ears were attuned. He disagreed with some of the positions of the Black Panthers, but he believed that the university should go on strike: "If the people at Yale find the storm threatening them . . . the wrath of the people is what is threatening Yale, not the Black Panther party." Following Mills was a black neighborhood-organization leader who condemned the treatment of Seale in the courts of Chicago; he also complained about Yale's patronizing study of the community: "No more research, no more human research, because we don't want it in our community. I don't want it and I'm not going to stand for it—no more!" The audience could easily, even automatically, applaud any knock at the university at this point and uproariously did so. Finally, a speaker for Women's Liberation called for the shutdown of classes and the realization that Yale women, too, were oppressed. She found a good deal of male chauvinism in the crowd. Her call for unity was not seriously considered and was followed only by this rally's loud equivalent of gentlemanly applause.

The preliminaries were over. Bodyguards appeared on the podium, most of them wearing dark glasses, some chewing gum, and all looking portentous, if not threatening. It was a false alarm. To the disappointment of the audience, onto the stage stepped a middle-class, middle-aged white man—Charles Garry. He clasped his hands over his head, smiled radiantly, and shouted "Power to the people! Power to the people!" He joked of defending Martha Mitchell if she were indicted by her husband for threatening to crucify Senator Fulbright. Most of the audience found his speech embarrassingly bland, but it was good-naturedly overlooked.

At last, with incongruous formality, Garry introduced Panther Chief of Staff David Hilliard. An earlier speaker had announced Hilliard's release from jail, and his appearance triggered a deafening eruption, joyous and total. Each "Power to the people!" offered in greeting by Hilliard was overwhelmed with a "Right on!" from an audience which sprang to its feet and raised high its clenched fists. To the crowd, for a moment fully united, Hilliard began to speak:

There is a very basic decision facing racist America as to whether we will allow this country to become openly fascist or whether we will wage revolutionary struggle to bring order to the disorder of this country. When black men are snatched out of courtrooms and taken to prisons, then brought before judges and reprimanded as if we were criminals to apologize for wrongdoings that were meted out against us, then I see that somewhat as a compromise. But there are distinctions between revolutionary compromises and reactionary compromises. That statement was necessary to allow us another day of freedom. But just because we were crafty enough to outwit the stupid, demonic persecutors of black people in this country, we're going to take the opportunity to say, "*Fuck the judicial system!*" Next time we're going to rot in jail rather than compromise! And that's my confession to Yale.

Some were relieved by this confession of revolutionary compromise—the fight against the trial would continue—but others could not grasp the difference between revolutionary and reactionary compromise. After much applause and a short pause,

Hilliard continued. For the many who expected stormy rhetoric building up to a strike call, a disappointment was in store: "We have a revolutionary brother in Berkeley [California]. The brother is charged with four counts of attempted murder of four pigs. And I don't think that's wrong. Because everybody knows that pigs are depraved traducers that violate the lives of human beings and that there ain't nothing wrong with taking the life of a motherfucking pig!"

Scattered applause was overwhelmed by loud boos as a large portion of the crowd reacted against the reference to killing a "pig." The unfortunate phrase was as natural to Hilliard as "If I am elected" is to leaders of other kinds of parties, but the fragile entente between Bulldog and Panther was almost destroyed by it. Hilliard was disappointed and angered. His inflammatory rhetoric had been booed before, but Panthers were accustomed to a warm response from student audiences. This crowd was comparatively cold and legalistic, and the Panthers would have been better served if Hilliard had confined himself to constructive suggestions for action. The Panthers were unwise to have him speak instead of Miranda, who was used to the romantic yet critical nature of Yale audiences, but as the highest-ranking-Panther-not-in-jail-or-exile, Hilliard had taken precedence. The last minute change came as a surprise even to Kenneth Mills, one of the organizers of the meeting:

The meeting changed in its tenor and in its purpose once the release of the two people in contempt was secured and they were coming to speak. The original idea was that blacks would just unfurl their demands, make known their demands, call for the moratorium, and that type of thing. The suggestion was, at that point from the Panthers, that Miranda would give a talk similar to his performance at Battell Chapel. Given the degree of manipulation involved, he would have been a more skillful articulator of certain themes that were appealing to Yalies. Hilliard had just come out of jail. He was in the incredible position, you have to remember, that he was not going to be publicly grateful to Yale—of all places in his conception of things—for his release. That would be to be mealy-mouthed to a degree that was incompatible with his general political stance. So, while owing his release, I think, in some measure to Yale's intervention, he had at the same time to take a sort of strong stand. He was hardly going to come there and tell Yalies, "You've been so lovely. You've been so wonderful. I thank you very much for having secured my release. You've been a divine audience." That sort of Duke Ellington wrap-up was not going to be Hilliard's performance that evening. So he was caught in that contradiction of owing his release to Yale, but damned if he was going to be publicly whore-mouthed about it. So he took this incredible stand of launching an attack upon Yalies. There is a degree of hideousness about race relationships in this society that was fully operative in that meeting.

Some have contended that Hilliard's subsequent attack on the audience was preplanned and calculated—as he later implied—to clear the air for a more secure and easy unity. The boos continued, curiously intense, and Hilliard went on: "That's the best thing that happened here tonight. Those boos. Because you give me room to tell you people my real feelings. . . . I knew you motherfuckers were racist. I didn't have any doubts." Louder boos followed, and Hilliard retorted:

Boo me right out of this motherfucker! Boo me right back to Litchfield jail! Go boo me again, racists! . . . Go back to your humanities classes, go back to your psychology classes, or your English 3, or whatever it is. Because we know this is a real situation—because we're suffering. We're dying in the streets; we're facing the threat of torture in the electric chair, and I say Yale has a long way to go if they don't think we're hostile and that we're not angered by the inactivity of a bunch of young, stupid motherfuckers that boo me when I speak about killing pigs. I say fuck you!

But the audience continued booing. Hilliard shouted back: "Boo. Boo. Boo. Boo Ho Chi Minh! Boo the Koreans! Boo the Latin Americans! Boo the Africans! Boo all the suffering blacks in this country! You're a goddam fool if you think I'm going to stand up here and let a bunch of so-called pacifists, you violent motherfuckers, boo me without getting violent with you!"

The crowd's anger abated. Hillard had attacked their complacency, an approach that they could more easily understand. He continued: "Because . . . because I understand that although you don't agree with what I have to say, you should be intelligent enough to tolerate that other than boo me." The black students rose as a group to applaud; scattered whites stood up as well. There was a feeling of relief, of release from that which, in their sense of guilt, the whites regarded as well-deserved chastisement. Hilliard made a statement about the inevitability of race war in the United States and then qualified it: "I think such a war might just be headed off, but that statement is supported when you all boo me. If there's any assassinators in the audience, if there's anyone crazy enough to come up here and supplant that booing by sticking a dagger in my back or shooting me in the head with a . . . magnum, then let's do that, because I know that will be the one spark that will set off the reaction that will civilize racists in this country and hopefully in the motherfucking world."

Hilliard broke off for a quick strategy conference, returning to the podium almost immediately. "Now you got me talking like a crazy nigger—you got me talking like your mothers and fathers talk to you. I've called you everything but long-haired hippies. . . . And now I want to compound my sin by calling you long-haired, hippie, crazy, Yale motherfuckers. Fuck you." All booing ended as Hilliard held out his arms: "I didn't mean any of that. I take it all back, everything I said to you. On the grounds that you repudiate your boos. Power to the people! Power to the people!" Most responded positively. There was even more intensity and unity displayed by those who rose and applauded than had been evident when Hilliard was introduced. Still, there remained patches of self-conscious silence from those who had felt the hand of manipulation, either explicitly or unconsciously. Many felt drained and exhausted by an emotional reproach which did not suggest any clear direction for action. Kenneth Mills, who did not altogether approve of the type of speech given by Hilliard, took a pedagogic view:

It's not my style, and I don't think it particularly generates any kind of possible rapprochement between blacks and whites who may at any point be able to work together on a particular thing. So, it's not a question of blaming Yalies or blaming Hillard, it's a question of recognizing the reality of racism in the United States. It makes it virtually impossible for the groups to get together in the context of that accumulated history of guilt, of fear, of masochism, of self-doubt, of just hideous and ugly emotions coming right out into the open. I don't mind the emotions coming out into the open—better they come out into the open than remain repressed. At the same time, their being made public does not detract from their horrendousness. I didn't feel I could function very much in that context that night, and I didn't think that it would lead Yale students to grasp any other issues involved. It would either lead them into an emotional intransigence, or an emotional wallowing in guilt, self-hatred, and those emotions that I find to be the most debilitating range of emotions that I know. Either way—either through intransigence or dismissing Hilliard with arrogance, or, on the other hand, saying, "Beat me, I'm guilty"—would not have made it possible for Yale students really to begin taking stock of themselves, of their environment and society—the kind of thing that I was more interested in.

61

After Hilliard's attempt at reconciliation, the audience witnessed some genuine violence which nearly turned the meeting into a riot. A white-shirted white man was caught in a circle of Hilliard's bodyguards, and the crowd to the rear of the platform stood up, shocked at what appeared to be the beating of a helpless person. One spectator has said that the man emerged from the crowd after Hilliard dared someone to come up on the stage to stab him, and the intruder was subsequently kicked and stomped about the head and stomach. Kenneth Mills intervened with some students to put a stop to it, while Hilliard announced that a "reactionary has just been prevented from taking over the platform." Some thought that Hilliard's dare had been taken seriously—or that an objection had been raised to the close control of the proceedings. Mills himself later explained that the vicious reaction of Hilliard's bodyguards was

a classic thing in miniature about the U.S. of A. What happened was that Hilliard was standing on the platform speaking. There was a degree of booing of him, and his counter-booing of his audience, and stuff like this. A person, white to all appearances, to the Panther bodyguard, starts making his way toward the podium. Now you must remember that, for most black people, Malcolm X had been shot at a public meeting; King had been shot. The history of violence, the history of interracial conflict, the history of fear generated in these people not paranoia, but what to my mind was justifiable, yet unfortunate, suspicion. They are not Yale intellectuals, they are just nitty-gritty people from the streets who responded, absolutely and spontaneously, to defend Hilliard from what they thought to be a possible attacker, and they just jumped on him. They were stomping him, in actual fact. *I* didn't think he was coming up to kill Hilliard, but my perceptions are not important, because my perceptions would be based upon a different experience from street blacks. They just reacted with the sense that this was a threatening situation to one of their beloved leaders and reacted very sharply.

The white man, released by the bodyguards, wandered around in a dazed and disoriented manner and the crowd continued to boo. Hilliard responded defensively: "I think that was a humane response to all those who try to block the legitimate struggle of black people in this country. I think that anybody who takes the opportunity to come up here and run me or any other individual off the platform deserves that kind of treatment—and if they don't want that, then keep their motherfucking asses down." Louder boos came after this, and Hilliard reminded Yalies that it was important in a democracy to tolerate other people's opinions.

He then began speaking in a lighter vein: "It's lucky I haven't been smoking any marijuana or LSD because I would have beat this motherfucker to death." This did not work either; a solitary, disdainful "boo" was the only reply. Hilliard responded in kind. Denouncing Yalies as false revolutionaries who only wanted to be entertained, he ended with a shout: "Fuck you! All power to all those except those who want to act like a bunch of goddam racists!" Aside, to his bodyguard, he added, "Kick *all* these motherfuckers' asses."

Kenneth Mills, in an attempt to salvage the rally, virtually took control of the proceedings. He was not entirely in step with any one portion of the crowd, although he appeared to be more the black radical than the Yale professor in this particular situation: "This meeting was scheduled by the Moratorium Committee. We did not schedule it as a debate." Mills was drowned out by cries of "Let the man speak," some polite and curious and some angrily mocking, but he was quickly able to regain the initiative: "Nevertheless,"—the pause had been short and the transition smooth—"this particular gentleman may speak and after that we shall get back to the business for which this meeting was called." Mills suddenly found himself a lonely mediator between the blacks around the podium and the white audience:

Once he [the white man] insisted upon speaking, I was aware, again, of a contradiction between the blacks sort of hating this guy's intervention and the whites reacting out of a very different perspective, which was: each person should be free to speak and to be heard, the constitutional right to free speech, that type of thing. It seemed to me just completely catastrophic at that point that the two things couldn't meet. Most of the black community people who ran that meeting wouldn't have had a chance. He might have lost his life. I was in actual fact the buffer zone between himself and the black group. Nobody expected the meeting to become a debate in that setting; however, one would let him speak. That was the point of my utterance—not to say that I was against debate, but simply that I didn't even see how debate could take place in a mass thing. Those meetings are not the places for debates.

Normally, most of the audience would probably have agreed with Mills. In this situation, the man was permitted to speak because the crowd felt the concession would compensate him for his rough treatment and enable them to discover from the victim exactly what had happened.

The intruder had to be helped up to the podium. He looked stunned. His clothes were torn and dirty, but he was not visibly hurt. After tearing up the papers on the lectern as Mills concluded his remarks, he simply stood there without speaking. After a few minutes of nonplused silence, jeers began. At one point, when he blew on the microphone, there was a little applause. More silence was followed by his scratching on the transmitter. At last he spoke, with a strong accent, audible only to some and understandable to fewer: "A small step for mankind, a big step for me—whatever that implies or means or invokes . . . ." Whispers passed through the crowd. There was uneasy, condescending laughter and then another strained silence, broken by the command: "Louder!" He answered with more rambling talk, something about his mother, and something like, "It's all happening again." Finally: "This is a privileged position I have at the moment. Of course, I'm hopeful that I'm worthy." It was very bizarre and very painful.

A thin, professorial man wearing glasses approached him—not Kenneth Mills this time, but someone from the audience. "I'm Ken Keniston," he said. "I'm a psychologist. I think this fellow is in trouble." In reply came one of the most trenchant comments of the evening: "I'm not in trouble," the man said. "I think it is you who are in trouble. I think it is all of you."

Keniston, a professor of psychology in the Yale medical school, was not convinced. He put his arm around the man and addressed the audience: "I'm going to ask all of you for the greatest understanding and sympathy at this point—and silence and respect—while we try to help this guy." There was a sympathetic applause and relief as the pair exited with a group of students.*

---

*Robert Brustein, dean of the Yale drama school, later attacked Keniston for not giving the man further psychological "help." Pointing out that Keniston's instant diagnosis could with equal justification have been applied to Hilliard, Brustein asserted that the action was motivated by "a desire to let the meeting proceed without interruption"—which made it "tactical" and "political." When Brustein called a few days after the meeting, Keniston explained that he had learned from friends of the emotionally distraught young man (who was a Lebanese architecture student) that they had been concerned about the student's psychological condition for weeks; he added that he had seen no evidence that any physical injury was the cause of the bizarre behavior on the podium. Keniston asked the student's friends not to leave the man alone, to take him to the hospital emergency room if

Professor Mills, undaunted, returned to the microphone to restore coherence to the proceedings and bring the strike to the forefront of everyone's attention:

> It isn't easy to deal with a situation of this kind, and it demands understanding and patience. I hope at this point we can be calm and get back to the business we are trying to deal with. . . . And that business of course for us here at Yale (my voice is going) is a consideration of what we are going to do about the defense of justice for the Panthers and to retain whatever humanity we still have left. A condition such as the one we have just seen is a kind of condition that can befall any of us at any time in a society like this. It really is in that sense something we should think about quite deeply. Yale is now the target and the question now is how to prevent that kind of holocaust and destruction that in many ways nobody here wants and yet that arises out of the nature of conflict and injustice in our society. I call for an acclamation that shows you are serious, and that the shutdown is *now*.

The crowd was not with him. Some took up the call of "Strike!" but there was no general acclamation. Another black speaker, as rousing as he could force himself to be, ended the program by calling for a university shutdown initiated through votes in the individual colleges.

Students slowly departed with shouts of "motherfucker" and "racist" ringing in their ears. For many it had been one of the most unsettling experiences of their lives—a nightmare and rude awakening combined—and it had offered no satisfactory resolution of a situation desperately in need of one. A number had seen their own emotional irrationality reflected in the behavior of the disturbed white man. There had been no strike vote—only a glimpse of brutal violence and David Hilliard's confusing rhetoric, along with Kenneth Mills's efforts to make it coherent. Mills himself was "so wiped out by that meeting, that I came back and went straight to bed, because I was horrified in some ways, and I just didn't feel that I wanted to deal with anything at all after that. I bolted the door with a chain, literally, and went straight to bed."

Such a meeting, in another time or place, might have led to an attack on the American Embassy or a Jewish ghetto. At Yale, violent extremism was prevented by several factors. The

he appeared to be a danger to himself or others, and to call Keniston if any help was needed. The student never sought psychiatric help, but he continued to behave in a bizarre manner and finally was hospitalized after trying to force his way into an art museum after hours "to look at a painting that reminded him of home."

moderates (in this case, the vast majority) not only were relatively dispassionate and critical; most of them sincerely believed in democratic procedure and debate. Only momentarily bemused by Hilliard's rhetoric, they regarded armed attack on putative symbols of evil as pointless. As a result, the rally, although it caused widespread confusion and some horror, had little effect on the advancing plans for a student strike vote. The twelve residential colleges—some of them now called communes—provided the opportunity for a decentralized operation by proponents of the strike. The common room or dining hall in each college was designated as the center for the community's decisions. College meetings thus held were a familiar thing: the afternoon before the rally, many of the colleges had assembled in their dining halls to discuss ways of preparing for the awesome May Day which loomed larger every hour.

A student strike was as broadly appealing as it was irrational. Considered as an action in support of the poor and oppressed, it eased guilt-ridden consciences. Moderates who were concerned about their lack of mature political feelings saw an opportunity for expiation. A strike also appeared to be the most practical way of staving off harm to Yale. Some moderates remained unconvinced, suspecting that the strike was called "to get out of school work," because of "a fascination with history and politics," because of "boredom," or because of "fear." Nevertheless, a large portion of them were sufficiently affected by the apocalyptic atmosphere to vote enthusiastically for a strike.

For supporters of the strike, the college referenda were crucial. Only a widely supported shutdown could attract the national publicity which both they and the Panther leaders believed was needed. They also recognized that, at Yale, it would be impossible to make a strike effective without a vote. The BSAY steering committee arranged for a "mobile unit" of its own members and other blacks who were "fairly fluent about the issues" to go to every college strike-vote meeting. Among white moderates there was no unanimity of feeling about the Panthers, so the students were assailed with more appealing themes—university military research, the Vietnam war, the draft. The blacks argued that the university had to go on strike, not only for the solution of local problems, but to focus attention on issues that affected all students. In short, the BSAY used every possible argument to help bring about a favorable strike vote.

In many cases blandishments were backed up with threats. College meetings were attended by a number of Black Panthers as well as an emerging group of radical white undergraduates who proclaimed the prostrike platform: "Yale disrupts reality!" "Shut it down, or burn!" "If Bobby dies, Yale fries!" Occasionally, a young Yale faculty member also turned up at a meeting and exhorted people to strike.

The conservatives were well organized, but they lacked the numbers and audacity necessary for using pressure as a tactic. Many who opposed the strike, including democratic socialists, were personally threatened by radicals, and they received little visible encouragement from faculty members who, except for the young liberals, rarely even considered attending a student strike meeting. The average student was confronted with peer pressure, threats, and concrete arguments from the Left; countered only by a muffled and defensive idealism from the Right, it was a difficult combination to resist.

At Berkeley College, the Ingalls Rink rally was followed by a meeting which bordered on hysteria. For the first time, moderates realized that "the blacks meant business"; radicals believed that their hour had come at last. One black girl in the college spoke in an attempt to tone down the sharp words of David Hilliard, hoping to salvage the votes of the more cautious idealists. After hours had passed, during which students seemed able to work through their confusion only in the form of rambling monologues, it became clear that no definite decision could be reached that night. A second meeting, the next evening, was attended by only one-third of the college. Conservative residents, especially, decided to stay away, suspecting that it was hopeless for them to try to exert influence. Most of those who supported the strike were present. Cries of "Right on!" and "Solidarity!" filled the room, but all students freely expressed their views. Robert Triffin, master of Berkeley, was distressed at the emotional oratory and stood up to speak. He was a short, graying man who spoke with a Belgian accent, and his voice showed the strain of the situation: "Do you know what you are doing? Do you all realize what you are saying? Revolution is not a game. You do not play revolution!" His words had little effect, and the strike vote was called. First, the chairman of the meeting called for a hand vote, which proved inconclusive. Next, he attempted to divide the voters, telling those who opposed a strike to proceed to one side of the room and the rest to stay where they were. This also was unsuccessful. The final expedient was to take a voice vote. The ayes in favor of a strike were sufficiently loud to put Berkeley on strike, with the vote count set at 101 to 30.

Throughout the weeks of crisis Branford College was widely assumed to be the most radical college at Yale. The master, J.P. Trinkaus, later stated that "the radical students in Branford were constantly in contact with the liberal and radical faculty, including myself." Trinkaus, a biologist, identified himself politically as a member of "The Movement" and once declared that the 1968 uprising in Paris was the most fulfilling moment of his career. Much of the radical policy during the strike originated in Branford; the college printing press produced many radical leaflets and posters, and Branford was the first college to be "totally liberated" and formally dedicated to the strike. Several Branford undergraduates who went from college to college presenting the radical case were frequently referred to as "the crazies." One of their most effective methods for winning over moderate   votes was to use the onus of unfashionable conservatism as a rhetorical weapon: "The people in this college are unbelievable! I've never seen such reactionary selfishness in all my life!" It is certainly true that they never saw such reactionary selfishness in Branford—where a favorable strike vote was a foregone conclusion. Almost every Branford resident voted, eighty percent of them in favor of the strike.

Branford was more radical and politically active than other colleges because the radical segment had long been encouraged by the black residents, by Master Trinkaus, and by several liberal-to-radical faculty members in the Branford fellowship, among them, Kenneth Mills. Mills had given talks at the college on university-community relations, and he and Trinkhaus had become politically prominent during the anti-ROTC agitation the previous spring. Formal and informal political discussions

68

were common at Branford long before May Day; thus, Branford radicals could approach the crisis with similar ideas about the forms that student politics should take and about how they should behave. Their attitudes were in sharp contrast to those of Yale SDS members.

The previous summer the national SDS had split into three factions—the terrorist Weathermen, Revolutionary Youth Movement (RYM) II, and Progressive Labor. Most Yale SDS members followed the policies of Progressive Labor, which was far more doctrinaire and tightly organized than the other two factions. The Branford radicals, because of their more easygoing, open approach, had something in common with RYM II, but they had no formal connection with the national group. Indeed, Branford radicals had begun to work together, in great part, because of disaffection with all SDS politics. Despite the joking name, "Branford Liberation Front," and a degree of Branford chauvinism, there was no tight political organization in the college; but their considered attitude about student political activity—rejecting such devices as building seizure, confrontation, and iron-clad demands—enabled the Branford radicals to take a leading role in the May Day crisis. It is significant that many Branford students, who would ordinarily have labelled themselves liberals or even apolitical, moved far to the left when they suddenly found their college in a dominant position.

An important influence on the college strike meetings were the frenzied reports of how other colleges were voting. This information was usually transmitted with the urgency of national presidential election returns—long before all of the votes had been cast—and often the results of one strike meeting had a strong effect on another. News of the Branford strike vote, which should have had less influence than any, interrupted the debate taking place in the Jonathan Edwards College common room. Several Jonathan Edwards students had been trying to formulate a specific statement of the reasons for striking, feeling that there should be a resolution stated before a vote was taken. One impatient coed at the gathering met this challenge as best she knew: "Why don't we just vote to strike tonight, and we'll decide tomorrow what we're striking for!" The notable conservative who had earlier tried to organize students against the strike stood up to answer her, but he was shouted down, and Jonathan Edwards eventually voted to go on strike.

The same trend prevailed in most of the other colleges. Feelings of anxiety and urgency predominated. Conservatives were ineffectual and radicals led the voting. The meetings, although many viewpoints were presented, were usually run by prostrike chairmen who gave the conservatives no encouragement and little opportunity. The prostrike majorities were usually large, but most colleges polled only about one-half of their members. Several of the strike votes were reported inaccurately, and a few large majorities were reported without mention of what a small portion of the college had voted.

Saybrook College initially took the same direction as the others. After the Ingalls Rink rally, about a hundred Saybrook students gathered in their common room to decide whether the college should go on strike. The meeting was confused and "tense." Radicals dominated the debate, trying to reconcile Hilliard's speech with the idea of a Panther-Bulldog entente. The outcome was the usual firm victory for the prostrike side. A few Saybrook students who attended were unimpressed; not content to accept the decision of such a small group, they drafted a referendum ballot and tried to word the questions as impartially as possible. The college was polled by secret ballot the next day, and those who did not respond were sought out and given ballots. The results were unexpected. Saybrook students voted against the strike, defeating it by a margin of 214 to 135. The decision of the rump meeting the previous night had been overturned by a kind of justice which was not unlike the justice for which so many believed they were striking.

Saybrook was quite alone among the twelve residential colleges. Nine meetings which cast prostrike votes the night of the Ingalls Rink rally were never effectively challenged; two other colleges voted in favor of the strike the next day. Out of 4,600 undergraduates, far less than half had voted to strike and not more than half had voted at all. These figures do not invalidate the radicals' claim that Yale College had voted in favor of the

70

strike. Those who voluntarily absent themselves from the polls have no right to complain about the consequences of their apathy. It is also entirely possible that a majority of those who did not vote would have supported the strike if they had been polled and abstained because they realized that their votes were unnecessary.

Nevertheless, it is clear that many of those who abstained from voting did not do so because of apathy. One aspect of the Yale strike is evident in the numerous political groups—such as the Party of the Right and the Young People's Socialist League—that felt compelled to take cover because of surprise, hopelessness, and fear. In the event, all of the strike votes were cast in the aftermath of an unsettling mass rally, amidst pressure dominated by radical students, Panthers, and, occasionally, radical members of the faculty. By Thursday, April 23, Yale College was on strike, whether it liked it or not.

DAY OF EQUIPOISE

Wednesday was the opening day of the flood of committee meetings, teach-ins, small rallies, marches, petitions, and picketing which would inundate the campus for the next ten days—and beyond. In spite of worked-up emotions and fears of violence, a festive spirit began to affect many aspects of campus life. Since the weekend, normal academic concentration had been impossible, but few feared that in ignoring classwork they were putting themselves at any great disadvantage in relation to their peers—which may account for the vacations taken by so many nonpolitical students. Panther-Bulldog tee shirts appeared and the mood of the strike took over.

The *Yale Daily News* carried Chauncey's statement that as many as three-quarters of the undergraduates were on strike. Teachers initiated political discussions and the BSAY interrupted every class it could. Yet education did not come to a halt. Elementary Organic Chemistry, an absolute requirement for premedical students, was attended by seventy-five percent of the class enrollment. In contrast—aptly enough—almost no one attended Professor Edmund Morgan's course on the American Revolution.

Although strike meetings were not confined to the undergraduate colleges, they were much less successful in most of the other schools. A new prostrike group organized by less than a hundred graduate students, the Graduate Student Collective, decided to coordinate its activities with the Yale College strike committee. The members of the Graduate Student Collective were far from unanimous in any of their decisions, but they did vote to strike and to urge teaching assistants either to redirect classes or not to conduct them at all. Graduate students in Spanish held a day-long teach-in during which they decided to "go into" the Italian and Puerto Rican communities of New Haven to discuss general problems of political repression. The drama school voted to "re-direct" its energies toward the same targets as the undergraduates. However, all drama and graduate school classes continued to be well attended, and the law and medical schools were almost entirely unaffected.

Wednesday afternoon, approximately a hundred people assembled in the common room of Dwight Hall. The outcome of their meeting was the formation of a new Yale College strike committee, which replaced the Moratorium Committee. It included representatives from each residential college, the graduate school, the law school, the drama school, and a hodgepodge of dissident Yale groups, including the Third World Liberation Front, the BSAY, the Coalition of Concerned Women, and SDS. This committee became the Strike Steering Committee (SSC), with William Farley, a black sophomore, as its chairman. It held its first meeting Wednesday night to decide more precisely on the reasons for the strike.

The resulting strike demands were based almost entirely on the recommendations of the BSAY. This is surprising, since the BSAY and the UFPD were maintaining their aloofness from the white strike committee and were satisfied with having Bill Farley as their only contact. The SSC remained unsuccessful in its efforts to attract more black members, and its obedience to the intermittent directives of the BSAY was an indication of the extraordinary credibility which blacks had among white students at this time.

The BSAY, and even the Panthers, wanted the white students to confine their demands to the trial and intra-Yale matters, leaving community issues to the blacks. Doug Miranda told a meeting in Dwight Hall on Wednesday: "Our first demand from you is not housing. We can take care of that. Your first issue is the trial, and everything else is secondary." The same day, the black community issued a statement which attacked the radicals at Yale and stated that from "their sometimes contradictory rhetoric and frantic posturing blacks can see that the white radicals are only different in method from their daddies and granddaddies in the callous manipulation of the lives of black people. . . . Their purpose is not our purpose and their goals are not our goals." Confused about its feelings toward the Black Panthers, the black community was confident in its opinion of student radicals.

Undiscouraged, the SSC hammered out its proposals on Wednesday evening and included a demand to stop university expansion into the community. The Moratorium Committee's statement calling for the immediate release of Bobby Seale was altered, and the SDS demand concerning Yale's apprenticeship program for the unemployed was replaced by a demand with more general wording. There were five points:

1. The New Haven Panther trial is taking place within the context of persistent and continuing repression of the Black Panther Party. The vicious and provocative attacks by federal, state, and local authorities upon the Panthers endanger us all. . . . We see any possibility of a fair trial . . . to be virtually nonexistent.

Therefore, we demand that the Yale Corporation call for the immediate dismissal of charges against the 9 Panthers and in so doing call public attention to the political nature of the trial. . . .

2. . . . we demand that Yale disclose all future plans as well as all land presently held by it or its agents for the purposes of . . . expansion. Furthermore, [we demand] that Yale pledge not to further deplete the New Haven housing market in any way.

3. Yale University shall establish adequate free day care facilities for her employees and the rest of the Yale community. . . .

4. Yale shall establish an adequate wage and workman's compensation and retirement plans for her employees.

5. Yale University shall cease and desist from all plans and construction of the Social Science Center and Institute.

Appended to the demands were several recommendations to the residential colleges: any group striking in solidarity with the demands should be supported; students' money should be donated to the Panther defense fund; Yale buildings should be "made available to the masses of people" coming to New Haven on May 1. These demands and recommendations were in some cases so extreme that the SSC would soon regret them.

The drafters planned to present the demands to the faculty meeting the next day, which was one reason they were formulated so quickly. However, they were also subject to the approval of Yale students, and when the SSC representatives brought the demands and recommendations to the colleges, there was a disappointing absence of university-wide support. The proposals were presented in common-room meetings and provided a basis for counterarguments which had not existed at the more "urgent" and simple strike meetings. The demand for an immediate dismissal of charges against the Panthers was regarded as outrageous by the conservatives and improper by most moderates; others questioned the validity of the tangential social demands coming in on the coattails of the trial issue. Countless concerned students, radicals and conservatives alike, objected to various phrases and spent hours rewording and arguing about the proposals on semantical as well as ideological grounds. Neither students nor the SSC understood that the BSAY preferred a vaguely worded manifesto that would exert a general pressure on Yale while the blacks devised more precise demands. The college meetings became a debacle of revolutionary solidarity. Some colleges voted "yes" on only some of the demands; others reworded them to their own satisfaction; still others gathered ten percent of their membership together and were able to vote unanimously for all of them. The SSC's first attempt to secure university-wide backing for a specific program had failed. The committee met again on Friday and Saturday to work out a remedy for this situation.

Earlier on Wednesday, April 22, a group of students had decided to publish a free daily report of campus events in coordination with the SSC. (Yale's radio station, WYBC, supported the strike, but the *Yale Daily News* was editorially opposed to it and remained so until after May Day.) The stated

74

purpose of the *Strike Newspaper* was to "provide a flow of information within the Yale community and from the Yale community to the outside media." The group established itself in Dwight Hall, where a printing press was available and where the newspaper's staff was welcomed. The *Strike Newspaper* began publishing on Thursday and issued a great deal of information in a way that encouraged the strike. Its very existence tended to give the strike a coloring of legitimacy, especially after the paper received positive support from the Council of Masters. Before long, other prostrike organizations were also assisted by the administration.

One long-awaited event of Wednesday—which many ecology-conscious Americans were celebrating as Earth Day—brought the Panther trial to greater national attention. The Yale Political Union, one of the few Yale groups that took any formal notice of Earth Day, had arranged a luncheon at which Senator Edward Kennedy was scheduled to deliver his first major address since the drowning at Chappaquiddick.* Well before the luncheon it became obvious that his speech would be interrupted by radical students, and the senator was forewarned. When the interruption actually occurred—before Kennedy had begun talking—it was anticlimatic for the organizers, though not for the audience. A number of the uninvited were readily admitted, their entry having been prearranged with the officers of the Political Union, while several hundred others were kept out.

Early that morning, a black junior named Kurt Schmoke had decided that a storming of the doors by SDS might be dangerous. Acting on his own initiative, he had called the president of the Political Union and offered to try to divert the crowd if some students were allowed inside to speak. The Political Union president chose to go along with Schmoke's plan, ignoring the objections of conservative members. A short banjo concert in Beinecke Plaza, followed by speeches by the law school dean and Chaplain Coffin, had been arranged as a way of diverting attention. With Coffin's help in using a bullhorn, Schmoke's method of averting violence was successful.

*Kennedy was still in danger of prosecution for that incident.

Inside the building, a group of black students, including Schmoke and Ralph Dawson, and two Puerto Ricans went to the podium. Dawson spoke about the usual issues—the Panthers, Yale-New Haven relations, political repression—and a mulatto student made a plea for a "free" Puerto Rico. Throughout these speeches and the pause that followed, the audience was extremely nervous and apprehensive. They were uncertain whether the labile campus was moving toward severe violence or an unwinding of tension—an uncertainty which they saw reflected on the podium before them. Earth Day and the national political issues surrounding it might never have existed. Kennedy, even more than Coffin, was clearly caught in a situation in which, liberal leader that he was, he did not feel comfortable. When Ralph Dawson had finished speaking, Kennedy tried to shake his hand. Dawson spurned him.

Kennedy began by announcing that it was "commendable these young people should be allowed to speak." After visible hesitation, he made an effort to face the complaints about political repression in Puerto Rico, but said he did not know enough about the Panther trial to comment. He did, however, strongly repudiate violence of any kind, declaring that he was an authority on that subject.

His condemnation of violence was delivered with such evident emotion that Kennedy easily succeeded in winning the sympathy of the crowd, and in a sense he instilled a feeling of relief. Regaining his composure, Kennedy delivered a truncated version of his original speech on Earth Day. The event is chiefly notable for its practical irrelevance to events on the rest of the campus. It was one more indication of the rising level of tension but had neither a positive nor a negative influence on the situation itself. National television featured the incident on the evening newscasts, and while most reporters concentrated on the interruption of Kennedy, they did provide some information about the turmoil in New Haven.

The same afternoon, Coffin called off his civil disobedience march to the courthouse, speaking to a disappointed crowd of 500 people who had come to Battell Chapel to organize the march. Brewster subsequently told Coffin that he, too, had been disappointed about the cancellation. A year later, Coffin said that he had decided to call off the march only after a long and painful debate with himself. He had "checked with some blacks in town, and they agreed that there was no real danger that we could not maintain discipline, be properly arrested, and go to jail. But the presence of people on the Green would attract the very volatile black high school crowd, and while we got carted off in a very orderly fashion, they might suddenly go wild, and heads would be cracked, and once again it would look like whites are getting off easy, and the blacks are getting picked on." Coffin did not concede that many people had disapproved of his symbolic march, but the indifferent reaction at the Ingalls Rink rally must have influenced his decision.

Coffin told his followers at the Battell Chapel meeting that Kennedy's speech, the student strike, and the *New York Times* articles had brought the trial to the attention of the nation. Furthermore, Seale's expressed hope for a fair trial and the release of Hilliard and Douglas were making the future look brighter for the defendants. Earlier in the day, during his address at the rally in Beinecke Plaza outside the building where Kennedy was speaking, Coffin had stated that the "atmosphere" had become more "moderate," meaning that a nonviolent approach was already gaining momentum. At the same rally, however, the law school dean's call for a fair trial and allegiance to the Constitution had been greeted by some immoderate hissing. Audiences sometimes cheered inflammatory rhetoric, sometimes booed it. Few people knew where things were moving. Most were biding their time.

Charles Garry, the Panthers' lawyer, was exceptional. He had had a hard day in the courtroom on Wednesday. In response to Garry's motion for bail for Bobby Seale, George Sams had described in greater detail his version of the murder and Seale's interrogation of Rackley before ordering the killing. Garry spent much of Wednesday evening in a local café with a group of Yale students, reconciling his statement to Judge Mulvey on Tuesday afternoon—in which he had expressed confidence in the court—with his usual vilification of American criminal justice. He now argued that his statement to Mulvey had been made only to free the two Panther leaders; any act that enabled one revolutionary to leave jail and be useful to the cause for one extra day was fair and just; even if the Panthers had killed Rackley, they should be freed by any means possible. When asked if the defendants were guilty of the killing, Garry made his denial without great conviction, contending that the question was trivial in the light of what he hoped to accomplish. Garry believed all words and deeds should be directed toward expediting the inevitable revolution.

Wednesday night there occurred another of the suspicious, multi-alarm fires which continued to plague Yale and parts of New Haven for the next ten days. There had already been fires at two colleges, Trumbull and Berkeley; neither had caused much physical damage, but they intensified the apprehension that was now gripping even the most level-headed undergraduates. Student paranoia was increased by the visible glow of fires in the "Hill Section" (a predominantly black area of New Haven) and by the smoke which sometimes drifted over the Yale campus. Who set these fires, and for what purpose, are questions with many possible answers. The most disturbing thing about them was that they were all unexplained.

For all its meetings and incidents, Wednesday was a lull between two storms. Most of Yale College had already gone on strike and nearly everyone was awaiting the faculty's reaction. During the morning, reporters from WYBC had asked President Brewster for a public comment on the events of the previous few days. But Brewster, too, was standing aloof, hoping that the students' fervor, which might be exacerbated by a public statement, would die down in a couple of days. In response to the reporters, he replied that, "out of respect for the integrity of the faculty," he would withhold any statement until after the faculty meeting. After the meeting, many members of the faculty felt that their integrity had, indeed, been compromised. However, they never openly blamed any one person or group, including themselves.

Chapter
5
The Faculty's Verdict

On Thursday, April 23, the Yale College faculty assembled in Sprague Hall to determine their response to the growing tumult. A strike against academic pursuits had been declared, and most teachers were coping with small classes and uncooperative students. Everyone knew of the predictions that upwards of 50,000 demonstrators would soon be swarming into New Haven. The demonstrators' attitude towards Yale would clearly be influenced by Yale's strength and unity or division and disorganization. It was clear also that there was a wider importance in the decision that would evolve at the faculty meeting—a decision which would define the premises for existence of a university threatened not only physically, but with respect to its academic principles.

Most faculty members recognized that similar meetings at other prominent universities had precipitated disasters, sometimes with long-term consequences. Brewster later explained this danger: "God knows, the tension was high, because it was just the kind of issue on which other institutions like Cornell, Harvard, and so on had split wide open, not only between faculty and administration, but within the faculty."* Yale faculty members were strongly opposed to any action that would damage their own integrity or that of the university as a whole. There was emphasis on Yale's survival, but survival without "too great" a compromise.

One measurable index of faculty attitudes had been evident at the regular meeting on April 16. That meeting had upheld a position of academic neutrality—or, as some called it, apathy. Little data on the evolving crisis had been available since then, except for the opinions of several deeply involved faculty members. The evening before the April 23 meeting, Dean May expressed his fear that the faculty might divide over the issues: "This danger has existed for a long time. I certainly hope that a split and polarization can be avoided. A slim vote on any issue runs the risk of leaving scars which will be difficult to live with in the future." Strangely enough, May did not expect the faculty to pass a motion on the strike: "Colleagues with whom I've talked understand some of the emotional reasons behind the student strike, but they simply don't understand against whom it is directed and what result is desired." Many of these colleagues must have represented the faculty members who were neither certain of what was going on nor interested in finding out.

The permanent Faculty Steering Committee, composed of three senior and three junior faculty members under the chairmanship of Dean May, had worked for four hours Thursday morning developing standards for conducting the meeting. The committee's chief concern had been to ensure that every faculty member with a strong view would have an opportunity to express it. It was decided to recommend at the outset that the faculty assemble as a "committee of the whole," so that a formal presentation of resolutions would not be necessary. Specific proposals could be voted on later in the meeting. The committee's second decision was to adjourn the meeting at 6:00, allowing the option to reconvene later if the faculty so wished.

*A year before, Harvard undergraduates had seized a university building and then were thrown out by the police; most other undergraduates immediately went on strike. At Cornell, black undergraduates had used rifles to occupy a campus building.

In the turbulent days before the meeting, two groups formulated resolutions for the faculty's consideration. One group consisted exclusively of the black faculty. The other group, composed of some twenty "liberal-radicals," was convened by Master Trinkaus at his house on Wednesday. A number of the liberal-radicals were among those who had deputed Triffin, Lifton, and Mills to see Brewster the day he appointed the Osborne Committee. After considerable discussion, a three-member committee, including Kenneth Keniston and Peter Brooks (a French professor), was asked to put together a specific resolution for the faculty's consideration. Before the committee was named, fragments of drafts had been scribbled down by several faculty members and suggested to the assembled group. Although he did not entirely agree with Keniston's views, Trinkaus proposed that Keniston be named chairman of the drafting committee.

Trinkaus's group reassembled at his house shortly before the faculty meeting to hear the resolution prepared by Keniston's subcommittee. They approved a carefully worded resolution supporting the cause of justice in the courts, condemning violence and coercion, and permitting faculty and students to modify class procedures and attendance until after May Day if they wished. Those present hoped to be in a position to mediate between the black faculty and the conservatives; none of them felt constrained to vote for their own resolution. As one member later summed it up: "We thought that we would represent a compromise, middle-of-the-road position. We thought that the right wing was going to be there in full force." Fearing that it was too radical for the majority to accept, members of the group tried to win adherents by spreading information about their proposal before the faculty met.

The preparations of the black faculty were more mysterious. Kenneth Mills, a member of both groups, attended the Wednesday meeting at Trinkaus's house and made suggestions about the possible content of the proposed resolution. In response to questions, Mills stated that, although the blacks intended to speak first at the meeting, insofar as he knew they did not intend to present a resolution. This misinformation may have

81

affected the policy of Trinkaus's group, but Keniston has said that he assumed there had been no duplicity involved—it was merely an indication of the frantic, last minute bickerings of the black faculty. Mills has explained that he was aware that the black faculty planned to meet on Thursday morning and suspected that they would agree on some resolution. However, he had not felt that he could speak for the group before they had made their position public: "Being noncommittal was a question of what I regarded as political responsibility to the group. It wasn't to obfuscate the matter, or to fool the press, or to lull anybody into a false sense of security. Politically one cannot, if one is a member of even a function collective, take on the responsibility of the group." Mills also pointed out that he did not actively participate in the framing of the Keniston resolution.

When the black faculty met on Thursday morning, they had a difficult time agreeing on a resolution. In addition to their concern for Yale, most members felt a commitment to a black community which deeply distrusted the university and to black students who they thought were caught in the middle. Brewster later characterized their situation: "I think that they had a hard time getting agreement among their own group on a single proposal, so I had no advance warning. They probably hadn't hammered out an acceptable compromise until the last minute." Despite their difficulties, the black faculty were able to put together a strongly worded proposal.

The misconceptions of Trinkaus's group about the conservative views of the white faculty and the widely believed myth of constant unanimity within the black faculty introduced a theme that was particularly evident at this faculty meeting—the confusion of stereotypes with reality. Most faculty members arrived at the meeting apprehensively certain that participants' behavior and personalities would be determined by their race and occupation; in nearly every instance this expectation was disappointed.

The final note in the prelude to the meeting was played by the students. At 3:00 p.m. they began to gather in Beinecke Plaza, half a block from Sprague Hall. The mood was tranquil as 750 people stood in light rain and listened to a speech by a bearded Panther named John Turner. Although Turner discouraged confrontation, he obviously was nettled by the reserved temperament of Yale students. "We're not out to provoke violence," he said. "The Black Panther party will not allow that to happen. . . . We'll let the faculty know that this is just the beginning of mass student solidarity—for the first time in the history of your gothic-style university." The demonstration had been planned to coincide with the faculty meeting, but since that meeting was not to begin for an hour, the students followed Turner to Brewster's house, where the Panther spoke again, this time from the top of a mail box. He was briefly interrupted by "Megaphone Mark" Zanger of SDS, who tried to interest the crowd in Yale's unjust apprenticeship program. Turner denounced Zanger as a provocateur.

After Turner had tacked the five newly formulated strike demands to a tree on Brewster's front lawn—campus police prevented a repetition of the original Protestant gesture of nailing them to the front door—the crowd paraded back to the site of the faculty meeting. Kurt Schmoke did his best to keep them calm. By the time the faculty had assembled, nearly a thousand students were gathered on the street in front of Sprague Hall and the city police obligingly closed the block to traffic. Turner spoke once more, deploring the absence of a proper strike atmosphere at Yale. He told the students to stop taking drugs and to "have discipline. It's the only way to become revolutionaries. There's no strike atmosphere here. The place looks like sixteenth-century Europe." Doug Miranda arrived and drew a fatuous analogy between the Panther trial and the faculty meeting: "The minority behind closed doors is again deciding something affecting the majority!" Though they sometimes chanted noisily, the mood of the crowd could best be characterized as expectant, curious, perhaps even respectful. On more than one occasion, the mob's attempt to drown out speakers inside the building was silenced by the majority of students at hand.

All moderates in the crowd hoped to exert pressure on the faculty, but their motives were diverse. Most of them now felt genuinely involved in the cause of justice for Bobby Seale and wanted Yale's official sanction for their involvement. Many also realized that the official faculty attitude would have a direct bearing on the May Day demonstrators' conduct toward Yale. Some, recognizing that faculty-administration relations during crises were always potentially explosive, felt a concern for the continued harmony of the university. Finally, and perhaps most importantly, a great many moderates were already uneasy about the strike which they had begun. They were waiting expectantly, hoping for an endorsement of their own suspension of academic work.

Inside, Dean May opened the meeting at 4:00 to a record attendance of over 400 people—approximately half of the Yale College faculty. He announced that the special meeting had been called so that faculty members could hear President Brewster's views and discuss the scope and limits of the university's institutional role with respect to current and pending matters in the community and state. May also said that only those who had received an announcement of the meeting were eligible to attend. It was clear to the dean that some of those present were not members of the Yale College faculty, but he deemed it imprudent to challenge them directly and immediately disrupt the harmony of the meeting. All but three of the blacks, who sat together in the front rows, were ineligible: one of them was Ralph Dawson, the undergraduate moderator of the BSAY; there were also some black leaders from the New Haven community. No faculty member addressed the chair in order to challenge these persons, although a precedent for such action had been established as recently as a year before. Dean May later judged it fortunate that everyone present ignored this obvious violation of the rules, for it was discovered that ineligible whites, less noticeable though more numerous, had also been present. The black faculty had decided to sit together to demonstrate what a small group they were, which they succeeded in doing despite their appendage of black students and non-Yale blacks.

As Dean May had entered Sprague Hall, Roy Bryce-LaPorte had asked him if the black faculty could have the floor immediately. The Faculty Steering Committee had earlier agreed that President Brewster, in accordance with custom, would have the floor first, but when May called upon Brewster, the president yielded and Bryce-LaPorte became the first speaker. Later,

Brewster assessed this move: "I realized afterward that theirs was a kind of tactic to try to get their resolution before the faculty before any other, given the fact that the black faculty were the most upset group." Perhaps Brewster agreed to let the blacks speak first in order to discover their position before committing himself to anything in his opening remarks. Most of the black faculty thought that their resolution would appear far too extreme for the traditionally conservative Yale faculty to accept. They were feeling quite jaunty, however, partly because of anticipated "theatricalities." After he took his seat, Kenneth Mills whispered to a friend, "We're going to be dynamite"—meaning that the performance would be memorable rather than effective.

Bryce-LaPorte spoke for just under thirty minutes, delivering a long and earnest preamble before reading the text of the resolution framed by the black faculty. He began by highlighting one of the problems which the black faculty faced at Yale: "Since my colleagues see me as the black person with the greatest 'prestige' on the Yale faculty, the choice of Bryce-LaPorte is an indication of the underlying problems at Yale. It would be more comfortable to sit with my peers and hear a senior, black, tenured professor with some administrative responsibilities, who could speak with the authority and security that this role commands." He went on to say that the Yale faculty, and especially the black faculty, was being watched by the black community. He outlined Yale's failings in the community and with blacks at the university, charging that the present crisis would not have developed if these concerns had been dealt with sooner. The principles of the American Revolution, as he understood them, were vitiated by Yale's aloofness in the midst of poverty. Obviously, Bryce-LaPorte was emphasizing community problems rather than the fair trial issue.

The resolution that followed included, in essence, the following proposals: (1) there should be an indefinite "suspension of the normal academic functions" of the university, i.e., "faculty members should suspend their classes"; (2) the university should not close its gates or take reprisals against students or faculty members who take advantage of this suspension; (3) a faculty fund should be established to contribute money to "financial aspects" of "the present situation"; (4) the faculty should give its support to the planned national conference of black organizations to be held at Yale; (5) Yale's relationship with the black community should be investigated by a commission that should include members of the community; (6) Yale should halt all proposed or existing land expansion programs not approved by this commission; (7) Yale should alleviate any further housing shortages caused by university expansion.

Although he did not use the threadbare word "non-negotiable," Bryce-LaPorte noted that his position was a composite one—representing several constituencies, some of them outside of the university—and declared that the black faculty were not prepared to negotiate away the substance of any of the proposals. They were not eager to win a debate by pragmatic concessions. They would prefer to lose the contest while holding to their principles: "Much of what is happening today is a part of the legacy of pragmatic compromises with regard to the status of blacks in the early American republic." Bryce-LaPorte repeated that the black faculty would prefer to see the entire resolution defeated rather than have it dissected and diluted. He implied that if it were voted down, the black faculty would leave for one of the ongoing community meetings, where they were expected to make a report.

Following this speech, the faculty, at Dean May's suggestion, voted to "adjourn" the meeting for five minutes while Kurt Schmoke addressed them. This formality was necessary in order to admit a student officially. May announced that a thousand students were waiting outside the door and that Schmoke would convey a sense of student opinion. Many faculty members had heard about the march to Brewster's house and some were frightened. "Whether the students were hostile, friendly, or something else, I did not know then and will never know," Alvin Kernan has said. "They did make a lot of noise, however, and hearing the roar of the crowd inside the room, sitting with the rest of the faculty, created some very strange feelings. 1789, I thought, must have sounded something like this."

When Schmoke walked down the aisle with Dean May, the room was absolutely silent. In Schmoke's own words: "Everybody just sat there. It was really eerie. When I walked in, there was total silence—all those people just sitting there. I had no idea what I was going to say." Contrary to all expectations, Schmoke began by thanking the faculty for taking whatever action had been necessary to allow a student to address the meeting and declared that he would not ask them to endorse any particular proposition. He made a simple plea for guidance, explaining that outside was a large group of dissident students who had marched from Brewster's house: "Many of the students in the group are committed to a cause, but there are a great number of students on campus who are confused and many who are frightened. They don't know what to think. You are our teachers. You are the people we respect. We look to you for guidance and moral leadership. On behalf of my fellow students, I beg you to give it to us." After he finished speaking, Schmoke went out and reported to the crowd of students in front of the building.

Since most of the faculty had expected an angry, militant student who would attempt to intimidate them, their response was overwhelming relief and loud applause. One professor remarked later: "When he finished, he was received with a standing, enthusiastic ovation, and he left in a very nice, pleasant way. My feelings at the time were: 'What a nice kid; isn't it extraordinary that Yalies can come up with a character like this in a situation like this,' for I remembered so well what types came along at Cornell." Schmoke's effectiveness among conservatives was largely the result of his contrast with a particular stereotype. Those who had expected arrogance and irrationality saw instead only respect. Dean May later claimed that Schmoke's speech was a "magnificent statement" and a "significant factor in the tone of the ensuing debate and the resolution that was finally passed."

As soon as Schmoke departed, Kingman Brewster delivered a prepared speech which included a statement that immediately became famous: "So in spite of my insistence on the limits of my official capacity, I personally want to say that I am appalled and ashamed that things should have come to such a pass that I am skeptical of the ability of black revolutionaries to achieve a fair trial anywhere in the United States."

When he had completed his formal remarks, Brewster reminded the faculty that the university could not contribute any money except uncommitted income to alleviate social injustice. Moreover, the university could not suspend regular classes and continue to maintain its educational obligations. Any action chosen by the colleges should be subject to these reservations; nor should anything be contemplated that might endanger university property. They were all under pressure, but if Yale set an example of coolness, the May Day events could be survived. Finally, Brewster said that his purpose in attending the meeting was as much to listen as to talk because he regarded the views of the faculty as important.

Brewster's observations were a critical influence on the faculty and, with their publication, on the national attitude toward Yale. His statement of skepticism about the possibility of a fair trial was at variance with his earlier call for academic neutrality. Brewster later attempted to clarify his new posture:

The [skepticism] statement was made in the context of two other statements. One was that the university had no business being a legal aid society for particular defendants; we could not contribute to a particular Panther defense fund, or whatever it was. Secondly, that to try to trash the trial was the worst way to get a fair trial. And having said those things, I didn't want anybody still to think that it wasn't because I didn't share their view that the chances of a black revolutionary getting a fair trial here are, or appear to be, worse than the chances of someone who is not a black revolutionary getting a fair trial.

He was attempting to tell the faculty that, although the university must not compromise its neutrality, he felt a personal concern for justice in the Panther trial. In taking this stand, Brewster was appealing to the entire faculty in a bid for unity: "I wanted to make it clear to those faculty members who felt that we ought to have a defense fund, or who felt that we ought to trash the trial, that the fact that I disagreed with both of those positions didn't mean that I didn't share their concern about the fairness of the trial. This was for the purpose of trying to convince, trying to unify the faculty." It may have seemed more imperative to Brewster than to anyone else that the faculty and the administration not fall into conflict. As president of the university, he bore the brunt of the responsibility for the safety of Yale, which seemed in greater danger now than on the previous

Sunday. Academic principles shifted to the back of his mind temporarily as he made his retreat in the face of a physical threat: "By the time of that faculty meeting, my principal concern was how to prepare for that hurricane in a way which would not invite successful attack upon the university from either inside or outside, in terms of its literal, physical survival, and physical harm to people."

Brewster returned to his seat amidst thunderous applause, after which Dean May explained the recommendations of the Steering Committee: there should be an informal presentation and discussion of resolutions; the meeting should adjourn at 6:00, reconvening later if necessary. May then recognized Kenneth Keniston, whose resolution had been distributed to the faculty as they entered the auditorium. Nearly half of the time allotted for the meeting had already passed, and the prevailing mood seemed far to the left of the Keniston proposal. This resolution and that of the black faculty were the only proposals presented at the meeting; as such, they became the focuses of attention during the two hours of debate which followed. The fundamental clash was related to two issues: first, the "shutdown" policy of the black faculty resolution versus the "redirection" policy of the Keniston group; second, the absence of a time limit in the black faculty's resolution, as opposed to Keniston's proposal that the university resume its normal business on May 4.

Conservative voices were strangely silent throughout the debate. A short conservative resolution written before the meeting was never presented, and no other conservative resolutions appeared; no one argued for strict academic integrity, repudiating any cessation of classes. There were some bad and several sufficient reasons for this restraint. Many feared that any hint of conservative intransigence would hopelessly divide the meeting, causing the black faculty to walk out and leaving the image of the university dangerously tarnished in the uneasy days to come. In fact, just before the end of the meeting, Kenneth Mills left his seat to inform Peter Brooks that if Brooks and his supporters persisted in their attempt to include a time limit in the faculty resolution, the black faculty would feel forced to leave the meeting.

Conservatives were also strongly influenced by the attitude of President Brewster, who had indicated that he wanted a solution more or less favorable to the blacks. Alvin Kernan has explained that "considerable pressure was exerted by the authority and the rhetorical power of the president himself, who swept along into this decision with him a lot of members of the faculty who probably, if left entirely to an absolutely free choice, would not have gone in this particular direction, but were almost certainly relieved to see the responsibility and the decision taken off their shoulders." Not only was there a tradition at Yale of giving the president a free hand and respecting his judgment in times of crisis, but many faculty members had never before attended a faculty meeting and did not know whom else to follow. Brewster himself responded agreeably to the suggestion that his influence had swayed the meeting. "Well, it would be nice if it were so. Sure, I think it was. I took the risk of much more of a steamroller approach than I ever had before on anything." Conservatives and liberals were taken by surprise when Brewster immediately yielded the floor to Bryce-LaPorte, who set the climate of the meeting. They were further amazed by Brewster's statement of skepticism.

A final, compelling reason for the conservatives' silence was the atmosphere of guilt and emotional politics which had leaked into the faculty meeting. All sentiment ran against any comment that could be construed as racist. The chairman of the classics department, Adam Parry, was a traditional, anti-Vietnam liberal who had risked arrest before it was fashionable, but even he felt restrained by the atmosphere: "It was a meeting controlled by fear. I suppose, frankly, I didn't speak out against the proposals because the feeling in the other direction was so strong that it seemed futile, and I suppose I was just afraid to." Although neither of the alternatives offered by Keniston and the black faculty was palatable to many faculty members, this widespread aversion had a negligible effect on the discussion.

The debate became a slow movement toward a compromise between the two resolutions. This began when a graduate student (who was ineligible to attend the meeting) pointed out the conflict between Brewster's statement—that, in keeping with the policy enunciated by Yale's Board of Trustees the previous November, classes should not be shut down—and the first clause of the black faculty resolution, which called for a suspension of academic functions. He then asked Brewster if he would not be likely to reject the black faculty resolution in light of this conflict. Brewster almost lost his stride. He riposted by declaring that he was there to listen to the faculty and not to impose his views. He added, however, that he would prefer not to issue a directive saying that the university could not carry out its normal academic responsibilities. On this point, it seemed to him, there was not much difference in spirit betwen the two faculty resolutions.

The debate continued, now in the direction of clarifying the black faculty's resolution. Bryce-LaPorte did his best to explain it, saying that Keniston's resolution emphasized only thought, whereas his emphasized action. *He* intended to continue teaching because *his* classes were relevant. A number of faculty members began to make statements that had little to do with either resolution. The Arnold Wolfers Professor of Political Science held forth at some length on the pros and cons of opening a university to outsiders. At another point, according to one witness, Erich Segal came "charging down the aisle as if he had been running around the block and happened to run into the meeting. Breathless, he ran to the front of the room and made a great emotional appeal; and breathless he ran back up the aisle." Like Kurt Schmoke, Segal insisted that the faculty take a definite position in order to guide the uncertain students. He did not express concern about the nature of the position.

Finally, Kenneth Mills rose to his feet and delivered an eloquent defense of the black faculty resolution, commenting on three aspects of it. Speaking of the Panthers, Mills pointed out that Brewster himself had expressed doubt about the possibility of a fair trial; it was unlikely, therefore, that fear of injustice would be dissipated merely by a pious resolution. Mills did not look upon the proposal for class suspension as a means of providing a holiday, but as a device for informing the public of the seriousness of the situation. With respect to the black community, Mills said that the Panthers and their posture were a direct outcome of slum conditions, which Yale must recognize and redress; the resolution's clauses concerning the community spoke for themselves. As for Yale's physical security, Mills said that an expression of concern for the jailed Panthers might prevent the university from becoming a target. That expression of concern, however, must not be a method of avoiding disaster without alleviating the existing problems. Therefore, the Keniston proposal was too passive to be compatible with Mills's aims. He concluded with an appeal to conservatives, assuring them that no one wanted to destroy Yale, but insisting that the faculty should keep its priorities straight.

Like so many of the influential speakers at the meeting, Mills did not meet his colleagues' expectations. His British diction and magniloquent style—combined with the fact that he had the substantial support of the black faculty—made him an extremely persuasive speaker. Moreover, he attained this stature despite the variety of roles which he felt compelled to play. He was one of the chief mediators not only between the black and white faculty, but between the Black Panthers and the Yale community and between the white students and the blacks as a whole. In this instance, it suited his purposes to give the black faculty resolution the appearance of moderation.

After Mills's speech, there was an interchange between him and Keniston which proved to be a turning point. Keniston remarked that there were differences, not contradictions, between the two resolutions; one of the differences was his declaration that students and teachers could hold classes if they wished. Mills, after visible consultation with his black colleagues, agreed that classes could be held, but held only to discuss the trial and related issues. This gave Brewster the opportunity for which he had been waiting three days. He said that he was heartened by Mills's statement that the black faculty did not wish to prevent other faculty members from using their classrooms as they thought best. He then suggested an amendment to the black faculty resolution, changing "suspension of the normal academic functions" to "modification" of "normal expectations" and altering the clause "should suspend their classes" to "should be free to suspend their classes." When Mills and Bryce-LaPorte accepted these changes there was thunderous applause from a once-again relieved faculty.

Despite the applause, many liberal faculty members continued to be upset at the prospect of subordinating academic work to politics. Unlike the Keniston resolution, which implied an emergency *interruption* of business, the modified black faculty resolution implied a *substitution* of political for academic pursuits. David Thorburn, a junior English professor, was the spokesman for the large block: "I beg my black colleagues not to put me in the position of having to say that my classes are irrelevant or are actually an obstacle to justice in this society; this is an intolerable position to put a colleague in. I ask you to reword this." Adam Parry felt even more offended: "A compromise was absurd. Either a university continues to operate as a university or it doesn't, and to say we shall stop being a university, but just for a while, compromises principles so much that it leaves no basis for existing."

Mills responded to the complaints by declaring that the black faculty was not attacking the integrity of anyone; whoever wished to teach could do so without fear of coercion, and the black faculty would accept a clause condemning violence and intimidation. Mills dealt pragmatically with the issue of the time limit. He suggested that it was in the interest of Yale's self-preservation to have an open-ended suspension of activities, since the university might find itself on a collision course if, for some reason, the students were not ready to return to classes at the predetermined date. He reiterated that the important thing was not to "get Yale off the hook," but to express conviction on the matter of racial injustice.

These suggestions made Mills's argument more attractive to many, including Brewster. They did not make it more attractive to David Thorburn, who had spoken in favor of a time limit. As Thorburn's speech had been interrupted several times by applause, Mills was aware that he had to mollify a considerable number of faculty members who agreed with Thorburn. Thorburn later recalled that

Mills immediately jumped up to respond to my objections, and he did it in a very careful, and I suppose you might even say a very cunning way. He began by referring to me by my first name. "I want to talk about David's concerns," he said. He spoke as if we were friends. (We are old friends in some sense. I was a

graduate student at Stanford when Mills was teaching there, and we spoke
several times from the same platform at antiwar rallies.) Mills claimed I was
misunderstanding the black resolution and their reluctance to put a time limit on
the suspension of classes. He said they certainly expected we would return to
normal academic pursuits at some point; he claimed he shared his colleagues'
concern for the academic mission of the university. But it would be dangerous
right now, given the inflammatory atmosphere in the community, to set a date
for our return to work. It was a very cunning speech, an effective one, and I think
that Ken was not being wholly honest. I think that even at this point he had some
expectations, not clear plans, but expectations of some kind that we might never
re-open the university that semester.

Long after May Day, Mills insisted that he had fully expected a
return to regular schooling after May 1, but he believed it was
tremendously important, in case some disaster occurred, that
there be no set date for a return to normal activities. The disasters
that did occur—the invasion of Cambodia and the Kent State
killings—were not, of course, foreseen at the time of the faculty
meeting. Ralph Dawson, maintaining that very few people
expected a return to regular classes after May Day under any
circumstances, suspected that Mills was debating tactically rather
than sincerely. Dawson may have been right. As early as the day
after the faculty meeting, Mills publicly urged students to
continue strike action indefinitely in order to encourage a fair
trial for the Panthers and proper treatment of the community by
Yale.

In any case, it is probable that Brewster had long since made up
his mind. As soon as Mills finished speaking, Brewster stepped to
the podium and declared that he was satisfied that Bryce-
LaPorte's amended resolution met the spirit of the meeting and
the needs of the present situation. He then took a step which was
rare for a president in a Yale faculty meeting—he called for an
end to the debate and a vote on the proposal.

Keniston, Brooks, and Thorburn refused to be silenced and
again objected to the lack of any time limit to the suspension of
normal university functions. Houston Baker opposed them on
behalf of the black faculty, and it was at this time that Mills
quietly informed Brooks that the blacks would feel forced to leave
the meeting if the issue of the time limit were pressed. Several
faculty members overheard Mills, but Brooks and the two others
continued to push for a definite date for the return to regular
schooling. George Pierson, the respected and sapient historian of

the university, also intervened to say that he had been caught short by the call for the question. He objected that items four and five of the resolution had not even been discussed and pointed out that many of the people present did not have a copy of it in front of them. He suggested that the faculty vote only on items one, two, three, and six of the resolution and reconvene later in the evening to finish the meeting. This was greeted by a chorus of disapproving shouts from the more impatient participants, the most prominent of whom, banging a cane on the floor, was President Brewster.

When questioned about his eagerness to end the meeting, despite the apparent haste or incompleteness with which the issues had been treated, Brewster gave an administrator's explanation: "It seemed to me that to have prolonged that discussion not only at that meeting, but to have held something over for another meeting, and to try to hold meetings between then and May Day, would have been a disaster, and would have taken us into May Day in exactly the condition I most feared, which would have been a kind of internal dissension and polarization. So there's no doubt at all that the steamroller or bulldozer effort was to avoid the necessity of having contentious faculty meetings between then and the invasion."

It was important to Brewster that a decision be reached, and he was willing to compromise the ideal of what a university should be in order to do what he believed necessary and expedient. Brewster subsequently declared that he had been delighted to hear Thorburn, only a junior faculty member, speak for academic integrity. Thorburn himself has commented:

I think Brewster acted wrongly by forcing a vote and accepting the inadequately amended black resolution. But it is important to see also that the primary responsibility for this mistake—I believe it to have been a grave moral and intellectual failure—rests not with the president but with the faculty itself. A president's view of the university and of his role is bound to be different from the faculty's view. Brewster's eagerness for a decisive action from the faculty in that meeting is appropriate to his function as executive head of the university, perfectly in keeping with his own temperament and character, and wholly unsurprising. It is the faculty that must be guardian of the university's moral and academic mission; its role ought to be that of adviser to the president. It ought to accept a responsibility to set limits within which the president should act in his executive capacity. There are times when a faculty can best serve its president by opposing him, by making clear that his inclinations in a given instance compromise the faculty's sense of what a university essentially stands for. I don't see why one should expect an executive officer to be more sensitive to such moral and philosophical issues than a faculty of teachers and scholars.

The faculty narrowly voted down Keniston's time limit amendment, to the surprise and disappointment of the young liberals who had supported it. It was no surprise to anyone when the faculty passed the rephrased black faculty resolution by an overwhelming voice vote. After the vote, there was some discussion about the meaning of certain sections of the resolution, and it was agreed that a committee should be set up to solve these problems. Thereupon, two-and-a-half hours after assembling, the faculty adjourned.

A sprinkling of students applauded as the faculty filed out of the building. Alexander Bickel, who was to defend the publication of the "Pentagon Papers" before the Supreme Court a year later, recalls having felt "ashamed" when he walked through the crowd of applauding students—because he had voted in favor of the resolution a few minutes before. Many other professors who had voted against the resolution felt that it had been railroaded through a meeting which was too large and too brief for proper deliberation. Master Trinkaus, however, was so proud of the faculty's action that he read the resolution to listening students on the steps of Sprague Hall.

What really had happened at the faculty meeting? Kenneth Mills soon asserted that the black faculty "knew what they went in for and by and large they got it. For several reasons the president of the university joined them, but this is not because he co-opted their efforts, but because of his own set of strategic plans." Mills was both wrong and right. The black faculty did bring about a disruption of the normal functions of the university. President Brewster did prod the black faculty toward moderation by having them alter the demand for class suspension. Whether the black faculty or Brewster had more impact, it remains obvious that the white faculty voted overwhelmingly to compromise the neutrality of the university. In response to intimidation, they had placed themselves in the hands of an administrator who, in the crunch, took a strictly pragmatic view of his duties as the head of an academic institution. It was an inevitable consequence of the faculty's narrow view of academic responsibility.

————————

Immediately after the meeting, Brewster and Chauncey hurried to City Hall to meet with Mayor Bartholomew Guida and Police Chief Ahern. One reason Brewster had been so eager to end the faculty meeting was that he had agreed to meet Mayor Guida at 6:00, and the delay of more than half an hour did nothing to soften the mayor's habitual hostility toward the university. Guida had told Ahern that it was extremely important to keep secret from Brewster most of the city's plans for the May Day rally, although few plans had been worked out or agreed upon by Ahern and the mayor. Just what interaction occurred between the two men remains uncertain, but neither of them was eager to cooperate with the other. They were together on this occasion to meet with Kingman Brewster.

When President Brewster, with his overcoat and cane, walked up to Guida, the tableau reminded Chief Ahern of "a medieval patrician confronting a frightened peasant." Certainly the mayor's apprehensions prevented any great progress during the meeting, but Guida made it clear that he held Yale partly responsible for the situation and insisted that any damage occurring in the city should occur at Yale. In other words, any unruly crowds should be pushed in the direction of the campus. After the meeting—the only time Brewster met with the mayor during the entire period—Ahern told Chauncey that, in view of the mayor's uncooperative mood, the best way to coordinate planning would be for Chauncey to remain in close touch with him during the next ten days.

Brewster went home to rephrase the faculty resolution and draft a general directive to the faculties of the university. He was assisted by Dean May and several black faculty members, including Houston Baker, who were the chief authors of the original black faculty resolution. One of Brewster's aides who was present was particularly concerned about the style of the resolution, fearing that, if the English were not elegant, Yale's reputation might be tarnished.

In his directive, which was issued that evening, Brewster stated that he had decided to "accept the recommendation" of the Yale College faculty "in the name of the President and Fellows." The following week should "be used to discuss and formulate propósals for action by Yale and its faculties and students to become more effective instruments for the improvement of the condition of blacks in America generally and the black New Haven community in particular." The directive emphasized that "there is no desire to urge, let alone require, any faculty to suspend classes." At the same time, Brewster released the text of his own "skepticism" statement about fair trials for black revolutionaries. It was immediately pounced upon by innumerable commentators throughout the country.

Earlier in the day, Judge Mulvey—after hearing Charles Garry's charge that the grand jury which had indicted Seale had been improperly chosen—suspended all courtroom proceedings until May 5. During the next seven days some Yale students and many New Haven residents silently withdrew. A great many others drew together and worked unceasingly to make the coming rally a peaceful one. Their efforts were not entirely successful.

Chapter
6
The Groundwork for May Day

The week between the faculty meeting and May Day was a period of relative calm at Yale. Many students, like the Panthers, were greatly surprised by the faculty's action and Yale's decision to welcome visiting demonstrators. Collective exhaustion produced a quiet weekend, after which opposing forces came together to prepare for the "invasion."

The preparation was marked by two signal characteristics: the continual vacillation of the general attitude toward May Day; and the movement toward cooperation among diverse groups. At one end of the spectrum was near panic at the prospect of widespread violence; at the opposite end was complacency, if not cynicism. The panic-stricken and the cynical kept to themselves or left New Haven, and a third of the students had departed by April 29. Most students, fluctuating between the extremes, joined the drive for cooperation with the Yale administration, the city government, and the black residents of New Haven, all of whom were eager to ensure a peaceful demonstration. Although the Panthers' policy was not yet clear, the black community had decided that a riot would not serve its purpose. This decision proved crucial.

May Day now absorbed the attention of all who had recently been caught up in the Panther trial. Despite constant teach-ins

99

and small rallies, the Strike Steering Committee could no longer generate interest in any issue beyond the big demonstration. The suspension of hearings in the Panther case contributed to the general abatement of a political fervor which had crested on the night of the Ingalls Rink rally. Whether they felt fearful, excited, or cynical about May Day, most involved moderates and a great many radicals were now preoccupied with the pursuit of pacifism.

As political fervor diminished, the number of persons involved in preparations for the rally steadily increased. By Thursday, April 23, a thousand students had offered their rooms to May Day visitors. Class attendance in Yale College was down by sixty-five to seventy-five percent, and many of the classes which were still meeting were devoted to inconclusive discussions of strike demands. On Friday, the art and architecture school resolved to follow the lead of Yale College and go on strike, but the graduate, law, and medical schools remained unaffected. Self-appointed committees had made frenzied but futile efforts to bring about some reaction in these schools and had arranged meetings for the next week to secure votes on the issues.

On Thursday evening, soon after the faculty adjourned, an old-fashioned, 1930s-style radical addressed a meeting of the Yale Political Union. Saul Alinsky's thoughtful discussion of the ways in which Yale students could react effectively to the Panther trial and improve the university's relationship with the community was a draught of cool, rational analysis at the end of a long week of emotion. Alinsky said that he suspected that there was an organized effort to eliminate the Panther party but conceded that his knowledge of the Rackley case was limited. He urged Yalies to work hard and in a practical manner on the large number of issues concerning the campus and the contiguous black neighborhoods, and he admonished them not to indulge in rhetoric and theatricality. The Panthers, he noted, had been guilty of this kind of destructive indulgence when, soon after Robert Kennedy's assassination, they had depicted the senator in their newspaper as a pig lying in a coffin. Alinsky felt that such extravagant vulgarities had frightened away many Americans who might otherwise have been helpful to the Panthers. However reasonable, Alinsky's low-key attempt at consensus radicalism, like Edward Kennedy's calculated evasiveness the day before, struck most of his audience as a far cry from anything that a racial, revolutionary group could accept.

Whatever the nature of Panther politics, the first constructive action taken by Yale students in preparation for the big rally was very much in the spirit of Alinsky's suggestions. A canvass of the New Haven citizenry was organized on Wednesday and Thursday and conducted for five days. This "teach-out" had little to do with the May Day rally in particular, but a large number of students supported it, perhaps in the hope that it would help bridge the yawning "town-gown gap" and have a cooling effect on May Day. Over the weekend, more than 500 people participated in the canvassing of citizens in the Westville section of the city (predominantly Irish Catholic, Italian, and Jewish) and in an affluent neighborhood near the divinity school. Canvassers were given specific instructions on how to do their job in an inoffensive and effective way; their methods included makeshift haircuts, "brushed-up politeness," and the devious tactic of having a girl speak first if a man answered the door. The stated purpose of the canvass was to inform the New Haven community about the Seale trial and the Yale strike, with emphasis on student preparations to insure a peaceful weekend. A leaflet was given out which read: "Yale students are not striking in anger. Rather we are striking to take time to reevaluate issues crucial to all of us in the New Haven community." Canvassers made an effort to discover the community's reaction to the trial and the Yale strike and to give the community a means of expressing its own concerns.

Results were compiled on Wednesday, April 29, and the organizers of the teach-out claimed to have reached no fewer than 11,700 families through the canvassers, many of whom were Yale faculty members and non-Yale people. A large majority of those interviewed expressed hostility toward the students, Yale, the Panthers, and the rally itself. Universities, they felt, subsisted on public generosity and should be less arrogant. They misunderstood Yale's role in the rally, and most of them assumed that the Panthers were guilty. They expressed "confidence in the judicial system" and much "disgust" over Brewster's expressed "skepticism" about the system. Canvassers discovered a strong undercurrent of racial bigotry, which the official report described as "unconscious." These local attitudes ultimately had little effect on events near the center of New Haven, but they bear no small resemblance to the attitudes expressed by the townspeople near Kent State University after the killings there a week later.

Brewster, meanwhile, was becoming an object of disgust for many besides the New Haven citizenry. The same evening on which he announced his "skepticism," telegrams and phone calls flooded his house, inquiring if "he really meant that." On Friday, the *New York Times* editorial that lashed out at Coffin also included an attack on the entire Yale community: "Those students and faculty members at Yale who are trying to stop a murder trial by calling a strike against the university have plunged campus activism into new depths of irrationality. Some are so enamoured with the Black Panthers' revolutionary rhetoric that they reject the legitimacy of any court that might try Panther Chairman Bobby Seale." The same day, Connecticut State Superior Court Judge Herbert MacDonald (Yale College '29) released an open letter in which he called Brewster's remarks "an awful letdown to the courts, the police and the people of the community in which Yale is located. . . . If what President Brewster says is true, it is in my opinion largely due to the agitation, unfair statements, and accusations that have been made." MacDonald indicated to news reporters that Judge Mulvey had always planned to commute the sentences of Hilliard and Douglas and merely wanted to take a strong stand to insure an orderly trial. This seems unlikely and would have been strange policy for a trial judge.

The next day, Brewster—in a letter beginning "Dear Hub"— replied to MacDonald's statement and apologized for being "distressing." He explained that "when blackness and revolution are combined in a criminal defendant in 1970 the prospect of his receiving objective treatment seems to me to warrant skepticism. . . . because of a politically prodded backlash against both blacks and radicals." Brewster added, in an afterthought, that his own skepticism did not "rise to the level of assertion that fairness for a black revolutionary is impossible." Judge MacDonald was not mollified.

MacDonald's letter was the first of a series of attacks from personages in the political and legal world. The second came from Connecticut Senate Majority Leader Edward Marcus (Yale College '47; LL.B., Yale '50), who was running for the United States Senate. Marcus questioned Brewster's competence in his job and proposed a national poll of all Yale alumni and students to determine whether Brewster should continue as president. In a letter to Brewster, Marcus wrote, "Your skepticism is unwarranted—your comment possibly disastrous. . . . In my opinion, your statement serves only to undermine the ability of the court to process this trial in a calm and judicial manner. . . . The flag of anarchy seems to be the new Yale mascot."

The *New York Times* had been so hostile to the striking Yale students in its April 24 editorial that Bill Farley, chairman of the Strike Steering Committee, responded the same day with a letter to the *Times.* Insisting that the editorial, "Murdering Justice," was based on misinformation in the *Times*'s news columns, Farley claimed that the Yale student reaction had indeed had an effect in reversing the unjust sentences of Hilliard and Douglas. He cited the alleged mistreatment of the imprisoned defendants and the slanted reporting in the *New Haven Register* as other examples of injustice, and he argued that the noncoercive strike was giving students an opportunity to examine important New Haven community problems. Chaplain Coffin, similarly irritated at the *Times* for its coverage of the strike, took more direct action:

I called the *New York Times* and said, "I want you to call Reston and tell him I'm really mad, and I want to talk to him right away." Ten minutes later Reston calls. I've never met him, but we've had long conversations over the phone. I said, "We've had pleasant conversations, and long ones. This one is going to be brief, and it's going to be angry. Frankly, you've got a horse's ass covering this thing up here. This is not like Columbia;* this is not like Cornell. As a matter of fact, it's not like anything else, because the university is not primarily the target for this strike, but the basis for this strike. The targets are elsewhere. You haven't understood this. You don't realize that the university is remarkably unified." So he said, "Well, you do sound very upset Dr. Coffin. What do you suggest we do?" And I said, "I suggest that you send up a decent reporter first of all, and secondly that you give John Hersey your spot on the 'Op-Ed' page." He replied, "A good idea. I'll call him." I said, "When are you going to call him?" He said, "I'll call him right away." I said, "Good. I'll follow up. I'll be over at his house in ten minutes."

*Two years before, most of the undergraduates at Columbia had gone on strike following a building seizure and police raid.

Hersey decided not to write the article, and the *Times* sent yet another ill-equipped reporter to New Haven. Coverage became more favorable to Yale during the next week, but the *Times* now depended too much on Coffin for information and continued to put an excessive emphasis on him in its Yale reports.

The mood in New Haven was becoming less hysterical. Mayor Guida announced on Friday his intention to maintain "a climate free of repression and violence for the citizens of and visitors to New Haven." The announcement was partly an outcome of the meeting with Brewster and Chauncey the evening before, although Brewster, in spite of a series of telephone calls to Richard Lee, the previous mayor of New Haven, remained frustrated in his efforts to find out what City Hall was doing.

Chauncey had already begun intensive preparations for the influx of demonstrators. On the day of the faculty meeting, he presided at a meeting of key members of the administrative departments—such as health, food service, and the campus police—in an attempt to coordinate preparations. On Friday, he met with student representatives from the SSC and the residential colleges and assured them that the university would try to cooperate with the students in every way in preparing for the May Day weekend. His extended comments covered arrangements for housing in the colleges, student marshals, campus and city police surveillance, out-of-town news coverage, and nonviolence. Three days later, Brewster released a statement which summarized the administration's public efforts to prepare for May Day. He outlined plans for the free housing and feeding of "guests" and placed the usual stress on the importance of preventing violence. Both Brewster and Chauncey were at pains to emphasize that any college was free to close its doors to visitors and that the university had no part in organizing the mass demonstration.

On Saturday, April 25, Yale students organized a "silent vigil" in front of the courthouse. Some 150 people assembled on the Green to set "a precedent of control for the week" and "to demonstrate that the hysteria going around is premature." Coffin, who was associated with the vigil because it had been his idea a week earlier, now disclaimed any connection: "I continue

104

to believe that the time is not ripe for any demonstrations or vigils." He had held this belief since Wednesday. In his sermon on Sunday, Coffin announced that Battell Chapel would be kept open during the rally as a place of "disengagement" if there were any violence.

Also on Sunday, a discussion of Brewster's faculty meeting speech took place between two Yale Law School professors who were interviewed separately by the *Yale Daily News*. One of them supported Brewster, arguing that publicity "prejudicial to the defendants" and a tendency to give more weight to police contentions than to the defense's case "affects not only jurors but the whole court apparatus." As for the assertion of the *New York Daily News,* in its Saturday editorial, that Brewster's "skepticism" statement constituted contempt of court, that was "nonsense." The dean-designate of the law school disagreed: "I see no evidence yet that [the Panthers] cannot get a fair trial here." The contempt sentences "may have been overly strict," but Mulvey had "corrected the situation very well. . . . That indicates as well as anything else the adaptability of the system."

Such scattered events give an incomplete picture of political activities which were flourishing in the residential colleges, mostly in the form of redesigned classes and teach-ins. Significantly, these gatherings were almost always arranged by people in favor of the strike, and during the week a few of them set up a "Liberation School" to coordinate teach-ins after May Day. Most of the discussions concerned such topics as Educational Reform and Student Dissent, Extension Studies and Night School at Yale, University Finances, Yale in New Haven, and the Communiversity. A teach-in on The Idea of the University posed many more questions than it answered, something that was true of most teach-ins. They fulfilled their purpose of encouraging students to think, but they gave little direction to the thinking and were confusingly intermingled with artistic activities, such as plays and concerts, which had no political overtones at all.

By the time of the Strike Steering Committee's Saturday-morning meeting, Chairman Bill Farley had met with Miranda and Dostou, as well as with Chauncey, and had reached a measure of understanding with all of them. Farley and his colleagues were not certain that the Panthers and the NHPDC would work effectively to prevent violence, since the NHPDC was still loudly advocating a militant demonstration. Nevertheless, the SCC, which had gained much authority, decided to allow the NHPDC to use college facilities for "political education" workshops during the May Day weekend, "provided such workshops dealt with no topic such as 'gun cleaning and maintenance.' " On Saturday, the SSC's subcommittee for the coordination of May Day activities moved into a room in Dwight Hall, and an NHPDC member, who was a senior at Yale, acted as chairman of the group.

Since the day of the faculty meeting, the SSC had been working doggedly to make its demands more palatable to the huge block of moderate students. Farley and many others were beginning to foresee an end to student enthusiasm after the big rally and recognized the importance of strike demands that might have lasting popularity. On Saturday, subcommittees were appointed to rewrite each of the five demands, and on Sunday, after approval by the central SSC, the revised proposals were released.

The major change appeared in the first demand, which concerned the trial. The wording of the demand was modified, almost certainly in order to pull in vacillating moderates. Instead of asking the Yale Corporation to call for an immediate dismissal of charges, the revised demand asked for an end to "injustice":

The Black Panther Party is and has been the victim of political repression and police bias. We the students of Yale University believe that these conditions subvert the legal system as an instrument of justice and preclude a fair trial for the New Haven 9. We call upon the Yale Corporation and the American people to recognize this and join us in demanding that the State of Connecticut end this injustice.

Other demands were changed only slightly. Day care requirements were elaborated, specific community housing plans—such as the suggestion that Yale provide a five million dollar revolving housing investment fund instead of constructing two new colleges—were outlined, and new demands were included which asked for the establishment of "adult education and high school teacher training programs" and an unemployment compensation program for university employees.

The SSC's hope that every college would immediately ratify the new program was disappointed. The revisions attracted significant additional support only from the Yale employees union, which was "surprised and encouraged" by the students' sudden interest in day care and unemployment compensation—particularly since undergraduates had broken a workers' strike two years before by "scabbing." For the moderate students, however, the demands became little more than debating topics, and meetings devoted to ratifying them were generally abortive.

The prospects for maintaining support for the strike after the big rally were dim. The SSC had vainly hoped that their encouragement of a proper political atmosphere during the bull sessions before May Day would strengthen the demand-oriented strike. Their attempts to control the direction of events by picketing uncooperative classes and setting up small rallies were also ineffective. In a final effort to regain the initiative, SSC leaders scheduled another mass meeting at Ingalls Rink for Wednesday, April 29.

ADVENT AND PROPHECY

The Yale community entered the pre-May Day week under the cloud of a serious fire in the law school library early Monday morning. Equally disturbing was the theft of $1,200 worth of mercury from a science laboratory. Mercury is used in the construction of bombs, and many thought that it had been stolen for this purpose. There was an easy black market in the chemical; a larger amount had been stolen from another Yale laboratory two months before. The Yale radio station (WYBC) carried reports on Monday of the robbery of a truck containing 280 bayonet-equipped riot guns and eighty rifles in North Branford, Connecticut; the truck was soon found empty in New York. WYBC also reported the theft of forty-three large-caliber guns and rifles from a sporting goods store in nearby Newington. Inevitably, the thefts and the fire contributed to the rising feeling of "uptightness."

A few hours after the law school fire, the dean of the Yale Graduate School announced that he would follow the lead of

Yale College in modifying "normal academic expectations"—
although the Graduate School Collective was reporting a
decrease of only ten percent in class attendance. The collective
met on Monday night, but neither then nor later was it able to
muster a clear majority for the strike in the Graduate and Professional Student Senate. Nearly all graduate, law, and medical
students continued to attend their classes until after May Day.
The divinity school, on the other hand, suspended its curriculum
for a week and initiated fund drives and "communication services" in support of the Panthers and nonviolence. The action in
the divinity school typified the zeal with which the New Haven
clergy of almost every denomination threw themselves into pro-
Panther activities. Individual clergymen involved in the events
ranged from Malcolm Boyd, a popular prayer writer, to Yale's
Episcopal chaplain, who soon eloped to Australia with his girl
friend from the NHPDC.

Monday's most important undertaking, the formation of the
Student-Faculty Monitoring Committee, was the work of
Chaplain Coffin, who hoped the committee would be able "to
judge whether adequate preconditions have been taken to insure
a nonviolent demonstration." The fourteen committee members
included Coffin, Kurt Schmoke, Peter Brooks, John Hersey, and
Kenneth Keniston. Setting its sights, the group announced that it
would be meeting with the SSC, the NHPDC, university officials,
local blacks, and students, and that it would soon release a
statement concerning the adequacy of peace-keeping
precautions. Within the next three days, members of the
Monitoring Committee talked with everyone who could assist in
keeping the peace. They began Monday morning with a visit to
NHPDC headquarters, where Coffin questioned Anne Froines
about arrangements for the rally. Unlike some other NHPDC
members, who made no secret of their contempt for Coffin,
Froines was willing to cooperate; she worked with a number of
Yale students to organize a force of student marshals which
proved crucial in keeping things under control throughout May
Day weekend. Important discussions between the marshals and
the police were initiated by the Monitoring Committee, since
Anne Froines and Chief Ahern had not been on speaking terms.

The Monitoring Committee was able to communicate with the entire spectrum of people involved in the rally because of the diversity of the committee members, yet these members were able to work together to produce a positive set of proposals and do a great deal of useful work. The energetic leadership of Coffin, who knew a wide variety of people, had a lot to do with this effectiveness. Eventually, the work of the Monitoring Committee became a general effort to track down the truth of rumors and subsequently communicate the facts to all groups, whether the NHPDC, the police, or the Panthers. Working in small groups rather than as a full committee, members of the Monitoring Committee continued to give constructive assistance throughout the weekend of the demonstration.

Most of the preparations for May Day took place at the residential college level. The preparations were coordinated by the Monitoring Committee, student representatives from the colleges, subcommittees of the SSC, and the Council of Masters. The Council of Masters was the only important white faculty group concerned with the May Day events. Although the council had little formal power at Yale, it did some high-level coordination of preparations, meeting several times during the final week—in the words of Master Trinkaus, "like a floating crap game." The college masters held widely differing political opinions,but in this situation they saw the profit in working as a unit and were particularly careful to discover the viewpoints of the students. The council and the administration—and sometimes radical students—worked on problems together and tried to reach decisions collectively. Chauncey was always present at the council meetings, and Brewster often attended, mainly to be briefed on student attitudes and how he might respond to them.

During the last council meeting before May Day, there was controversy over Brewster's decision to keep Phelps Gate closed during the weekend. Phelps Gate was the main entrance to the Old Campus quadrangle from the Green and the symbolic entrance to the university. Several radical students were asked into the meeting; among them was Bill Farley, who assured the masters that he didn't want to "mess" with them and that he appreciated what they were doing. Following Farley, another student made an eloquent plea to have Phelps Gate remain open, saying that a horde of tired, hungry people coming from the Green would be aggravated by a locked gate. Yale must be open in every sense of the word.

This convinced most of the masters, but Chauncey looked doubtful. "You don't get blood out of a turnip," Trinkaus later observed. "Chauncey's approach was that of a careful and conservative person who was more concerned with security than liberty. He took a characteristic law and order stance, with little understanding of the political issues involved." Several masters were irritated that administrators like Chauncey had apparently arrogated the power to make major decisions. Chauncey has since explained that he had already decided, on the basis of Chief Ahern's advice, that Phelps Gate should be kept open. In order to have bargaining power, he did not tell the masters that his decision had been made until they reached the same conclusion. Brewster, meanwhile, retained the right to close any gate at any time.

The Council of Masters held useful discussions with students about housing, medical aid, and the marshals—but when they moved beyond administrative matters, the masters were less prudent. Representatives of the *Strike Newspaper* showed up at one council meeting and asked for $600, arguing that the *Strike Newspaper* carried impartial news of college activities, kept people informed, and prevented the spread of false rumors. The masters offered $300 from the colleges' discretionary funds and from their own pockets. They were able to obtain another $500 from student social funds, which were released with the consent of college student committees. A further $2,800 from student social funds was diverted to buy food for the visiting demonstrators. In its zeal to promote "communication," the Council of Masters implicitly supported political propaganda by an improper use of students' money. At the same time, the council made no decisions that were positively foolish, and it probably short-circuited a number of dangerously extreme suggestions.

Financial contributions came from a variety of other sources. The Yale baseball team contributed the proceeds from their Saturday match to the BSAY; a group of undergraduate poker players began giving the Panthers a portion of every kitty; John Hersey initiated a Panther Defense Trust, for which a benefit concert was held by the Yale Russian Chorus. Faculty members contributed $2,000 to their Fund for Justice, and the residential college system facilitated the gathering of $1,000 for Dwight Hall and the Panthers. In one college, after requesting $200 from a group of students, Doug Miranda said, "If any of you think this is a stickup, say so, and we'll talk about it." No one spoke up, and the money was granted.

Activities in individual colleges were too extensive and promiscuous to recount in any detail. Every college except Berkeley committed itself to feeding and housing visitors. Enough nonpolitical leaders emerged to make the necessary arrangements, and most of the masters gave these leaders a completely free hand. Information centers were established in nearly every college; all-night patrols of the basements were organized to guard against fires, vandalism, and bombs; illicit drugs and other valuables were carefully hidden or hastily consumed. There was a great deal of practice for emergency procedures which might be needed over the weekend, and a wide variety of people participated in multiple efforts to defuse the situation. Some were primarily concerned lest the demonstration be discredited by successful acts of terrorism; others only wished to ensure the physical safety of Yale. A large portion of the undergraduates remained in residence for no purpose except to share in the romantic aura of danger and revolution.

Initially, students asked for a medical station and a doctor in every college. The administration's representative for medical preparations pointed out that this would be a foolish watering down of available resources and persuaded students to concentrate their efforts on "comfort stations." The Yale-New Haven Hospital suggested that the Yale medical staff be assigned to the Department of University Health building—which was close to the Green—rather than to the distant Yale Infirmary. This was done. Medical centers were also located in a Senior Society building which faced the Green and in Pierson College. Davenport College announced that it was converting itself into a child care center where children could be left for safekeeping during the May Day demonstrations.

An important characteristic of the May Day events was the absence of any individual, innovative, student political leaders. The strike was run by groups and committees, and the few people who stood out performed their roles in businesslike, methodical ways. Kurt Schmoke, generally a lone wolf who was not an active member of the BSAY, calmed tensions, clarified the confusion, and participated in a lot of things, but he initiated very little. Bill Farley, another black who was of little account in the BSAY, accepted the position as titular head of the strike mainly because he could thus serve as a means of communication with black students. He saw himself as a moderator and a liaison, rather than as an inspirational type of leader, and he viewed the job of the SSC as an administrative one. The resulting political vacuum was never filled by any person or group.

The vacuum persisted, not only because of the moderates' preoccupation with the approaching May Day, but because of the continued, deliberate aloofness of the BSAY and the UFPD. The blacks spoke at public meetings, but these were usually their own teach-ins and panel discussions. They maintained a low profile, partly because they knew that bringing the BSAY-Panther differences into the open would only harm both groups. They also preferred to bargain with Kingman Brewster on their own, leaving the SSC to apply additional pressure. Primarily, they kept their distance because of the ideological diversity, theatricality, and political dilettantism of the whites. Prophesying that white political enthusiasm would soon burn itself out, black students refused to be drawn into the flurry of nonpolitical preparations for May Day which they feared were obscuring the basic issues.

Kenneth Mills, recognizing the probability that political activity would diminish, if not disintegrate, after the demonstration was over, had said in a speech on Friday, April 24, that the faculty resolution had not resolved the debate surrounding the strike and that after May Day there should be continued strike action on the "wider issues." These wider issues concerned Yale's relations with the black community, rather than just May Day and the Panther trial, and the BSAY and the UFPD were quietly preparing a detailed set of demands to be presented by the black community to Brewster after May Day.

William Kunstler
addressing Yale students
at Woolsey Hall on
April 13

Doug Miranda pauses
during a speech at a
meeting of Yale students

Bill Coffin delivers the first speech at Ingalls Rink on April 21; Kenneth Mills sits on the stage behind him

David Hilliard, accompanied by his body-guards, harangues the crowd at Ingalls Rink

Yale Archives

Yale Archives

Ralph Dawson rebukes the Yale
Political Union after interrupting
Senator Edward Kennedy; Kurt
Schmoke, holding a bullhorn, stands
behind the senator

Students demonstrating in front of
Sprague Hall during the faculty
meeting

A student receives a haircut in preparation for canvassing the New Haven community

Charles Garry speaking at an assembly of Yale students

Master J. P. Trinkhaus

Kingman Brewster holding his press
conference on April 30

Demonstrators receiving food on May Day weekend

Abbie Hoffman promotes his book during the Center Church press conference on May Day

Kenneth Mills points to the courthouse
during a speech on May Day weekend

Bill Coffin confronting a National Guard
officer after the May Day demonstration

Police Chief Ahern monitors the nighttime disturbances on May Day weekend.

National Guard troops advancing up a street during the nighttime riots.

Yale A●

Mills and other black faculty members continued speaking in the same vein at various meetings throughout the week, while the UFPD and the BSAY urged that constant pressure be put on Yale to make commitments to the black community.

A puzzling question remains. Why did the blacks not take drastic action, as the blacks at Cornell University had done the year before? Yale blacks disapproved of compromise and were goaded by the Panthers, yet by remaining quiet after the faculty meeting they unintentionally exerted a moderating influence. In part the black students were restrained by the attitude of New Haven blacks, who deplored the trial but were not strongly pro-Panther. Several times during the week it was publicly remarked that Panther aims and community interests were not identical. Physical clashes had broken out between New Haven blacks and Panther party members, many of whom were recent arrivals from other cities. Warren Kimbro's involvement with the party had caused great ill feeling in the community. At least one black community leader thought that the Panthers were a destructive influence on teenage blacks; high schools had scarcely been able to operate because of disruptions during the previous week. However reluctant they were to admit it, it is unlikely that many leaders of the black community felt any great solidarity with the Black Panther party during the May Day events.

One black undergraduate, who was a social democrat, later explained the important effect on BSAY attitudes of the black community's concerns. Black students, he said, "did not have that much affinity with really radical white groups, because they knew, and they also shared the same concern that I had, that if violence came, the forces of law and order, or repression of disorder, were going to hit the black community." He was also suspicious of the Panthers' concern for the black community. "I think the trial was quite necessary. The reason is that the Panthers as a group are rivals for political power and political prestige within the black community. They are rivaling one trend, which we might call the integrationist trend, and the other trend, which we might call the separatist or nationalist trend. If the Panthers were to learn that they would not be tried when suspected of a major crime like murder, what would stop them from starting a

113

reign of terror in the black community against their rivals?" Kurt Schmoke made a similar observation: "The community itself didn't want this thing. If violence had started, they realized that the repression would come down hardest on members of the black community. I don't think the Panthers have that much voice in community affairs." He went on to say that the BSAY worked with the community blacks far more closely than with the Panther Party during the week before May Day.

As a result, the BSAY never let itself be pushed to violent extremes by the Panthers. Not everyone kept his head—in one emotional meeting a BSAY member suggested that all black students drop out of Yale—but blacks had been listening to Miranda all year. Not only were they immune to the sudden enthusiasm which gripped the whites, but many blacks had been alienated by Miranda's politics. The BSAY cooperated as much as it could with the Panthers in political preparations and the channeling of money; full cooperation was impossible.

Finally, the blacks at Yale had an outlook different from that of their counterparts at most other universities. On April 19, at the nearby University of Connecticut, a white undergraduate had been beaten with steel bars by some black students for saying, "I hope Seale gets executed." Yale blacks were seldom subjected to such provocation and they tried to make it clear what kind of behavior would provoke them. Unlike conservative students, blacks did not feel disenfranchised by the Yale administration, for President Brewster apparently cared about their concerns. Their aim was to encourage a strike—though without always calling it a strike—and to control it—though without actually appearing to control it. In large part, they succeeded.

On Tuesday, April 28, there was another Beinecke Plaza demonstration, called on this occasion for "strike solidarity and action!" The BSAY moderator, Ralph Dawson, played an important part in the demonstration, and his statements reflected the black students' perspective on the immediate situation of the Panthers and the trial. The safety of the black community was the BSAY's overriding concern, and Dawson warned the 600 demonstrators that black students would "deal some serious political consequences" to anyone who provoked incidents over the weekend. He emphasized that work in the black community should be left to black students, promising that the BSAY would continue to push its demands after May Day. An SDS speaker complained that some classes were still meeting. "The classes are not going to be stopped by physical force," he said. "But that doesn't mean we are going to let them continue."

The supporting speech by an SDS member attests the variety of those present at the plaza rally. The previous day there had been a similar, though much smaller, rally at which some 200 people had listened to the SDS jug band. Overall, the Yale SDS continued to be unimportant and unpopular. The Panthers forced one SDS leader to leave town, but other SDS members may have been deliberately disassociating themselves from the May Day events, which did not emphasize the Marxist class conflict. This had been the attitude of the Progressive Labor SDS in many recent upheavals on American campuses. Progressive Labor often regarded blacks as a hopeless *lumpen proletariat* which was not worth helping. Perhaps the weakness of SDS at Yale—and elsewhere—was that it never understood the futility of imposing its particularistic program on people. Unlike the SSC, which had modified its five strike demands, SDS was not flexible enough to try to build up a coherent popular front.

The SSC met Tuesday afternoon to make specific plans for the second Ingalls Rink rally, scheduled for Wednesday night. The committee arranged an elaborate agenda of speakers, to be followed by a discussion of the five revised demands. It was decided not to risk taking a vote on the demands at the Wednesday-night meeting because, judging from the college discussions, committee members feared that there would be insufficient support for approval. Rejecting a student's suggestion to drum up support by a building seizure, a black community representative announced that the blacks strongly opposed the occupation of buildings, considering it a futile gesture which was no more than an end in itself.

Professor Ogilvy, a faculty representative on the SSC, provoked the liveliest discussion at the Tuesday meeting when he proposed that the committee try to reach an immediate understanding with Brewster concerning the strike demands. Because the students were still out of class, because there was enough of the semester left to make it worth saving, and because the potentially disastrous weekend had not yet arrived, Ogilvy argued that the SSC was in a much stronger bargaining position than it would be in after May Day. He believed an early agreement with Brewster would enable the SSC to call off the strike immediately after the demonstration and thereby block any attempt by the president to undercut the committee. If the committee members could overwhelm Brewster—Yippie style— by embracing him, the SSC would appear quite reasonable to moderates, while Brewster would look almost radical in comparison. "If," said Ogilvy, "we play our cards correctly, we can co-opt Brewster into the radical student movement. He gave us a strike; we will give him back his University. In so doing it is we who retain the initiative." Ogilvy showed some sympathy for Brewster: "We must show the nation that Brewster's statement on the trial was the correct statement to make, and that Yale is not just 'one more University down the drain.' "

The discussion that followed Ogilvy's proposal revealed some reluctance to be allied with Brewster at the expense of compromise and betrayal of constitutents and of the UFPD. A committee member referred to one of Brewster's chameleon-like qualities: "He's such a slimy bastard, he'll just flow with the slime." Nevertheless, the committee passed a motion to accept the "spirit" of Ogilvy's proposal and establish "negotiating subcommittees." These subcommittees did not begin negotiating until the strike demands were presented to Brewster on Thursday, which was far too late to obtain any answer from Brewster until after the weekend. By May 1—after the invasion of Cambodia— there was every likelihood of the strike continuing, but over an entirely different issue. Events verified Ogilvy's prophecy, and Brewster retained the initiative, displaying his usual guile in delaying his replies to an SSC which became increasingly weak and isolated.

Attacks on Brewster from critics outside the university buttressed his support among moderate students, who also felt besieged. On Tuesday a petition supporting the president's policies and leadership was circulated throughout the university in response to State Senator Marcus's criticism of Brewster's "skepticism" statement. Harsher criticism was to follow. Connecticut's Governor Dempsey said on Wednesday that although Brewster's statement "shocked me, as I think it did a lot of people in the state," the question of resignation should be left to Brewster's own conscience. United States Senator Thomas Dodd (LL.B., Yale '33), who was running for re-election, stated that he had "information and evidence that clearly indicates that the administration of Yale University and some of its students have been led into the position of helping a national conspiracy that seeks to wreck the legal process in the United States and to threaten the very existence of an American city and indeed of our whole American free society." Eric Sevareid, pontificating on a nationwide television newscast on Tuesday evening, declared that "a fair portion of [Yale's] student body now feels the springtime urge to prove their manhood. . . . They apparently know in advance of the evidence that the defendants are innocent, by some intellectual alchemy denied to lesser mortals. They have been aided and abetted by their president, Kingman Brewster."

Vice President Spiro Agnew's speech on Tuesday night solidified Brewster's popularity among moderates for the duration of the strike. Speaking at a Republican fund-raising dinner in Florida, Agnew said that he could

well understand the attitude of the majority of the student body at Yale University when most of the Yale faculty vote to endorse a strike in support of members of an organization dedicated to criminal violence, anarchy, and the destruction of the United States of America. And when the president of that respected university describes the election of a president of the United States by the people of the United States as a "hucksterized process" under which they could not expect much better, "whichever package was bought or sold," it is clearly time for the alumni of that fine old college to demand that it be headed by a more mature and responsible person. President Brewster of Yale has also stated that he does not feel that black revolutionaries can get a fair trial within our judicial system. I do not feel that students of Yale University can get a fair impression of their country under the tutelage of Kingman Brewster.

Shortly thereafter, Bill Coffin, in a moment of candid geniality, summarized his feelings about Agnew. "I pray every night for the safety of the president," he quipped. In this instance, evidently, he meant President Nixon.

Wednesday, April 29, was the last day of radical statements and press releases before the weekend deluge began. A student committee ordered food for 140,000 meals. Other arrangements for Yale's arriving "guests" were completed, policy concerning the strike and forthcoming demonstrations was determined, and self-righteous invective had one last fling.

Sporadic fears of violence were reinforced by reports of the arrest of two people early Tuesday morning for possession of explosives. There may have been a connection between the explosives and the theft of mercury three days earlier. The police had found smoke grenades and "chemical compounds prepared for explosives" in the apartment of the individuals arrested, and the two were held under $15,000 bond each. One of them was a former Yale student who claimed he was an ex-Weatherman. Another suspect remained at large.

At 9:00 a.m., between sixty and eighty members of the national media attended a press conference held by the SSC in Dwight Hall. Bill Farley read a statement entitled "Misconceptions about May Day, the Yale Strike, and Related Events," which emphasized that the strike was a reaction to the "injustices" suffered by Bobby Seale and the New Haven Panthers and to "the history of suppression and mistreatment" of all Black Panthers. Farley referred to the issues concerning Yale's relationship with New Haven that had been raised in the strike demands. He pointed out that the demonstration "was not initiated or planned by any members of the Yale community," although he stressed the general effort among Yale students toward cooperation and nonviolence. Calling upon the news media to be "fair and truthful about the events in New Haven and the motivations behind them," Farley concluded with the apocalyptic observation that this was, "hopefully, the beginning of a new day that will see the American Reality approach the American Dream."

At an SSC meeting Wednesday afternoon, the members discussed proposals for an undergraduate grading policy which would allow for work stoppage during the strike. They concluded that it was a matter which should be considered by the faculty rather than the administration. Some in the SSC felt that a revised grading system was irrelevant—that strikers should be willing to "put themselves on the line" for the sake of the strike demands—but they overcame this scruple and agreed that the proposal for temporary grading changes should be read that evening at the Ingalls Rink meeting. The students' sense of the importance and uniqueness of what was going on at Yale became evident during this committee meeting. Several spoke of the need for competent "historians" to compile a careful record. This is typical of the self-consciousness in most student politics; it is also typical that no one implemented the suggestion.

The best-publicized event of the day was President Brewster's acceptance of the petition of support signed by 3,000 students. The initiator of the petition presented it to Brewster in front of Woodbridge Hall, and a crowd cheered as he emerged from the building. Brewster, slumping with fatigue, could scarcely respond. After declining to make a statement about his detractors, he thanked the students for having "poured out such energy, common sense, and goodwill, not just to protect the university but to try to improve it." He added, "If we can get through this weekend, hopefully we can respond constructively to our long-range responsibilities as well." Brewster, at this point, was almost certainly more concerned about those long-range responsibilities than was the average undergraduate.

Yale students were not alone in flocking to Brewster's, and Yale's, defense. Prominent faculty members publicly supported Brewster, and several Connecticut politicians lent a hand. Joseph Duffey, who was running against State Senator Marcus for the Democratic nomination to the United States Senate,* spoke to students at Ezra Stiles College on Tuesday and denounced the statement of Senator Marcus on the ground that it inflamed "an already irrational situation in a dangerous fashion." Contending that all members of the Yale community were working for nonviolence, Duffey said that he hoped in upcoming speeches "to highlight the strike, not the demonstrations, and show that the general temper here is not as it is widely felt to be." Thayer Baldwin (Yale College '62), a congresssional candidate in the

---

*Duffey, a Congregationalist minister and the national chairman of the Americans for Democratic Action, defeated Marcus for the Democratic nomination but lost the election to Lowell Weicker.

May 5 Democratic primary,* observed that "to the greatest possible extent, peaceful protest is warranted in assuring a fair and open trial for Bobby Seale and the other Panthers. Protests, in the best interests of the defendants, should include all elements of the community dedicated to nonviolence." William Horowitz, a New Haven banker who was a member of the Yale Board of Trustees, sent a condescending letter to Agnew in response to

unjustified, irresponsible, and self-serving remarks about Kingman Brewster, Jr. and the Yale community. . . . It is perfectly clear that your Florida speech is a continuation of your systematic campaign to inflame popular passions against anyone dealing constructively with the problems confronting American society today. . . . I frankly do not believe that your experience as a president of a P.T.A. Chapter qualifies you to evaluate the contributions to education by the most distinguished University President in the United States.

The suggestion that attacking Brewster meant agreement with Spiro Agnew was sufficient to discourage many of Brewster's critics, but the prevailing mood remained hostile to Yale. Many newspapers around the country were more interested in responding to Agnew than in supporting Yale's president. The *Chicago Sun Times,* published by a Yale alumnus, closed its April 30 editorial, entitled "Agnew Off Base Again," with a crude declaration: "We submit that Agnew uses his mouth too much." Between April 27 and May 6, more than 1,500 telegrams and letters were sent to Kingman Brewster. Those supporting him numbered 1,012, those critical, 501; the alumni favored Brewster by a margin of 4 to 1. The White House was unimpressed; Brewster's name was put on Nixon's "enemies" list.

The common theme, by April 29, was planned pacifism. Even the Panthers came out as a group against violence. At a press conference, Big Man observed: "We don't want anarchists to provoke the pigs. We don't want a lot of pigs running around amok." Continuing, he read a collective statement, purportedly written by the jailed New Haven Panthers. The statement included the following:

We can't be anarchistic and emotional, we have to be clear headed and organized. An example of this type of clear headedness is the fact that Yale

*Baldwin lost the New Haven primary to Robert Giamo, who called Baldwin's supporters "a small clique of extremists." Most of Baldwin's strength came from wards which were heavily populated by students and blacks.

students cut their hair and took the time, to go into White middle-class communities to rally support for this trial and for the cause of justice in the United States. Breaking windows and snatching pocket books will never lay a foundation for the long, hard struggle ahead; politicizing and educating the various segments of the young, the open-minded and the concerned will.

The *New York Times* began to report student efforts to avoid violence: "Student emmissaries have gone to Cambridge and New York to plead with violence prone radicals and Weathermen: either stay home or come in peace. . . . All Yale student elements, including blacks, are apparently determined to avoid violence."
In spite of these assurances, said the article, the campus police were organized, a secret command post had been established, and plans had been made for a fall-back position in case the forward area was overrun. Yale's vital records and most valuable works of art were removed to new locations for safekeeping. Asked during the week what kind of formula was being used to determine policy, Chauncey replied, "We will protect human life first, essential services second, buildings third."

The Student-Faculty Monitoring Committee published its findings on Wednesday night. Stating that no known groups or individuals involved in the rally openly advocated violence, the report noted that there were still a number of serious organizational difficulties and warned of a dangerous absence of communication among some groups. The participation of large numbers of children and high school students was expected to add another unstable element. The Monitoring Committee was particularly fearful that police pursuit of individual demonstrators would not be abandoned after the demonstrators left the immediate area. There were hints that the Yale campus would not be considered a sanctuary from the New Haven police, and all were aware that during the Harvard Square riot two weeks before, the police had pursued students inside their dormitories. Although Chief Ahern refused to commit himself to any policy except an attempt to maintain a "low profile" during the rally, he later claimed that he had made careful plans for his department. A crucial factor in these arrangements was the position, next to the Green, of the Yale campus, which Mayor Guida had insisted should bear the brunt of any serious damage caused by rioting. In the event of violence, the demonstrators would be pushed in that direction, which Ahern hoped would minimize direct contact between the police and any troublemakers and result in fewer unnecessary arrests. When serious offenders entered the Yale grounds, the police were to regroup and arrange for any necessary arrests to be made later by plainclothes officers or campus police.

Ahern may have exaggerated his efforts to "educate" the police force to be cool-headed and neutral during the rally, but his arrangements were closely coordinated with those of the campus police, and low visibility was carefully planned. Noting that in the Boston riot the worst trouble had occurred after the crowd had left the Boston Common, Ahern decided to concentrate on dispersal routes. He attempted to keep a close control over his men, and for mobility and secrecy he assigned large numbers of them to sit in vans parked on side streets and in garages.

On Monday, April 27, Ahern had granted the NHPDC a permit for a large demonstration on the New Haven Green during Friday and Saturday afternoons. Also on Monday—in response to Mayor Guida's request to Governor Dempsey— the Adjutant General of the Connecticut National Guard had announced that 4,000 guardsmen would be "standing by" during May Day weekend; three days later Mayor Guida said that the guardsmen would be deployed on the streets of New Haven. The announcement came as a disappointment to much of the Yale community. Ahern said that he could not recall any other occasion when the guard had been deployed in Connecticut before disorders took place, and he stated that he was "confident that the vast majority of individuals planning to attend the events here this weekend are committed to a non-violent and peaceful expression of their dissent." Nevertheless, Ahern met with National Guard and state police officers to work out safety procedures, and two weeks later he said that the prior deployment had been a good idea. This points up the unusual advantage which Ahern and other Connecticut officials had in their efforts to prevent mob violence—time to prepare.

Ahern had grown up in New Haven, had studied for the priesthood before going to college, and had risen through the ranks to become New Haven's chief of police. He was hard driving and egotistical. He was also innovative and reasonable and

122

stood for an enlightened approach to law enforcement; he was soon to turn down the offer of an FBI job, having little use for Nixonian methods of preventing crime. Ahern's reasonableness was shown by his willingness to cooperate with Coffin regarding the proposed march to the courthouse. His egotism was demonstrated by his eagerness to belittle almost all of the other government officials involved in the May Day events. He portrayed Mayor Guida as incompetent because the mayor played such a small part in the May Day preparations. Although Ahern's protrayal has some merit, it discounts the mayor's concern with a great many problems—such as the high cost of the preparations and the very real danger of a political backlash.

A serious disagreement over their May Day strategy erupted between Ahern and the state police commissioner. Ahern wanted one person in command and low police visibility, whereas the commissioner preferred a separation of authority and a dramatic "show of force." The two men decided to have their differences arbitrated by Governor Dempsey in Hartford. When they met with the governor on Wednesday evening, William Ruckelshaus, an assistant attorney general, was present with some other members of the presidential "strike force" for civil disorders. Ruckelshaus made the surprising announcement that President Nixon had arranged to put 4,000 marines and paratroopers on the alert in Rhode Island and Massachusetts. This decision was purportedly based on an FBI intelligence report predicting widespread destruction in New Haven. Ahern later claimed that the strike force members at first refused to let him see the report. When he finally did secure a copy, he became seriously alarmed "about the quality of information that results in crucial government decisions. The report was almost completely composed of unsorted and unevaluated stories, threats, and rumors that had crossed my desk in New Haven. Many of these had long before been discounted by our Intelligence Division. But they had made their way from New Haven to Washington, had gained completely unwarranted credibility, and had been submitted by the Director of the F.B.I. to the President of the United States."

Ahern has pointed out that these inaccurate reports may have been sent to the president only because of the president's demand for information, and he has plausibly suggested that Nixon may have alerted the federal troops for political reasons. Nixon must also have feared the possible effect which his announcement of the invasion of Cambodia would have on a group of demonstrators. It is unclear, in any case, who first asked for federal troops. Public announcements on Thursday stated that the troops had been requested from Attorney General Mitchell by Governor Dempsey.

Governor Dempsey may have welcomed the federal alert, but in other respects he approved of Ahern's low-key approach. He took the risk of giving the New Haven police chief wide authority, and the arbitration meeting ended with an order by the governor that, during May Day, both the state police and the National Guard would be under Ahern's command.

The activities of Monday, Tuesday, and Wednesday culminated in the second mass meeting at Ingalls Rink on Wednesday evening. Approximately 2,500 students arrived to hear more about the plans for May Day, more discussion of the SSC's demands, and a new emphasis on the importance of continuing the strike after May 3. Kurt Schmoke, who co-chaired the meeting with Bill Farley, began the proceedings with an attack on Agnew's attack on Brewster. He followed this with a reading of Horowitz's letter to Agnew and the presentation of a petition calling for the vice president's resignation. Both letter and petition—which Schmoke said could begin circulating the next day—elicited a great deal of cheerful applause, especially when Brewster's name was mentioned. Bill Farley then read an SDS petition which asked that the meeting depart from its carefully planned agenda and allow open discussion. When Farley explained that there would be open discussion before the end of the meeting, the SDS petition was overwhelmingly defeated by a hand vote. Sobriety and order were definitely gaining the upper hand.

The first speaker, John Froines, was a member of the Chicago Seven and a group called the Conspiracy Eight—the Chicago Seven plus Bobby Seale. Throughout his speech, which condemned the violence of President Nixon and his ordering of troops into Cambodia (for most of the audience this was the first news of the invasion), Froines emphasized the Conspiracy Eight's desire to avoid violence. He maintained that he felt "tension in New Haven," but "I don't understand the tension when people are afraid of their own brothers and sisters." According to Froines, the chief aim of the May Day demonstrations was to "help free Bobby," and this goal could only be accomplished through peaceful demonstrations. "Until Bobby Seale is freed, the strike cannot end here!"

Doug Miranda, who followed Froines, promised that the Black Panther party would not be the cause of violence on May Day weekend. The police, he opined, were the chief perpetrators of violence in America, and he stated that the local police had surrounded the Panthers' New Haven headquarters. "We have very good reason to believe the police will move against us. You who are willing to put your bodies on the line should come over to 35 Sylvan Avenue and help us defend what we believe." Rumors had been circulating for days about such a police raid, and several Yale students were helping the Panthers to fortify their household. Few people at the rink, however, took Miranda's request seriously; to most, it seemed extremely unlikely that the police would be so foolish as to stage an attack that would trigger serious violence before the weekend.

After Miranda's speech, the rally took on the overtones of another teach-in about May Day and the strike demands. There were the usual features of that sort of meeting—including Kenneth Mills. The radicals had lost most Yalies on the trial issue, but Mills's vehement presentation of the first demand received the greatest applause of the evening. Urging the audience to "forget your semantic distinctions on the demands and start dealing with the issues," he pointed out that the wording of the first demand called simply for a stoppage of the trial: "There is one clear and simple demand—that is, 'Free Bobby, free the Panthers.'" Mills emphasized that the Yale strike must continue until this goal was achieved. "You have to keep the strike going past Monday; you can't leave your black brothers out on a limb," he pleaded. "We aren't going back. We want to see justice done; we intend to see justice done." Over half of the audience rose to applaud him.

Despite Mills's pleas, a marked exodus began with the discussion of the five demands. Weary of speeches and talk, people were interested in little except the coming weekend. Finally, Schmoke read an SSC resolution—directed at Dean May—which suggested that students be allowed to take "Satisfactory" or "Unsatisfactory" grades based on their term's work thus far or be given extra time to make up work missed during the strike. On this auspicious note the meeting broke up.

Kenneth Mills thought that the second Ingalls Rink rally was a good idea, since a certain strike momentum had to be kept up by the SSC. He was glad to assist in maintaining this momentum but has claimed that his chief concern was to promote a broader social awareness among Yale students. Schmoke's comments reveal a different perspective: "I thought the meeting served a good purpose in the long run by actually getting people to question their own involvement and thus not be carried on by the fervor. I thought the fervor was bad. Students were manipulated to a great extent, and I'm glad they reacted to it." The end of the fervor—and the questioning of personal involvement—had already led to a general spiritlessness which was obscured only by May Day. Two weeks was the customary limit for generalized student frenzy; Yale moderates were already showing their deficiency in one prerequisite for sustained political action—imperviousness to boredom.

MAY DAY EVE

Thursday, April 30, was a day of waiting. Faculty approval of Brewster, especially in response to Agnew's attack, continued to be expressed in the form of petitions from various departments. On Thursday afternoon Brewster was given a petition signed by 438 members of the university faculty, who expressed their "support" for him in the face of Agnew's efforts "to bring external pressure upon the operation of autonomous institutions."

At a morning press conference with more than sixty reporters, Brewster re-emphasized that Yale had nothing to do with the demonstrations on the Green: "The rally was not promoted by, sponsored by, Yale or any Yale group." He claimed that Yale was being hospitable mainly to prevent violence and warned that it was a mistake to analogize the situation with rebellions on other campuses: the disturbance at Yale had started as a strike and had become a moratorium of regular classes during which faculty and students could conduct relevant discussions. He wondered how much support the SSC had and contended—rightly—that few people at Yale now wanted the trial stopped. His and Yale's main concern was legal and social justice, particularly with respect to the New Haven community. When questioned about the propriety of his "skepticism" statement, Brewster responded that he had made it as an individual and not as president of the university. A few hours later, Brewster was presented with the SSC's five demands.

The Black Panthers also held a press conference at which Big Man, David Hilliard, and "Sister" Carol spoke. Big Man repudiated media reports that the Panthers intended to incite violence: "We are calling for a peaceful mobilization, and we want to make that very clear." Brother David added, however, that if violence was initiated by the police, "we will resist that, because we believe in self-defense." The Panthers were genuinely fearful of a police bust. Big Man stated that Panther headquarters in Baltimore were "under siege by the pigs," and no one doubted that the New Haven area was crawling with the forces of law and order. In addition to the local alert, on Thursday the National Guard, the state police, and the federal troops stationed in Massachusetts and Rhode Island were given deployment orders by their commanders and authorization by Governor Dempsey. Anticipating the worst, a speech prepared for delivery on Friday by President Nixon deplored the violence in New Haven.

Despite the extraordinary efforts made to calm things down, it would be difficult to exaggerate the mood of fear which gripped not only the Panther party but most of New Haven the evening before May Day. Black Panther rhetoric and adolescent hysteria had penetrated every section of the city. Visionaries predicted a bloodbath, a violent showdown between culture and counterculture. Wild stories were heard everywhere, and nothing was too fantastic for credibility: the Hell's Angels were coming; armored tanks waited in the next town; Minutemen were booked into local motels. The master of Calhoun College was reported to have assured some students that the FBI was installing machine guns behind Calhoun's battlements, and several other faculty members have admitted that they had not been so frightened since facing enemy fire. While teams of medical students worked full time to prepare themselves, the Yale-New Haven Hospital reminded the police that it was required to report only four types of injury: gunshot wounds, knife wounds, "proven" rape, and dog bites.

Fear of right-wing violence was as intense as fear of radical violence, putting almost every group on the defensive. Afro-America House, where many black coeds were housed for the weekend, was closely guarded. The BSAY advised its members to stay off the streets or leave town entirely. Many people took their wives and children out of town for the weekend, and some New Haven residents armed themselves. The Black Panthers and their henchmen were repeatedly accused of purchasing guns and explosives, but there was also great worry about violence from fanatics of no particular political persuasion. Mysterious gun robberies were prominently reported; several other universities had recently been shaken by arson and firebombings; a number of homemade bombs were found at Yale.

Brewster had been trying to prepare for the threat from extremists by seeking advice from other universities. He went to a picnic in Massachusetts with Harvard Law School Professor Archibald Cox, the chairman of a commission which had investigated the Columbia University uprising. Cox was also a policy-maker in discipline and security at Harvard, and he buoyed Brewster's self-confidence as they discussed the problems of their universities over white wine and chicken. "They had had that trashing of Harvard Square on April 15, after Abbie Hoffman's speech," said Brewster later, "and we were somewhat relieved to find out that they really were somewhat less sophisticated than we were. But their problem, of course, was much greater." Another expert whom Brewster contacted was Cyrus Vance, a Yale trustee who came to New Haven a few days before May Day to be present during the rally. Brewster was grateful for the help which Vance was able to give before the rally began:

128

The Groundwork for May Day

I was quite well aware of the fact we might fall flat on our faces, and I wanted some trustee around who was relatively expert in these things to be able to be an objective witness about what happened, and what we did wrong, and what we did right, and what we tried to do. Vance had been President Johnson's special assistant on urban disorders after the Detroit riots, and later the Washington riots. So he, poor guy, was going to some daughter's commencement in Colorado, and I said, "No, you've got to come here." So he came here Wednesday and reviewed all our procedures and checked immediately with the Secretary of the Army [Stanley Resor, Yale College '39; LL.D., Yale '46] and then with the White House to find out who their personal representatives in town were. It turned out he knew them both very well in past associations, so he immediately got a hot line. One general and Mr. Ruckelshaus were here for the White House, and this really gave us a very high-level hot line as far as avoiding the confusion of command. Sam Chauncey's relationship with Ahern was the other. We all met together. Williamson was the general's name—Butch Williamson. It was a great relief to me. Oh, Butch Williamson! Williamson, I think, was practically afraid to be in the same room with me lest he be tainted by my radicalism. He was very funny. He looked very leery of having me in on the act.

Thursday night, an after-midnight meeting at Brewster's house was attended by Brewster, Vance, Coffin, Fitt, Trinkaus, Tom Hayden (a cofounder of SDS), Anne Froines, John Froines (M.S., Yale '64; Ph.D., Yale '67), and David Dellinger (Yale College '36). Brewster was concerned because there did not appear to be any single person in charge of overall planning for the demonstration, and he hoped to gain a better understanding of what might occur by speaking with one of the Chicago Seven. Coffin's Monitoring Committee had already stated that arrangements for dispersing the crowd were insufficient, but Coffin had been unable to discover anything more about the rally plans from the Froineses. David Dellinger was expected to be the moderator of the demonstration, and Brewster had attempted to get in touch with Dellinger through William Kunstler:

We thought [Coffin and the Monitoring Committee] were holding out on us, but they really didn't know. They really had no plans. So I said, "Well, damn it, I'll call Bill Kunstler," who is a friend of mine, who was a classmate here, and of course he was said to be coming as one of the speakers. I had a hard time getting his number, but he finally called me back and I said, "Now, I hear you're going to be up here raising hell tomorrow. What is this all about?" And he said, "Yeah, that's what I read too, but I'm not going to be there. I've got to go out and argue a motion in the court in Chicago." I said, "Oh, come on now, this is nuts. We're not trying to tell them how to run this meeting. All we want to know is how they plan to run the meeting so we can take that into account in our own security

129

arrangements. If they don't have anyone running the meeting, that's the most dangerous thing in the world because it can be taken away from them no matter what their motivation, and with so many uglies coming to town they can't guarantee that they [the uglies] won't just take it over." And he said, "I think you've got a point." And I said, "If you can get in touch with anyone, tell them to call me."

Dellinger, meanwhile, was meeting with the Froineses and Tom Hayden at the Branford College Master's House, where Dellinger was spending the weekend. A call came, not from Kunstler but from someone in Brewster's house, informing Dellinger that Brewster wanted to see him. Dellinger did not immediately respond, but shortly after midnight he and the others decided that they should speak to Brewster because of their own worry that the National Guard would be stationed in provocative positions. One of the most alarming pieces of information turned up by the Monitoring Committee was a report that the guard was to be deployed around the Green with fixed bayonets. Keniston had called Daniel Patrick Moynihan in the White House, but to no avail, and Dellinger, the Froineses, and Trinkaus hoped that Brewster would intercede with Governor Dempsey to have the guard removed to a more discreet location. They did not realize that Police Chief Ahern was now in command of the guard. Brewster later described the conversation:

I got this call from Dellinger, another alumnus, and I said, "I just wanted to solicit you for the Alumni Fund." And he said, "Well, I'll give you twenty-three cents." And I said, "Well, that's better terms. What the hell goes on? You're rumored to be the moderator of this thing tomorrow." Dellinger answered, "Well, maybe I will be." And I said, "If you can tell us what you are going to do. . . ." And he said, "Well, I want something from you too. I want you to get the National Guard out of town." I said I couldn't get the National Guard out of town. He said, "Well, I'd at least like to have them pulled back from the Green. The plan was to have them surround the Green, and that's going to be too provocative." And I said, "I agree, but I can't do anything about it. You tell us what's bothering you, and I'll tell you what's bothering us." So, in fact, we had already worked it out with the guard not to be around the Green. We had heard about that a day or two before, and thanks to Vance and Ahern that had already been changed. But I had to have some bargaining power with Dellinger, so I said, "Look, Senator Dodd is already announcing that he's going to have a senate investigation about me, so don't leave me alone. You've got to be here for protective coloration."

Dellinger and Trinkaus left for the president's house in one car, while the Froineses went in another car to collect Tom Hayden, who had gone home earlier. Soon after they had all arrived at Brewster's house, Coffin also appeared, uninvited, having heard about the meeting from his own sources. Brewster had asked Vance to be present as a witness, in order to prevent Brewster's indictment as a coconspirator if there were violence on May Day. Vance had already met some of the Chicago Seven during the Vietnam peace negotiations in Paris, and he was able to greet them as an old friend.

To some of the radical group, Brewster also seemed reasonable and receptive. He indicated that he would get in touch with Chauncey, who was close to Ahern, about the National Guard. At the same time he seemed pessimistic about any attempts to influence Governor Dempsey, pointing out that he was in bad odor politically because of his "skepticism" statement of the week before. As Brewster saw the meeting:

There we were Thursday night, giving the radicals a lecture about how we ought to get charge of ourselves and about running this rally; and they telling us we ought to get the guard off the Green. Our perception was that the greatest danger for the defendants in the trial, for Seale and his codefendants, would be to have this thing blow up. We thought they had an obligation which only they could discharge: to try and convince their supporters and listeners that they were dead set against violence. It was also in our interest, but I don't think that was cause and effect—they felt that way anyway. They agreed that they would adjourn the rally and give people instructions about how to disperse, and so on. So I think we had some effect.

None of these arrangements was known to the average demonstrator—or to some 5,000 jittery Yale students. That night, in a televised speech, President Nixon confirmed the news of the invasion of Cambodia, and a report appeared about the arrest in Baltimore of eighteen people—described as Black Panthers, sympathizers, and associates—in connection with a murder of the previous July. If any of the "uglies" coming to town wished to start a riot, they had a sufficient accumulation of pretexts to do so.

Chapter
7
The Opening of Yale

Few Yale students or arriving demonstrators knew about the fragile web of communication among the police, the Panthers, the army, the administration, and the Chicago Seven. A large number of them would have been disappointed to hear of it; to them, this was a time in which the people had the power, unaffected by the machinations of leaders and organizers. Most of them did not want violence, but they wanted that decision to be theirs and no one else's.

The city awaiting this peaceful anarchy waited quietly. Even police sirens were forbidden. Struck by the eerie stillness, the associate university chaplain recorded his scattered thoughts the night before May Day: "I walked around the New Haven downtown and met virtual silence: shops were mute and boarded, the streets deserted. If someone was walking, an intense look of direction marked his face. Police cars with tell-tale green lights swept silently through the avenues, but the usual night sounds and rhythms that gave me my bearings, these were absent. New Haven bred a heavy silence that night, rooted not in peace but fear." Late in the evening, a fire truck drove to the flagpole on the Green. Firemen tied the halyards twenty feet above the ground and applied a coat of grease to the bottom part of the pole to prevent any demonstrators from lowering the American flag.

133

Friday, misty at first, was bright and beautiful by noon. By 9:30 in the morning, less than 600 demonstrators had officially checked in at Yale's residential colleges. Since thousands were expected, many were disappointed by the early registration figures, but the vast majority of demonstrators came later in the day. Beginning in the middle of the morning, food was available in all colleges—purple fruit juice, milk, and granola. Some of the arrivals had little interest in the Panthers; they had come to New Haven out of sheer curiosity. Their frivolous attitude was summed up by one of them in a few words: "Man, if you keep serving us this shit, you're gonna have a *real* revolution on your hands." Many Yalies who remained in their colleges were even less involved in Panther politics. As Kurt Schmoke has remarked, "Those that did show a lot of fervor for the Panthers may stand out in people's minds, but those who stayed around and worked, dishing out the food, working in the courtyard with children and babies of the demonstrators, and those that manned first aid stations—those kids were not motivated by an overzealous commitment to the Panther party." Their primary motive was to appease the visiting radicals.

The leaders of the rally met during the morning at the Branford College Master's House to discuss and coordinate speeches for the afternoon. All of them, the Chicago Seven plus Miranda, Big Man, and Master Trinkaus, were in various states of exaltation, expecting great events in New Haven. The more sober among them, such as Tom Hayden and David Dellinger, recognized that they were guilty of some arrogance in coming to New Haven to speak without having participated in the May Day preparations and without any base in the university or New Haven communities. They felt that if some speaker from Yale joined them on the platform, it would add an air of legitimacy to their presence. When Dellinger asked Trinkaus who might fill this role, Trinkhaus suggested Kenneth Mills and called him over to the meeting. Mills had not been planning to speak at the rally and was reluctant to do so because of the possibility of violence and the unwillingness of the Yippie leaders, Jerry Rubin and Abbie Hoffman, to take a strong stand against mob action.

The Chicago Seven [Mills has recalled] were not a political collective with collective responsibility for each other at all. Supposing I had spoken at the Green and somebody there had exhorted the crowd to riot, which I disagreed with—if any summons had been handed down, they would have been handed down to almost everybody who spoke there, knowing the way things actually work out. What would have happened thereafter was that I would have been roped into a common situation with them; and if I had then broken ranks with them and denounced them, I would have been seen as denouncing them in order to save my skin, whereas the denunciation in fact would have been correct because I never really agreed with their politics.

Despite his misgivings, Mills was persuaded to speak. Dellinger and Hayden, knowing that the success of the demonstration would be in large part the result of Yale's efforts, felt that it was important to include a man who had been part of those efforts. They also understood that Mills, as a Marxist black, could openly condemn violence without losing face. Rubin and Hoffman were loath to make any sort of "cool it" speeches themselves, lest they lose what they considered their revolutionary credibility as "bogey men for the bourgeoisie." Rubin, who had not been at Kingman Brewster's house the night before, was convinced that Brewster had trapped the radicals into neutrality. Nevertheless, it was agreed that, while the speeches would be militant, all would avoid any references that might stimulate violence.

In order to call attention to the problems of New Haven minorities, representatives of more than thirty black and Puerto Rican community organizations held a morning press conference at the United Church on the Green. Speakers revealed that for more than a week, neighborhood patrols had been working to keep blacks and Puerto Ricans informed "by monitoring our neighborhood and by providing guidance for those of our people who attend the rallies on the Green." Fearing serious threats from right-wing whites, vigilante groups, and the police, whose reconnaissance had been unusually heavy, the patrols also worked to prevent violence from outsiders. This neighborhood solidarity produced one fortunate outcome which the Panthers may have abetted—many violence-prone high schoolers were kept away from the rally.

At the Center Church on the Green, a better-attended press conference was held by Hilliard, Big Man, and the Chicago Seven—

who were insisting that they be called the Conspiracy Eight in association with Bobby Seale. This attempt to close ranks with Seale points up the main reason why the Chicago Seven were in New Haven: "They were into being the Chicago Seven, of course," a Yale radical has remarked; "but on a more serious level, they were coming to New Haven to show their solidarity with the Panthers and to show that they were sorry that they hadn't brought the Chicago trial to a halt when Bobby Seale was gagged and strapped to his chair. After the trial, all the white people were free on bail, but it was Seale who stayed in jail." That Seale alone was still in jail seemed to demonstrate that only blacks bore the full brunt of oppression in American society, and this intensified the guilt feelings of many whites. Hoffman's and Rubin's reluctance to condemn violence arose not only from their adventuristic politics, but from their need to compensate for their whiteness by being more militant than the Panthers and as radical as any black.

The Center Church press conference was unusual in that most of the reporters were "very militant folks in their own way, and they applauded the Chicago Seven as they spoke. As you looked across the room, you saw a lot of long hair, and a lot of 'Right ons,' and some critical responses by the reporters to other reporters' questions. That's the first time I've ever been in a press conference where there's been that kind of tension and that kind of internecine quarrelling going on among the press." Presumably, many of the reporters were from underground papers. The conference had been called for the purpose of outlining the rally goal of the Chicago Seven—free all political prisoners—and was more than a little repetitive, with Dellinger, Hayden, and Hoffman doing most of the talking. Hilliard and Big Man contributed a report of the "Baltimore Bust" and asserted that it was one more step in the government's plot to exterminate the Panthers.

After the press conference, those interested in hearing more proceeded to Woolsey Hall. Jerry Rubin, resplendent in baggy, wine-colored pants and a tie-dyed tee shirt of yellow, turquoise, and red, stood at the podium. Flanked by an array of Yippie flags and Yippie underlings, Rubin delivered a high-pitched eschatological harangue before an audience of over a thousand:

The Opening of Yale

America is a place where everything is upside down—the people who build this country are poor and the rich don't work! We know what work is—a dirty four letter word. Things should be free! . . . We are everything they say we are. International? You're damn right we're international! I don't believe in state lines. My brother is a Chinese peasant, and my enemy is Richard Nixon. . . . We're destroyed in the first eight years of our life, and what we're trying to do is regain those years. Don't give me age as an excuse: Bertrand Russell had his first sit-in at ninety. I don't know anyone more Yippie than Dave Dellinger and Bill Kunstler. Let's face it: we're never, never gonna grow up. . . . Fuck rationality! We're irrational and irresponsible. I haven't taken a bath in six months. . . . Julius [Hoffman], you're the nation's number one Yippie, because you've incited more riots than we ever could. The evening I got into jail and heard the Bank of America in Santa Barbara was burning, I knew we were going to be free. . . . If Bobby Seale had been in that car with Mary Jo, he'd be hanging from a tree. He'd be lynched! . . . We're a religion with our own ritual. A joint is communal, a ritual. Arresting us for smoking dope is like arresting Jews for eating matzos. We're going to get stoned with our kids. We're going to take acid with our kids. We'll turn the Pentagon into an experimental LSD farm and the White House into a crash pad—and paint it black!

Television camera lights flared, boos were heard, and Rubin started long "Fuck Richard Nixon!" and "Fuck Kingston Brewer!" chants. The bright lights went off; applause was followed by calmer rhetoric; television lights reappeared; more obscenities were shouted; the lights again faded; once again there were cheers. It had become a game. Rubin was screaming, his voice almost gone:

If TV had been in the Chicago courtroom for one hour, there'd have been an insurrection in the streets! . . . I ran into Walter Cronkite in the street the other day and said, "Right Walter, you can announce the revolution on TV!" . . . Yale is a place where they separate the rich from the poor. . . . Under that definition, Yale is criminal. . . . What kind of sickness is that when you feel good because you get better grades than someone else? . . . Number one on the Yippie program is kill your parents, who got us into this mess in the first place. . . . We are a new race of people; we don't want a Yale degree; we don't want to be professors, judges, prosecutors. Everything that exists in the university is stolen, because there is no such thing as ownership. . . . We've gotta keep Yale closed forever. . . . A new nation is born today—the Youth International Party. . . . Don't say, "Right on." Do it!

Elated or appalled, the crowd streamed out of the exits, most of them returning to the colleges. Chaplain Coffin later recalled that Robert Jay Lifton and some other psychiatrists took extensive notes during the speech, particularly when Rubin complained about his childhood traumas.* A historical prototype for Rubin's behavior can be found in medieval millenarianism, but few radicals thought about such precedents. To them, May Day was part of a new era, not an old pattern.

By midday, in the college courtyards granola had given way to white rice mixed with soy sauce, salad served by plastic-covered hands, and sliced loaves of bread. There was a small fracas over requested contributions for food, because a number of visitors thought that the money was going to Yale, rather than to the revolution. In fact, a large part of the food money ultimately found its way to the Black Panthers.

Attention shifted to the New Haven Green—the same Green where Kingman Brewster, not yet president of "that fine old college," had marched with New Haven community blacks in support of the civil rights movement many years before. There was no sign of him there this afternoon of May 1. Six years of radical student activism had pushed his sort of liberalism off the stage. At noon, approximately 3,000 people were assembled on the Green to hear a replay of that morning's press conference at the Center Church. Restaurants near the Green that had remained open were doing a roaring business. Except for some twenty uniformed and plainclothes officers who stood in front of City Hall, the police were scarcely visible.

Binoculars and a pair of movie cameras protruded from the newly manned FBI headquarters on the fifth and sixth floors of a bank building overlooking the Green; observers had reported continual activity there for nearly a week. John W. Dean was seen walking around, and there were a number of well-founded reports about police agents and "long haired pig-provocatoo-ers." The police and Dean were probably on the lookout for alleged criminals and conspirators: three Weathermen involved in the recent townhouse explosion in Greenwich Village may have attended the demonstration; Timothy Leary was rumored to have floated into New Haven for the weekend; and a notorious white-slave trafficker was said to be in town, contributing his profits to the Panther defense fund.

---

*Dr. Lifton has commented that he was interested not in the speech's references to childhood traumas, but in certain phrases that Rubin used.

Police strategems prevented some would-be demonstrators from reaching New Haven. Several buses scheduled to bring demonstrators from the Boston area had been cancelled after the FBI suggested that the passengers might be carrying guns. Later on, during the rally itself, a cavalcade of motorcyclists drove along the street next to the demonstration, but the New Haven police took quick action to prevent a larger influx of mounted, right-wing gangs. Stopping motorcyclists on the outskirts of the city, policemen were able to find violations of motor vehicle statutes on every machine—the arrangement was that drivers who turned back would not be arrested.

It is unlikely that these efforts thwarted anyone determined to come to New Haven. Six hundred journalists had arrived to chronicle a holocaust; a brigade of 200 sugarcane cutters had returned from Cuba in time for May Day; and more and more visitors poured in as the day wore on. There is no reliable information about the number of outsiders who were in the city for the weekend, but by the time the rally started about 15,000 people had gathered on the Green. Mixed in with the throng were several hundred undercover marshals—including a large contingent from the black community. They and the regular marshals—mostly women and graduate students—had a noticeable effect as they circulated through the crowd and cooled down arguments. The yellow headbands of the organized student marshals, which Anne Froines had feared would be provocative, were regarded as merely pretentious. The Dwight Hall general secretary was functioning as a marshal, and he noted that "people seemed relatively passive. There wasn't much talk about trashing—the weather was nice, the day was sunny—but as it got closer to evening you could feel the tension beginning to mount, and the question was always: 'What's going to happen between the end of the rally and nightfall?' "

Chief Ahern, who monitored the Panther walkie-talkies, claims that he heard a number of high-ranking Panthers give orders to stir up action in the crowd. His own agents moved about and attempted to calm small groups who appeared to be dangerously impressed by the rhetoric of Panther provocateurs. The Panthers frequently engaged in such covert instigations, and

139

not until later in the weekend did they undertake a wholehearted effort to keep the peace. On Friday afternoon, Ahern prudently refused to challenge their nonviolent public posture.

Less than an hour before the scheduled start of the rally, the Yale SDS attempted to initiate the first action of the day. From the SDS office—which faced the Green—a group of chanters emerged: "Free Bobby Seale! Out of Vietnam, Laos, Trinidad, Cambodia, Thailand, and New Haven!" Others joined them as they made their way across the Green towards City Hall. During this miniature march, bands continued to play and student marshals worked to prevent demonstrators from joining the SDS crowd. By the time a few hundred people had reached the other side of the Green, marching under the SDS banner, the leaders decided not to attempt to cross the street. Instead, an SDS speaker lectured the crowd through a bullhorn, creating a separate rally of several thousand people. He delivered one of the short, racy speeches in which SDS members excelled, contending that Brewster and his ilk tore down proletarian dwellings to make way for expressways and Yale buildings: "Down there where the superhighway comes through, thousands of people were cleared out so the rich people from the suburbs, the bosses and their families, could come into the city real fast without having to look at any of the squalid effects of the oppressive system that's making them fat. They just zip right downtown to shop for all their expensive shit and then zip right back to their posh homes." Student marshals broke up the SDS audience before the scheduled speeches began at 4:00 p.m.

WYBC broadcasts of the rally, which could also be heard through loudspeakers placed in some of the colleges, put the radio station's license in jeopardy for transmission of obscenity. The first speech, written in French by Jean Genet and read by Big Man in butchered English, was fairly described by Peter Brooks, a professor of French literature: "Genet's preposterous inanities, which Big Man struggled through in translation, reminded me of the hopeless superficiality of most French analyses of American society. But they also brought home just how impossible it was to articulate to the outside world what was going on." David Hilliard, who spoke next, had learned something from his experience at Ingalls Rink ten days before. This time he praised Yale students, with no hint of mockery or resentment. Describing New Haven as an armed camp, he declared that the rally had already made its point: the American government could control its own people only by the threat of massive violence. Finally, he underscored the Panther theme of the day: there should be no violence on the part of the demonstrators; violence would be no victory; it would only get people hurt.

An editor of *Ramparts* magazine arose and offered his impression of the country's creeping fascism: "What we have in this country right now is an all-out war of repression to depoliticize the climate, to turn the clock back to the fifties, and to destroy a generation that is engaged in free-thinking and revolution and is on the verge of taking power in this society. The Black Panther party is bearing the full brunt of that repression because they have been in the vanguard of that struggle." The *New York Times,* he said flatly, was attempting to turn the weekend into a bloodbath. He was followed by a black speaker and then by a proponent of Women's Liberation, who supplemented her message with a leaflet rallying the sisters in jail to continue the struggle; on the back of the leaflet was a picture of Ericka Huggins.

The next three speakers—Dellinger, Mills, and Hoffman—were the heart of the rally. Terming Bobby Seale "the real hero of the Chicago conspiracy trial," David Dellinger assured the crowd that Seale had not been involved in planning the Chicago demonstrations and declared that it was the federal government which was provoking violence in New Haven—by arresting innocent Black Panthers in Baltimore and sending troops into Cambodia. Dellinger, a pacifist, received a standing ovation when he insisted that violence was too easy a response; there were "more ingenious ways to off the pigs." Kenneth Mills's accent was more out of place than usual when he announced that "the determination to be nonviolent is the determination to be militant." Welcoming everyone to New Haven, Professor Mills emphasized that no one in the city wanted a riot. Abbie Hoffman, the most militant speaker of the afternoon, expressed his agreement with Brewster's "skepticism" and shouted the crowd to its feet with the promise that the Chicago Seven would not quit New Haven until Bobby Seale and his fellow defendants were free.

The speakers who followed Hoffman were almost bland— perhaps deliberately. Among them was a representative of a Quaker group who, like Mills, gave a speech which was well delivered rhetorically but ill designed for the ragtag multitude before him. Mills, returning to the microphone, warned the departing crowd not to be provoked by the nearby National Guard. With this final, cautious note, the demonstration came to a quiet close. Frisbees began to soar; a few demonstrators bent over to pick up trash or play leapfrog; most returned to the colleges to eat more granola.

Coffin assured one journalist that May Day had established "a new kind of political process." Kurt Schmoke, however, viewed the afternoon with some ambivalence:

I didn't think that the rally was going to free the Panthers. I thought having the demonstration in New Haven was an important thing if for no other reason than it showed the conservative factions and those on the Right who had already condemned the Panthers that the Left was just as vigilant as they were and that these people were here to demand true justice and not the kangaroo court like we saw in Chicago. There were some things that were good about the demonstration, and some things that were bad. A lot of people turned it into a circus. I think the radicals were a small group. The ones right around the podium—the Yippies that were whooping it up with Abbie Hoffman—their politics were so extreme, you call it non-politics. There were a lot of concerned people that wanted their bodies down there so that they could show their concern that the Panthers didn't get railroaded, so that that group was a silent majority of the Left. There was a Woodstockish element. It was an amazing conglomeration of people.

Except for the blacks, the speakers had been as motley a conglomeration as the audience. A French playwright, a journalist, a feminist, a pacifist, an intellectual, a Quaker—all were middle class; none had any roots in the local community; each had an entirely different axe to grind. The Panthers stood for almost none of their causes, and their only common theme was an ephemeral tribute to the Black Panther party. The principal lesson of the May Day demonstrations was already apparent: serious revolutionary parties in the United States have to tread a narrow path between particularism and diversity; the Panthers, in inflating the issue of the New Haven trial, had veered into diversity to form a loose coalition which had no enduring strength or purpose.

The Yale administration had monitored the rally from a secret command post in Alumni House, an inconspicuous building half a block from the speakers' platform. Already furnished with extensive sleeping and cooking facilities, the house had been stocked with equipment for any likely May Day emergency— especially firebombing. An elaborate telephone system included telephones with secret numbers known only by the college masters, the SSC, the National Guard headquarters, the mayor, and the FBI. Chauncey received all the campus-police radio communications and was in constant communication with Ahern. As a result, Chauncey could arrange the movements of campus police and student marshals as advantageously as possible and even could influence the positioning of the National Guard. There was a fall-back command post on the other side of the campus which could be used if evacuation from Alumni House became necessary.

Despite these elaborate contrivances, for a time it looked as if there might be trouble because of the high visibility of several National Guard battalions only two blocks away. Twenty-five hundred guardsmen had been deployed, shortly before the rally, around the vicinity of the Green and at utility plants in the city; groups of 40 to 150 men each had been stationed about one block apart. Their principal weapons were tear gas canisters and rifles with sheathed bayonets. One company had loaded rifles and a few of the soldiers had brought their own ammunition, but in spite of some harassment from civilians, the guardsmen were generally friendly. The commander of "Task Force Bravo" was Brigadier General Edward Wozenski, who spent most of the day in a "red, white, and blue unmarked helicopter."

As the crowds left the Green, one person called the White House and another went to the National Guard headquarters, but in Chaplain Coffin's judgment it was largely because of his and John Hersey's efforts that the most conspicuous troops were

143

moved out of sight before the departing crowd reached them. Keniston has described Hersey's success in shifting one of the units:

John Hersey, ex-war correspondent, novelist, and Master of Pierson College at Yale—a tall man of great moral strength, sensitivity, and distinctive bearing—walks up to the commanding officer of the Guard unit, introduces himself, and says, "I must ask you to move these men back one block immediately. They are obstructing the movement of our visitors. Please contact your superior officer." The officer, surprised, goes to the radio in his jeep and returns in a few moments saying, "They will be out in three or four minutes." The Guardsmen then shoulder arms and march down the street, to the applause of the gathered crowd.

I call President Brewster's office to inform one of his aides that the Guard unit has moved. The president's aide laughs and says, "But John Hersey shouldn't get all the credit for things that Kingman has arranged."

The presidential aide may have been Chauncey, although Chauncey himself gives most of the credit to neither Brewster, nor Hersey, nor Coffin: "I know who moved the National Guard—it was Chief Ahern. In response to some request of mine, Jim did move National Guard units." The guard was gradually withdrawn, and an hour after the rally there were only 400 soldiers left in the city.

The crowd soon spread itself out within the campus, drawn by the lure of concurrent rock concerts at the Old Campus and Ingalls Rink. Allen Ginsberg also sang his "May King's Prophecy" at the Old Campus, and the Chicago Seven were scheduled to give speeches in the courtyards of the various colleges at 9:00 p.m. These distractions prevented disturbances for several hours.

———————

At 10:00, an incident in the Branford College courtyard helped to ignite a small riot. A black youth claiming to be a Panther interrupted a speech by Rubin in which the Yippie leader spoke against violence. The youth announced that two Panthers had been arrested on the Green (Ahern had ordered the Green cleared by dusk), and he exhorted the crowd to go to the prisoners' defense. A group called Youth Against War and Fascism may have been responsible for the interruption, since its members raised their banners in a preplanned manner when the crowd began to move out of the college courtyard. The war-painted

Yippies also responded enthusiastically, and Rubin made an ineffectual attempt to stop them. Part of the crowd moved in the general direction of Ezra Stiles College, where Abbie Hoffman had been speaking to an audience which included Kingman Brewster.

Brewster had spent the earlier part of the evening at his house. There had been fewer people at the rally than he had expected, and he returned for a relaxed dinner with his wife, two aides, and Cyrus Vance. After some consideration, Brewster decided that it would be safe to move around the campus to demonstrate his leadership and gain an up-to-the-minute sense of the prevailing mood. Brewster and Vance arrived at Ezra Stiles College at the tail end of Hoffman's speech and narrowly escaped involvement in the ensuing action. A student reporter has described the outcome of Hoffman's tirade:

He cracked a few jokes, yipped a lot, and suggested Yale be destroyed. Toward the end I got bored, went to take a piss, and came back to find someone announcing something, and the crowd standing up, and then all filing out of the Stiles entrance. There were a fair number of people chanting "Free Bobby" and, around me, much talk of burning a bank. A fellow next to me asked where the nearest bank was—I thought he was joking and said that there was a small branch of the First New Haven right across [the street]. I then discovered he was carrying a big mother of an axe and a black flag. He called on people to rally round to head for the bank. I told him there were guards with shotguns outside, and he said he'd be careful.

A number of spectators have claimed that Hoffman encouraged violence in his speech by innuendo and that a group of Yippies and Weathermen stirred up the crowd to march into the street. Nothing came of the movement to burn the First New Haven National Bank, although some minor damage was done to nearby stores. The crowd coming out of Ezra Stiles joined the crowd from Branford, and the entire throng moved across the Green chanting, "The streets belong to the people!" Many who had left the Ingalls Rink rock concert joined them, swelling the crowd to over 1,500.

The gradual emptying of the rink was an event of unparalleled good fortune; two hours later a bomb exploded inside the building. Dean Wilkinson left the concert a few minutes before the explosion and went into his house near the rink: "I heard the screams after the roar had stopped. It seemed to go on for ever and ever—one of those suspended moments that occasionally happens in a movie. I thought my own house was on its way down, and I heard people running out the back door to my back yard."

Brewster and Vance, who had made their way to Alumni House, were more calm, although the weekend would have been a disaster if there had been any deaths. One of Brewster's aides has reported:

I don't think we actually heard a blast. I think we heard on the police frequency that there had been a disturbance at the hockey rink, an explosion. They radioed back, factually, that they were going in to look for survivors—just that one phrase gives you a sense of mangled bodies all over the place. I went to the phone and called the associate provost and asked him to go down and give me a firsthand impression. But there was a gap there for about twenty minutes when we didn't know what was going on. My impression is that Mr. Brewster and Mr. Vance sat on the couch, side by side, in the Alumni House and didn't say a word until they knew there had been no serious injuries. They just sat there. There was tremendous composure.

To stem widespread panic and discourage other terrorists, Chauncey quickly called newspaper offices and radio and television stations to report that there had been an explosion but that no one had been hurt and the situation was under control. Radio stations cooperated by not announcing the explosion at all or by reporting it in an understated, precise manner.

Shortly after the blast, which occurred just before midnight, four youths were seen running away from the building; they were not captured. The police immediately sealed off the area and found that the explosion had been caused by two small charges which had done serious damage. No one was ever convicted of the bombing. The "most likely suspect," according to the city police, was a leftist. An extreme rightist would appear to have had more rational motivation for the deed.

Few of those who had gone to the Green learned of the explosion that night. The steadily increasing mob, led by the Youth Against War and Fascism, advanced across the Green. Student marshals formed a human chain to prevent anyone from clashing with the line of police in front of City Hall, and reinforcements were summoned to assist the 400 guardsmen who were still in town. Kenneth Mills and David Dellinger, who were about to address a meeting in Silliman College, received a message asking that they come at once and assist in calming the crowd. When Mills asked the gathering in Silliman to carry on their own meeting while he and Dellinger went to the Green, a member of the audience promptly denounced him for "holding back the people's fighting spirit."

Although a great many students did remain in the college courtyards, the crowd on the Green continued to swell. Pressed by the police, they began a slow retreat toward the Old Campus, the line of police following them as they withdrew. Police released tear gas after a few demonstrators hurled rocks and bottles, and Ahern claimed that bricks, pipes, and chains were also thrown. By this time the entire campus had been alerted. Large clusters of people, including camera crews and news reporters, assembled near Battell Chapel to witness the confrontation and enjoy the thrill of being lightly gassed.

The associate chaplain later recalled the ending of a performance in Battell Chapel of Euripides' *Orestes,* involving the kind of aesthetic coincidence which could only occur on a college campus:

With the Furies on stage watching over the collapsed House of Atreus, there came forth, in the real distance, sounds of tear gas canisters going off. The audience shifted nervously, not realizing where the play ended and some outside reality began. Apprehension mounted, reinforced by the glare of theater lights in a church where white cloths shrouded all the familiar spaces. The play finished, actors appeared for their applause, tear gas canisters again sounded, and the doors of the chapel opened suddenly, followed by crowds of people and whiffs of tear gas. Audience and actors merged with crowds escaping the gas, and the church-playhouse became a sanctuary for the frightened and overwhelmed.

The SSC quickly reported the new trouble to the NHPDC, which in turn alerted Panther headquarters and spread word that the rumor about two arrested Panthers was untrue. Panthers were dispatched to avert violence in several different areas, including the black community; Artie Seale reassured many New Haven blacks who were upset by reports of violence in the center of town. Coffin and Mills, meanwhile, tried to persuade people to

147

leave the Green. When Coffin introduced himself to one group, he was received with shouts of "Fuck you, Reverend!" Others responded with indifference. Mills, as Coffin has related, was no more effective:

I wasn't getting anywhere, and they were putting on their gasmasks, and they had their oxygen. So I grabbed Mills, whom I saw there, and I said, "You try!" So Ken comes striding up in front of them—most of them were about five foot three or four, and Mills goes up to about six foot two, and then he keeps on going with his afro. You know, he's a pretty fearsome looking character. He strode up and down in front of them, and these guys stopped short out of tremendous respect for this black giant, and they lifted their gas masks and listened to him, and Ken said in his best Trinidad accent, "This nonsense must stop! This is not the way to make the revolution!" You can imagine what was going on for poor old Mills. His accent did him in and the rocks started to fly.

Phelps Gate did turn out to be important. Policemen began to collar people outside the Old Campus, and Chauncey became aware that a campus policeman "lost his cool and started to close the gate, and it was essential to move fast enough to keep that from happening, because that would have then become a hostile act that would have resulted in just the kind of thing we were trying to avoid. I fortunately was monitoring the radio at the time and heard him giving the order to close it, and I told him not to. This was no particular judgment on my part; anyone should have known better than to close the gate. Gas was being thrown and people were moving back." However, as soon as Phelps Gate was opened, many in the Old Campus quadrangle abandoned safety and poured into the streets. They were met by two companies of guardsmen standing with fixed bayonets, and marshals and Panthers struggled to move the crowd back to the Old Campus. Exremists threw rocks and bottles at the guardsmen and more tear gas was released by the police.

Doug Miranda, supplied with a bullhorn by the campus police, attempted to persuade people to stay inside: "You motherfuckin' pi-i-igs in civilian clothes. You motherfuckin' pigs in civilian clothes. . . . Get back in there, get back into that Ol' Campus, you motherfuckin' pigs!" He continued, "If niggers can have discipline, then so can you!" Allen Ginsberg sat chanting on the Old Campus bandstand while students applied wet towels to his face to alleviate the effects of tear gas. A bystander was involved

148

in one revealing episode: "I went back into the Old Campus and there was Tom Hayden. And he said to me, 'What's happened?' I said, 'Nothing, they just put down some tear gas.' And he said, with some vehemence, 'I don't believe you!' I thought at the time, 'Wow, he sounds disappointed.' " When tear gas seeped into Alumni House, the atmosphere noticeably lightened. In Chauncey's words, "I picked up the direct line to Ahern. He was obviously very harassed. I said, 'Is this the local gasman?' and somehow it just broke him up."

Finally the crowd quieted down, and the evening degenerated into a two-hour vigil during which police and demonstrators glared at each other across a twenty-foot no-man's-land along the streets bordering the Yale campus. At 1:30 a.m., a final burst of excitement was generated by a fire which had been set, symbolically, in the jury box of the Yale Law School moot courtroom. Damage was minimal. Thereafter, the crowd gradually scattered, and except for continued reports of broken windows, the campus and surrounding streets were quiet.

The police department later reported seventeen arrests and two injuries. Prior to nightfall, it had been one of the quietest days in the department's history; only one arrest had been made, entirely unconnected with the rally. The National Guard reported no arrests at all. The Yale-New Haven Hospital, which had geared its emergency room for a holocaust, treated three minor injuries.

The night offered moderate Yale students everything they had been waiting for. There was every conceivable sort of action between the police and the demonstrators short of outright violence. May Day was entirely successful in the sense that the work for nonviolence had had an effect—yet not so great an effect as to make the weekend a dreary anticlimax. It was almost artistic.

———————

Saturday morning brought with it a sense of relief that the weekend had been acceptably uneventful—thus far. The relief was accompanied by a rising fear of real violence during the second day; it seemed impossible to maintain the balance between complete calm and outright attack that had been the temper of May 1. Rumors continued to circulate that the Hell's Angels were coming to town and that the National Guard had been given orders to "shoot to kill." Late the night before, Keniston had run into Kenneth Mills, looking worn and depressed. Mills said to him, "They no longer will listen to us. They no longer respect us. I fear for tomorrow." Mills also remembered the encounter:

I was depressed because people wouldn't listen, they wouldn't respond, and I just saw that if that was going to be the mood and nobody was going to take responsibility the next day for telling people to cool it, then we were in for trouble. It seemed that we had come so far and were nearly home, and for trouble to break out right at the end would just seem a wipe out. But I think on Saturday morning the Panthers had pulled themselves together and were going around the college courtyards and everywhere with their bullhorn asking people to restrain themselves, and they were taking a very clear lead in so doing. I really had been getting disgusted at that point at some aspects of radical politics—a lack of political discipline, a lack of collective discipline.

Mills felt disgusted not only by the Panthers, but by the Chicago Seven's movie-star radicalism—a peculiarly American characteristic of the student movement. The Chicago Seven came into a city, created as big a stir as possible, and departed. They showed no constructive interest in organizing strong, permanent followings in the numerous places they visited.

Other weaknesses of the Chicago Seven were apparent even to themselves. On Saturday morning, at another meeting with a few Yale people at the Branford College Master's House, the Chicago group made it clear to at least one observer that they were reluctant to make any more public speeches in New Haven because

virtually anything they said would implicate them in conspiracy. The law reads that if you said that a crowd ought to trash a building, even if the building were not trashed, you would be subject to conspiracy. That was one problem. The second problem was that the Chicago Seven didn't want to say things which were less militant or ideologically watered down, or which did not represent their politics. They didn't want to get out there and be a sham in order to avoid the conspiracy charge, so they were really boxed in. Yet each of them saw a kind of constituency out there which they wanted to do justice to.

The second of these problems was primarily the problem of the Yippie leaders, Hoffman and Rubin. May Day had demonstrated the limitations of their usual tactics. Yippies expected that their leaders would always sound the note of a commander leading troops into battle. In New Haven that note was not wanted by

150

the Black Panthers, and Hoffman and Rubin, fearful of losing their martial image, found themselves unable to harmonize with those on whose behalf they were speaking.

Traces of tear gas lingered on the Green on Saturday morning, and police officers directed traffic wearing face shields and carrying gasmasks and long truncheons. A Black Panther sound truck amplified an appeal for nonviolence. Behind the courthouse, generally unnoticed, was a blue Yale shuttlebus containing one of the toughest collections of last-resort policemen ever seen in New Haven. The "Yale University" lettering on the bus had been blocked over and special lettering put on the roof to facilitate helicopter identification. The Youth Against War and Fascism tried to make trouble during a small meeting in Branford College by calling the Black Panthers "bourgeois" and "counterrevolutionary." The Student-Faculty Monitoring Committee relayed this information to the Black Panther headquarters, and in ten minutes there were three Panthers in the courtyard telling the crowd to "cool it." One Youth member rejoined, "We're more oppressed than you are because of our long hair." This puerile contention destroyed any rapport between the group and the Branford meeting, but many other visitors were still eager to take part in a rampage. Kenneth Keniston encountered "a girl from Cornell, a heavy girl, not attractive, with lanky black hair. By herself, she looked lonely. I had gone up to her to ask where she was from. She told me, and when I asked her why she was here, she said, 'I heard this was going to be the biggest riot of the year—so I came.' "

The morning was a welter of meetings and rumors. Such diverse subjects as Women and Imperialism, The Church as an Agent of Repression, and Ecology and Health were hashed over in seemingly endless workshops, while one group went off to "Rap with the Guard." The only visible reminder of the National Guard was a jeep which was patrolling the area around the campus, but students went to a parking lot four blocks away where 400 guardsmen had been deployed. National Guard headquarters on the Southern Connecticut College campus received an anonymous telephone call about a secret cache of bombs. The police, unusually responsive to any tip, investigated at once but turned up only three Coca-Cola bottles filled with gasoline.

At 2:00 in the afternoon, the Panthers and the NHPDC held a press conference at NHPDC headquarters. Earlier in the day, the NHPDC had released a circular condemning Friday's "confrontations for the mere sake of confrontation." Dostou now supplemented this, stating that his group did "not advocate violence" and hinting that the explosion at Ingalls Rink was staged by local right-wing extremists. Doug Miranda supported Dostou's stance against violence and declared that the weekend was "a political education course—one of the correct tactics for revolution is to educate the people." Furthermore, said Miranda, the unidentified black youth who had announced the arrests of Panthers the night before was a "liar and a police agent." The Panthers were particularly resentful of white rioters, who apparently were permitted to break the law without ever paying the penalty.

When the rally began at 4:30, the crowd was smaller than it had been on Friday afternoon. Marshals had quelled a few dangerous incidents around the Green earlier in the day, but people were now quite calm. Two sky-written peace symbols floated overhead and marijuana was passed around openly. Miranda, who spoke first, was as angry and compelling as he had been at the morning press conference: "Spontaneity leads to suicide if you don't organize it and you don't discipline it. . . . The major task, the major contradiction confronting those in white America who want to move in a revolutionary fashion is how they're going to organize." He concluded with a startling variation of the usual salutation: "All power to the people. And when the word is given, all power to the good shooters!" Militants had not abandoned revolutionary violence, but the moment for action was not yet at hand.

Miranda was followed by a speaker who attempted to enlist volunteers for political and agricultural work in Georgia, and after a spokesman from the New York Gay Liberation Front had decried the oppression of homosexuals, Jerry Rubin again took center stage. Rubin gave another febrile rendition of his Woolsey

Hall speech, scrambling the sentences into a different order but failing to conceal a repetition that bored listeners who had enjoyed it the first time. His "Fuck Kingston Brewer" chant evoked no response other than an echo from the walls of the surrounding buildings. Kenneth Mills's speech, in which he attacked the Vietnam war and domestic oppression, was more cogent. Appealing to students in other American universities, Mills employed a thereafter much quoted line: "Shut them down to open them up to reality!"

Artie Seale, wife of the incarcerated Panther chairman, came to the podium amidst cries of "Free Bobby Seale!" Instead of addressing the crowd directly, she played a tape which she had made three hours earlier in the Montville Correctional Center by concealing a recorder in her pocketbook. Through a miracle of modern technology, Bobby Seale was able to announce to thousands that his stand in the courtroom ten days before had been misunderstood. He now stated that he did not believe he could have a fair trial, because the American judicial system was racist. Nevertheless, he averred, the basis of the Panther ideology was in the hearts and minds of over fifty percent of the people in America; those who pledged allegiance to the flag did not pledge allegiance to a government which behaved like the government of the United States. The Seale tape was a dramatic reminder that the May Day rallies had been organized in pursuit of a specific object.

After another digression, this time by two spokeswomen for Women's Liberation, Doug Miranda returned to the podium to solicit donations to the Panther legal defense fund. Tom Hayden backed him up: "You do not give money to the Black Panther party on a philanthropic or humanitarian basis. You invest money . . . because it is part of an investment of money in your own revolution." Hayden then announced the outcome of a meeting organized by a Brandeis University sociology professor and a group of his students—a call for a national student strike. (Held earlier in the day at Dwight Hall, the meeting had been attended by almost 2,000 people and resulted in the formation of the National Student Strike Committee.) Kenneth Mills, who conveyed the news of the strike call to the speakers' platform, had some difficulty persuading Hayden to announce it to the rally. "Hayden," Mills has explained, "is a very uptight guy on some things. He had written his speech out, something I never do, and he was *not* going to deviate. It was really very funny. I went back about three or four times, and then *finally* he agreed to put it into his speech. He was associated the next day in the *New York Times* with the authorship of the national strike, although he was actually a reluctant purveyor of information."

However reluctant, Hayden read the demands which had been agreed upon at the Dwight Hall meeting: the United States government should end its oppression of political dissidents and release all political prisoners, such as Bobby Seale; the government should immediately withdraw all of its forces from Southeast Asia; universities should end their complicity with the American war machine by an immediate end to defense research, ROTC, counterinsurgency research, and any other warmongering programs. The strike would start on Tuesday, May 5—coincidentally Karl Marx's birthday—and would continue until the demands were met.

Hayden's prepared speech, the last of the day, was based on a doctrine which few had dared to enunciate: "Facts are as irrelevant in this case in Connecticut as facts are irrelevant about Vietnam. . . . A lot of educated people are going to have to be convinced that the facts are irrelevant!" Emphasizing that the hour had come to begin organizing the revolution, he closed with a personal farewell: "That's why really it is not a time any more for talk, and this is about the last speech I'm ever going to give." He was, apparently, about to go underground.

The crowd on the Green was not visibly stirred by Hayden's announcement of a strike which would soon arouse the entire country. The activities of the weekend were obviously losing appeal, and the Sunday program was cancelled—according to one speaker, because of the difficulty of preventing violence after news of the renewed bombing of North Vietnam. Schmoke has offered a different interpretation: "I don't think that is true. I think what happened was that everybody who was involved with the rally sort of felt the crowd out and saw that people were drifting away. If you looked at the crowd Saturday as compared to the first one you could see that there just weren't that many people and if you tried to have something the next day there would be nobody around. I think that for political and publicity purposes they didn't want to have the second round."

Thousands were leaving New Haven; still, concern about the government's latest bombing activity had some justification. A number of universities had gone on strike immediately after the invasion of Cambodia, and on Saturday night striking students at Kent State burned their ROTC building to the ground. Scores of other universities saw the national strike demands announced by Hayden as a signal to stop all classes, sometimes with concomitant violence. At Yale, the primary impact of the national strike was the disruption of the existing disruption and the distraction of many Yalies not only from resuming their classwork, but from rectifying those local injustices which they had been discussing for over two weeks. The ease with which Yale students were diverted was an inevitable result of the radicals' attempts to win adherents by opportunistic and manipulative methods; these tactics reduced the moderates' choices to aimless, hysterical radicalism or no radicalism at all.

Those who remained in town after the demonstration drifted back to the campus for more granola and more meetings. Much of the talk now focused on long-range problems, such as the national strike and Education for the Revolution. Abbie Hoffman was seen warmly embracing Kingman Brewster in the Ezra Stiles College courtyard, and the crowds were calmer than they had been the previous night, but there was still some concern about the possibility of new nocturnal disturbances. A few small fires were reported in the colleges early in the evening, most of them in wastebaskets, and there was a brief scuffle between firemen and a handful of demonstrators outside Branford College.

A more exciting fire occurred in a building less than half a block from the courthouse. At 8:45, large amounts of smoke poured out of the "New Politics Corner," a clearing house for liberal and reform-oriented politics which had been converted to an information center for the weekend. Minutes after the smoke appeared, hundreds of spectators gathered. Ahern asked student marshals to move people from the courthouse steps, which they

155

were able to do without any difficulty, and as the crowd grew larger the police asked people to leave the street and sidewalk and move onto the Green. Panthers moved down the street in a green panel sound truck, telling the crowd that the fire was the work of a provocateur and urging them to leave the area. It seems probable that the fire was deliberately set, although the fire marshal later said that it was not of suspicious origin and had been caused by a faulty oil burner in the basement.

As the fire was brought under control, most responded to the Panthers' continuing pleas and returned to the Yale campus. National Guard troops, backed by a row of policemen, lined up between the courthouse and the Green, which was populated by less than a hundred people, many of them marshals and medical aides. A few rocks and bottles were thrown at the guard, and Chief Ahern was hit in the chest by a champagne magnum. As he staggered back, his officers wanted to respond immediately, but Ahern delayed calling for tear gas "to avoid giving the men the impression that I had reacted out of personal anger." The police and the guard eventually did launch their canisters, and by 10:00 the gas fog was so thick that marshals and medical aides had to help those caught in the barrage to escape through Phelps Gate. The police were wearing gasmasks, which gave them the look of outer-space creatures—or "pigs."

The few people remaining on the Green, by now mostly reporters and demonstrators who had gasmasks, continued to resist efforts by the police to make the Green uninhabitable. Some sought refuge in the Center Church, but that, too, was thick with gas, and they were forced to retreat to the Old Campus. A score of policemen gathered near Phelps Gate and switched on a gas-spreading machine, which took several minutes to warm up. The roar of the motor drew people back to the Green out of curiosity, and a few marshals asked the police to turn it off. They received a brief reply: "If they want war, let them come."

Policemen responded to another barrage of rocks by methodically moving up the streets bordering the campus, dispersing onlookers and releasing gas in an effort to isolate the university from the surrounding city. They fired a number of canisters on streets within the campus, and the leaded windows of Yale buildings proved ineffective sealants for the rooms. Most people sought shelter in attics or on roofs which were too high to be affected. The Old Campus was completely deserted. Requests to stop releasing so much gas went unheeded, and traffic to the Connecticut turnpike was diverted from the center of the city to a roundabout route which went by President Brewster's house.

As soon as the gas subsided slightly, a good many people returned to the streets and sat before the platooned guard, singing "We Shall Overcome." When the guard warned them to move, they rose to their feet and began to sing "America, the Beautiful." The guardsmen responded with a final volley of tear gas, and at least a dozen more canisters were fired before the crowd dissipated. As the gas faded away, the last stragglers were helped—or urged—off the streets near the campus and first aid was administered to the few who needed it. The National Guard began to leave, and officials were notified that the federal troops were no longer required. Soon after midnight all the intersections of the city were open, and Ahern proudly released his summary of events.

The few examples of terrorism and vandalism which had occurred on campus since the eve of May Day were headed by the Ingalls Rink bomb, the spray painting on the walls of one common room, and some trashing in Branford College. Except for these incidents and some scattered fire damage, there was little destruction of Yale property. On Sunday morning, WYBC was able to report that during the two days of demonstrations only one Yalie had been arrested. He had been taken into custody for sitting in a car in which another passenger was brandishing a loaded water pistol.

Chapter
8
The Closing Down

Sunday morning brought rainy weather and a sharp sense of disassociation from the episode known as May Day. A few hundred guardsmen remained in town and state police stayed on to protect the courthouse, but most people were no longer fearful of an outbreak of violence. Thoughts quickly turned to the distant future—distant, that is, compared to the outlook of the preceding week, when no one had thought of anything beyond the demonstration. Any future strike activity would have less intensity: it would no longer be related to a specific Yale-New Haven event, the semester was almost over, and too much had happened already.

The morning included one customary feature, a sermon in Battell Chapel by Bill Coffin. "We should rejoice," he declaimed. "We did a hell of a job. We did a Christian job. We practiced Christianity. We took a Christian chance, and it paid off. We licked 'em with love." He reaffirmed his earlier contention that the Seale trial was perhaps "legally right, but morally wrong," and he criticized Nixon's assertion that the United States must not become a "pitiful, helpless giant." The danger, said Coffin, was that the country might become a mindless, heartless giant: "Violence is a denial of manhood. President Nixon set a dreadful tone when he suggested that manhood is for a giant to behave like a giant. That is the most perverted notion of manhood that has been heard from high places in a decade."

Coffin asked for comments from the congregation, and after several others had spoken, Professor Emeritus Harry Rudin, who had taught history at Yale for thirty-nine years, rose to his feet. Rudin spoke with an air of sadness. He doubted that the rally for the Black Panthers had brought Yale closer to the community. Warning of a rising wave of anti-intellectualism in the country, he predicted that "the backlash here in New Haven will be anti-university." Universities, said Rudin, stood for the concept of rational inquiry and the task of identifying problems and working to solve them. They were, perhaps, the last hope for improving American society. To strike against the university and to take the attitude that classes and intellectual labor are irrelevant to society's problems or to justice was more than foolish; it was dangerous.

Throughout his life Rudin had been known as a man who supported the underdog and the unpopular cause, and it must have been difficult for him to take a seemingly conservative stance. But like many other Yale professors who had long considered themselves in the avant-garde, Rudin found himself unable to sympathize with the radicals of May Day. Kurt Schmoke, himself a minister's son, probably spoke for the majority in the congregation. He saw little of value in Rudin's statement:

The gist of Rudin's speech was that our actions in the past few days were attacks against the president of the United States and they could be considered un-American activity. He went on to say that at the university you should confine yourself to academic pursuits and forget about what's going on outside the ivy walls. Rev. Coffin had called me the night before and said that if I'd like to come down and say something during the service, I was welcome. I didn't plan to say anything. I was tired. But when I heard that professor I just couldn't believe it; so I got up and said that students could not just sit around and grind it out, although that was one of the things we should be doing. Because we are given four years in which we are relatively free of responsibility, except for passing in papers, we have a responsibility to our brothers and sisters who are outside of this situation, who are working and dying in the streets and dying in wars, to do something about today's problems. I said this was as much our responsibility as academic pursuits. I also said a sort of second grade thing, like "Nixon is a very bad man." By then I was really worked up. This professor had really got to me. I was tired and started crying. I couldn't think of any more to say, but, finally, I got myself together and was able to finish up.

Some of the congregation wept with Schmoke, although it seemed to others that there was a sense in which both speakers were right.

An hour after this service, Brewster held a press conference at which he expressed "admiration and gratitude to everyone concerned with the exception of the small group of roving willful troublemakers. They were the challenge." Brewster thanked all who had helped, from Chauncey and Police Chief Ahern to Doug Miranda and the Strike Steering Committee, and he announced that he would be meeting during the afternoon with the SSC "to respond to the so-called 'demands' generated by the week's discussions." Alluding to the government's "new provocation" in Indochina, he commented on the nascent national student strike, declaring it an "irrationality which results from the inability to find any other way of shaking the regular political system into its senses. I personally share the students' feelings about the war; but I hope we are smart enough to devise a better way to demonstrate our distress than to curtail education." He would suggest an alternative a week later.

Throughout the following week, Brewster received reams of favorable publicity because of his association with Yale. Headlines reflected the admiration of the press: "How A Marathon Effort Cooled Yale's 3-Day Weekend"; "Confrontation, But The Mood Was Polite." *Life* magazine, contrasting the May Day weekend with the Kent State killings, stated that "Yale Proves Dissent Doesn't Have To Turn Out That Way." A few were not so adulatory. At a press conference on Monday, Mayor Guida thanked everyone except Yale for keeping the peace, and one notable, conservative alumnus—William Buckley—continued to publish his more outspoken disapproval. Pointing out the inconsistency of Brewster's various stances, Buckley wrote in his newspaper column that the president of Yale was "a prime example of what the mob can do to a leader. . . . Brewster emerges, sounding for all the world like the last days of Alexander Kerenski . . . wooing the cheers of the mob." Another conservative alumnus was caught up in the excitement of the weekend. As a trustee of the Yale Corporation, William McChesney Martin was engaged in a survey of the faculty on the question of whether Brewster should retain his presidency for another seven years. After May Day, Martin wrote the alumni that, while Brewster had his failings, he deserved to be reappointed. President Nixon expressed more reserved approval, telling Governor Dempsey that he was "pleased to see that everything went well in New Haven."

Reactions within Yale were surprisingly mixed, reflecting the incoherence of the events following May Day. Trinkaus felt that, "thanks largely to our effort, Yale is now in the vanguard of a great movement in this country. This is one of the greatest events in this college's history." A student called the events "an indication of moral bankruptcy on the part of a university ready, and even eager, to abandon its teaching role for that of the radical political activist." When questioned about May Day a year later, an editor of the *Yale Daily News*, who was about to go to work in the White House, blurted out, "It is my confirmed belief that students here are full of shit!" Still others claimed that a difficult time had come and gone without any significant effect. Coffin was disappointed because "so much energy was expended preventing something negative that afterwards we haven't been able to cook up any comparable energy to promote something positive." One black student said that the strike "brought the blacks at Yale together for the first time." A white prep school coed also took a nostalgic view: "Friends were made and lost, and now people can always reminisce." A year after he made his postrally speech expressing "admiration and gratitude," Kingman Brewster himself was more critical:

I don't think society appreciates it when a university has to acquiesce in the suspension of its normal activities, which are carried on in public interest, and has to put something else ahead of its stated purpose. I don't think that's what we did, frankly, but that's the way it was perceived. The second thing is that I think in a way that probably [May Day weekend] gave some people more a kind of therapeutic satisfaction than they deserved, in the sense that it didn't accomplish a damn thing in the serious sense, and people use a kind of group therapy bash like that as a substitute for really doing the hard work of making the world better.

The most important interaction during the post-May Day period was between the administration and the students. After the rallies, the undergraduates' immediate concern shifted to their own academic requirements, and it soon became obvious that the UFPD and the Strike Steering Committee had had only a tenuous hold on their attention. In the farrago of speeches during the demonstrations, no mention had been made of the SSC or its program. Sunday afternoon, meeting with an SSC which he knew had little power, Brewster made a "preliminary" response which proved to be final. He stated that several of the SSC's demands "overlap issues called to my attention by the faculty vote of April 23; but this is not intended to be a full response to that resolution." He promised to ask the Yale Board of Trustees for a ratification of his statement that "institutional neutrality [does] not inhibit Yale from committing itself to the achievement of fairness in our local criminal courts." Concerning Yale's role in the New Haven community, he said that he would recommend to the trustees the authorization of Yale's participation in the "creation of a joint Yale and community housing and economic development corporation" to be controlled by the community, and he promised that a hitherto unrestricted pledge of a million dollars would be used as initial capital for the venture. He also promised that Yale would match any funds raised for the Calvin Hill Day Care Center, but he postponed comment on unemployment compensation until a "legal analysis" and further cost studies were made. As for the final demand, Brewster differentiated between the Social Science Center building and the programs of the Institute for Social Sciences. Arguing that the institute could be a way of "loosening up a purely departmental and theoretical approach to human, social, and policy matters," he proposed that a four-member student group meet with the institute's interim governing board.

The Strike Steering Committee found Brewster's replies "completely unsatisfactory." His answer to the demand concerning the trial was called "inadequate" and "an evasion"; his reply to the day care demand addressed "only part of the demand." The proposal concerning the Institute for Social Sciences was described as "unclear and inadequate." "We do not," stated the SSC, "want to be merely consulted about our views while hiring and architectural plans go forward." Brewster's response to the unemployment compensation demand

163

was "equivocal," and his commitment to community housing was termed "unclear," although the pledge of a million dollars was a "step in the right direction." Fighting to maintain a grip on its ever weakening bargaining position, the Strike Steering Committee urged students to stay in New Haven, "assisting community groups [to] work out the priorities of these programs," in order to "insure the implementation of these demands."

The BSAY and the black faculty were no less dismayed by Brewster's position. He had, they felt, ignored the faculty resolution and failed to take into account the needs of the black community. They warned that they would continue to apply pressure. On May 8, they sent Brewster a letter which included an elaborate set of demands which the UFPD had been drafting for more than two weeks. Brewster knew, however, that the UFPD had even less support than the SSC within the university, and he parried the UFPD with a noncommittal response. He reaffirmed his pledge of a million dollars for the community; he appointed a committee to look into some of the UFPD proposals; and he dismissed the other proposals as irrelevant to his view of the university's purpose—which was "to educate."

———

Sunday evening, May 3, after meeting with the SSC, Brewster released a major statement, the heart of which is found in this excerpt:

Much that has been achieved by the outpouring of energies during this period would be lost if we had to choose between social responsibility and academic responsibility. It is not an either/or choice.

The five demands of the Strike Coordinating Committee [sic] do not seek the abandonment of the university's academic goals. Rather, they urge that the assumption by Yale of widened community responsibilities will in fact make it a better place at which to be educated.

If I read the mood of the faculties and students correctly, there is a widespread urge to restore academic expectations. . . .

It is quite clear to the Deans of Schools in which academic activities were suspended that their faculties should make every effort to see that no student is handicapped or penalized in the grading of or the credit for his courses because of any suspension of an academic activity last week.

In a statement released simultaneously, Dean May announced that his concern was "to insure a just and orderly return to the normal academic expectations of Yale College." He presented four grading options to the students: work could be completed in the normal manner; the grade of "Incomplete" could be taken, with the understanding that the work was to be made up during the summer; students could withdraw from any course through May 13; if the instructor agreed, the grade of "Satisfactory" or "Unsatisfactory" could be elected, in place of the regular grade, for work done through April 26.

Two aspects of May's announcement merit special attention. First, the faculty was never consulted about the return to "the normal academic functions of the University," although there had been an implicit understanding at the meeting on April 23 that the faculty would reconvene to determine its next step. Second, all academic changes were the prerogative of the faculty, yet the Yale College faculty as a whole was not consulted about the changes in the grading system. The decision was an administrative one which had been under consideration for some time. Long before May Day, a group of black faculty members had called on Dean Wilkinson and asked him, very firmly, to consider modifying grading requirements for the year. They argued that it was of great importance for many black students, half of them freshmen, who were at a serious disadvantage compared with the whites because they had been under strong political pressure since early April.

Despite the failure to consult the faculty, the statements of Brewster and May partially appeased both political extremes in the university. The official recall to regular schooling pleased the conservatives, while the generous grading options were agreeable to white radicals and blacks—as well as to the many students who had no strong political motivation but whose academic work had suffered badly in the preceding weeks. Brewster later conceded that the decisions were an attempt at unification by compromise: "And so we really gave with one hand and took away with the other—we said that the moratorium business was over, but the completion of academic requirements could be based on any work done to date if they would settle for a Satisfactory grade." In the same pragmatic spirit, Brewster decided not to leave the decision up to the faculty: "Georges May and I decided just on our own that to reconvene the faculty would be again to invite total division and, although some people might resent our using the dictatorial directive, the resentment would not be anywhere near as bad for the institution as the divisiveness that would come out of a faculty debate, and so we just took the bull by the horns and said [banging the table] this is it—which softened it."

However high-handed, the action was not the decision of one man. Brewster, May, and Kernan had sounded out many faculty members and administrators and received strong support in several quarters for the final statements. In the Faculty Steering Committee, however, the proposal met considerable resistance. The six members were divided evenly and the session was a stormy one. Two of the junior faculty members took the academically conservative stance. David Thorburn was one of them:

I opposed the grade reform very strongly on two grounds. First, I felt it entirely wrong for the dean and the president to impose a new grade by fiat. This is clearly an area in which the faculty as a whole must have authority. By compromising or ignoring the faculty's right to create new grading categories or to decide what constitutes acceptable work, the president and the dean were implicitly saying they had no confidence in the wisdom and reasonableness of the faculty. Second, I opposed the proposal to grant a Satisfactory grade for work done prior to the interruption of classes because there seemed no possible justification for such a decision. If we had decided to permit students to make up their work over the summer but had also insisted the work had to be done in order for students to receive credit for the semester, we would have succeeded in doing something that no other college in a similar crisis had been able to do: we would have affirmed our belief in the importance and value of the intellectual enterprise that universities stand for and are supposed to protect. I nearly resigned from the Faculty Steering Committee because I was so disappointed, even outraged, by what seemed to be a real (and also wholly unnecessary!) crime against the very idea of the university.

Dean May did not disagree. Although he broke the Faculty Steering Committee tie and issued the grading statement, he later confessed that he and Brewster had "cheated." May considered the decision a painful compromise of academic integrity which could be justified because it was essential to the preservation of the university. He was troubled less by the substance of the

166

decision than by the failure to submit the question to the faculty for debate and approval, but he felt that, in this instance, the good of the cause justified the "wickedness" of the means.

It is possible that May acted in response to strong pressure from Brewster to issue a directive on grades at the same time that Brewster issued his statement on the return to normal academic functions. During the long meeting of the Faculty Steering Committee, Brewster telephoned Dean May at least three times, presumably to urge him to stop consulting and produce the directive. Before May left to see the president, he decided that he could issue the directive only with the statement that he had "consulted" the Faculty Steering Committee. He could not say that the committee had "supported" the directive, and he later told a colleague that he agreed with those who had objected but was torn by his loyalty to Brewster.

One pressure on Brewster, and therefore also on Dean May, was the opinion of the Yale trustees. Most of them had supported Brewster's "skepticism" statement, and he had been making decisions in their name. Thus far, however, they had been in touch with him only on an individual basis, not as a group. Brewster explained the situation later: "We also had the trustees coming to town that following weekend, and it was very clear to me that while I could justify the moratorium in the face of external attack, I could not justify the moratorium as a strategy of just plain politicization, which was what the shut-it-down guys were after." May Day had cost Yale over $25,000, but Brewster's arguments were persuasive. On May 9, the Yale Board of Trustees gave him a resounding vote of confidence for his handling of the crisis.

<hr>

On the Sunday evening that Brewster and May called for a return to normal academic expectations, a Yale national strike committee was formed and arrangements were made for increased picketing of classrooms to discourage student backsliding. The next day, while many continued to boycott classes, there was a discernible trend toward a resumption of school work. Undergraduate Yalies, radicals and moderates alike, were weary of their two-week bout with political idealism. Despite the passionate protest of more than 300 campuses against the invasion of Cambodia, the new strike call probably would have failed at Yale if National Guard troops had not killed four students at Kent State University on Monday afternoon.

The impact of the killings at Kent State on students at Yale is difficult to assess. Even the most jaded undergraduates were not only shocked by the tragedy; they were acutely aware of their own closeness to it. Yet Yale College was no exception to the rule that student enthusiasm could not be sustained much longer than two weeks. The strongest supporters of the national strike at Yale were older students, who had hitherto held themselves aloof. The Graduate and Professional Student Senate overwhelmingly endorsed the new strike. More than a thousand students from the graduate, law, and medical schools quickly followed suit. On Wednesday, the *Yale Daily News* finally caved in and published an editorial in support of the strike. Undergraduate support, however, lacked its former intensity. Dramatized by Kent State, the national strike commanded Yale's attention; it did not revive concentrated fervor.

Nevertheless, Yale became a focal point for the national strike. The university had acquired considerable prestige among radicals as an institution which knew how to engage in restrained political agitation which avoided a backlash. Tom Hayden, in a long magazine article, said that the New Haven trial should serve as a point of departure for black liberation and praised the May Day rally for securing the inclusion of a "political prisoners" clause in the national strike demands. Soon after May Day, Kenneth Mills, Bill Farley, and several other Yale political figures began addressing strike rallies at other universities. On May 13, conscious of Yale's current mystique, a national strike conference convened in New Haven to establish lines of communication among the hundreds of striking colleges. On Yale itself, the conference had no appreciable impact.

The diffusion of political energy was encouraged by Kingman Brewster's scattershot suggestions. On Thursday, May 7, he proposed a national drive to promote congressional candidates "who commit themselves to bring a prompt end to the war in Southeast Asia." He also announced that he would travel to Washington at the head of a group of Yale students, faculty members, and trustees who wished to discuss ways to halt the Vietnam war with members of Congress—especially those who were Yale alumni. In Washington, four days later, he announced his support of the "Princeton Plan," which could permit students two weeks off in the autumn to campaign for political candidates. The plan, however, was never adopted. When it was submitted to the faculty for approval in June, a number of conservatives had recovered their voices, and it was only narrowly approved. Meanwhile, Brewster's enthusiasm had waned; he pointed out the legal obstacles to the plan, and when the graduate school faculty rejected it, he seized the opportunity to veto it altogether.

While white Yale returned to its bourgeois concerns, the blacks and their closest allies developed problems among themselves. At a meeting with members of the Yale administration the week after May Day, Doug Miranda castigated the BSAY for "jivin' and half-steppin' " and failing to follow the Panthers' lead. It was the last straw in a long series of Panther criticisms directed at the BSAY; at a meeting held shortly afterward, a majority of the BSAY voted to break off all negotiations with the Panther party, causing the more radical blacks to walk out in anger. On May 23, the national conference of black organizations called to discuss the Panther question met belatedly at Yale. Reluctantly sponsored by the BSAY, the conference turned out to be an unproductive "fizzle" (Bill Farley's word) which only illuminated the shift from outrage over the Panther trial to the less specific, less passionate anger over national and local racial injustice.

Deprived of the immediate focus of the May Day rallies, recently formed organizations disintegrated rapidly. The SSC broke up into small groups. Its program was overshadowed by that of the national strike committee; not even the SSC demand concerning the Panther trial could any longer attract significant attention. The NHPDC lost the spirited leadership of Tom Dostou—who reverted to drug-taking—and its activities became aimless and desultory. The New Haven police recommenced their harassment of the group when the summer vacation began, but most NHPDC members were too disillusioned with both the Panther party and all revolutionary politics to respond as an organization. In conformity with another national trend, at least three of them became Jesus Freaks.

169

Yale's cooling enthusiasm soon turned to ash. The *Strike Newspaper*, after doing all it could to create interest in the summer Liberation School, announced on May 18 that publication would be discontinued until "energy, enthusiasm, and the need return." The organizers of the Liberation School, still hoping to discover how Yale might become closer and more helpful to the community, proposed that the administration keep three colleges open for the school during the summer. As Dean Wilkinson has reported, "the Council of Masters said no to that emphatically. Part of our strategy was just to sit back and let these plans wither on the vine. We knew they would as soon as the end of exams approached, and we knew that more and more students who thought they wanted to stay would get sick of it and would want to go. It finally ended up, I guess, with a dozen or so students who stayed in the Master's House in Branford, which, of course, was the master's prerogative." Almost all other students, including the blacks, departed by the middle of June.

———

A year later, Bobby Seale and Ericka Huggins were freed because of a hung jury and the prohibitive cost of empaneling another impartial jury. By 1975, no low-income housing had gone up in New Haven at Yale's expense, and plans for the Social Science Center remained stalled only because of insufficient funding. The Calvin Hill Day Care Center for the children of Yale employees had opened, but it was suffering from lack of money. New legislation had forced Yale to pay unemployment compensation.

Did the experience of May Day generate reforms? Kingman Brewster has answered: "Oh, some, yeah, yeah. But I think there was a kind of romanticized self-congratulation, which is not undeserved in many cases. One thing it didn't accomplish, really, was getting down to the serious business of improving the world. People accept the therapeutic bash as a substitute for hard work." If Yale's quiet rejection of the spirit of the demands was also an evasion of "the serious business of improving the world," neither the students nor the faculty nor the president has remarked it.

Chapter
9
Conclusion

May Day and the national strike were the last manifestations of a movement which had made headlines for over five years. The national strike ended at the beginning of the summer vacation, and the universities remained quiet when students returned in the autumn. National organizations died the same death as that of ad hoc committees at Yale. SDS, which had been disintegrating for more than a year, all but disappeared by the end of 1970. No similar group replaced it, and campus radicals quickly dropped out of politics and the public eye.

Several pundits argue that the prevailing calm on American campuses conceals new radical tactics, that student activists have merely renounced violence in accordance with the "Yale Doctrine." In fact, campuses are quiet because moderates are uninterested and radicals are demoralized and depleted. The nonviolence at Yale—which often concealed coercion—gave new direction to no more than a few remnants of the movement. Underground radicals are as violent as ever, but they are without influence on a student generation dominated by apathetic moderates.

The prevailing apathy is in part the result of developments outside the universities. The Black Panther party, always closely associated with students, began to decline soon after SDS, and its claims of government persecution were largely discredited. Inflation, shrinking university endowments, reduced federal assistance, and a dismal job market have altered priorities for everyone. Younger faculty members and students are greatly concerned about their careers, not at all concerned about war and conscription, and only abstractly concerned about social injustice.

Yale reflects all of these changes. New Haven's black community has been unable to exert organized pressure on the university since May Day. The faculty and students, by all accounts, are working much harder than in 1970. Yale's relative poverty has forced the administration to accommodate conservatives, especially conservative alumni. In 1972 Brewster told a group of Old Blues that he was inclined to doubt the wisdom of his 1970 decision to allow "students and faculty to make an independent choice as to whether to suspend classes." It had been, he said, "a degree of freedom extended in the area of the expression of private political opinion" which the university was no longer granting. He also conceded that his journey to Washington with a group of student lobbyists had been an act "verging on the edge of what is academically permissible."

The aura of the Black Panthers made it difficult for any traditional liberal to retain his political compass during the May Day events. Brewster's transmutations reflected this difficulty, but Brewster himself never lost control. He won his duel with Kenneth Mills by moving from the center to the far left before finally embracing the moderate right. Luck played a part—he was greatly assisted by Yale's resistance to an attack on the university and by the relative weakness of the Yale strike—but few could have maneuvered so skillfully.

Many liberals lost their bearings. Chaplain Coffin, especially, foundered in his attempt to control the direction of events. Self-effacement was hard for him, but when he found himself unable to lead a movement which developed on his home ground, he was compelled to join less vocal liberals who were trying to prevent violence and injury to Yale. Activists like Coffin, Trinkaus, and Hersey present a paradox. Though they resembled students in neither age nor occupation, they reacted to the Black Panthers with the naive excitement of undergraduates. Nearly all of them were administrators and functionaries in the academic community. It was their vocation to interact with students, which may explain their indiscriminate enthusiasm for the passing fashions of the young.

The excitement and confusion of white liberals was a predominant characteristic of campus agitation everywhere. Three other characteristics which pervaded the student movement were also highlighted by the Yale experience: the ambush of the conservatives, the superficial radicalization of the moderates, and the inherent weaknesses of the radicals. Surprised conservatives gave way without a murmur; the conversion of the moderates was shallow and transitory; the radicals were divided, vainglorious, and manipulative.

Conservatives collapsed under radical pressure because of their caution and uncertainty. Few in number, rightist students were often disliked and occasionally subjected to physical intimidation. They projected an unfashionable rationalism which encouraged others to dismiss all of their proposals. Yet today, conservative student groups are remarkably vibrant. The experience of unpopularity and the intolerance shown them during the sixties may have assisted their resurgence.

Moderates at Yale were converted in a highly charged and sometimes hysterical atmosphere. The emotional environment was created by a real or imagined outrage—the Panther trial and the imprisonment of Hilliard and Douglas—and was intensified by paranoia, proselytizing, and pressure. The hysteria was encouraged by reactions outside the university, reactions which also gave Yalies an exaggerated feeling of self-importance. Given the superficial nature of their conversion, it is not surprising that the failure to achieve instant results caused moderates to abandon radical politics within three weeks.

The radicals who engendered the campus upheavals had little more staying power. As seen at Yale, their tactics were not only artful; they were irrational and unrealistic. The strike was run by organizations which rarely worked well together. United only on the issue of the Panther trial, they distrusted one another. Some radical groups, such as SDS, were opposed to the course of events or were not taken seriously; others, like the BSAY, were suspicious of the moderates and kept to themselves; the SSC was slow and unwieldy; and the "Branford Liberation Front" was scarcely organized at all. A student strike is a dubious political strategem under any circumstances. Dissension and disorganization among the leaders ensure its failure.

The blacks would not, or could not, create unity. Community blacks had little direct influence on white students, while Dawson, Rochon, Bryce-LaPorte, and Farley were no more than temporary, almost bureaucratic heads of their respective organizations. Doug Miranda was a superb crowd-rouser, but the higher-ups in the Black Panther party constrained him. Kurt Schmoke emerged as a leader, but for no clear purpose except to prevent others from clashing or going to extremes. The most important black leader was Kenneth Mills. Very effective for a time, Mills was too dilettantish to apply continuous pressure. He has stated that he supported the SSC's demands reluctantly because his primary aim was the Marxist education of Yale students during a moratorium of academic work. However, Mills turned without a backward glance from the dying moratorium to the flourishing national strike.

Mills's easy abandonment of the fading moratorium exemplified the fundamental weakness of a movement which would soon have expired, regardless of the course of the Vietnam war and the financial pressures of the seventies. Always capricious and undisciplined, campus radicalism appeared vigorous and widespread because it passed from one uninitiated college to another, encouraged by the national publicity which greeted each new disruption. Even a capably led, soundly organized radical movement would have faced formidable obstacles. Not only is the United States too large and diverse to be seriously affected by student politics, but the students of the sixties had neither extreme inequities to complain of nor a strong radical tradition to sustain them.

Most participants will remember the years of "The Movement" with nostalgia rather than embarassment. For the others, the memory may be made easier to bear by a consideration of similar upheavals in a more distant past. The "people's crusades" of medieval Europe consisted of disaffected aristocrats, unmarriageable women, nonconformist priests, and peasants, yet they bore a notable resemblance to the American student movement. Anticipating an egalitarian paradise, their ragged processions usually began with sporadic violence and invariably ended in disappointment and failure. The principal historian of medieval millenarianism concludes his study with a reminder that, "stripped of their original supernatural sanction," such movements still persist in "certain politically marginal elements in technologically advanced societies—chiefly young or unemployed workers and a small minority of intellectuals and students."

The "marginal elements" that dominated American campuses in the sixties were often inspired by a sense of decency and compassion. But no movement succeeds because of the virtue of its motives. In action, student radicals exhibited so much self-indulgent intolerance that their reforms were transitory, their allies were estranged, and their entire generation was diminished.

Chronology

Organizations and Participants

ORGANIZATIONS

BSAY	Black Student Alliance at Yale
NHPDC	New Haven Panther Defense Committee
ROTC	Reserve Officers' Training Corps
SDS	Students for a Democratic Society
SSC	Strike Steering Committee (the SSC replaced the Moratorium Committee on April 22)
UFPD	United Front for Panther Defense (a conglomerate of representatives from the BSAY, the black community, the Third World Liberation Front, and other groups)
WYBC	Yale Broadcasting Company

UNIVERSITY ADMINISTRATORS

Kingman Brewster Jr.	President of Yale University
Henry ("Sam") Chauncey Jr.	Special Assistant to the President
The Reverend William Sloan Coffin Jr.	University Chaplain
Alfred Fitt	Special Adviser to the President
John Hersey	Master of Pierson College
Alvin Kernan	Acting Provost of Yale University
Georges May	Dean of Yale College
Ernest Osborne	Chairman of the Yale Council on Community Affairs; brother-in-law of Warren Kimbro
Cyrus Vance	Trustee of the Yale Corporation
John Wilkinson	Dean of Undergraduate Affairs and Associate Dean of Yale College

FACULTY MEMBERS

Houston Baker	Assistant Professor of English
Peter Brooks	Assistant Professor of French
Roy Bryce-LaPorte	Assistant Professor of Sociology
Kenneth Keniston	Professor of Psychology (Psychiatry)
Robert Jay Lifton	Professor of Psychiatry
Kenneth Mills	Assistant Professor of Philosophy
James ("Jay") Ogilvy	Assistant Professor of Philosophy
David Thorburn	Assistant Professor of English
Robert Triffin	Master of Berkeley College and Professor of Economics
J.P. Trinkaus	Master of Branford College and Professor of Biology

179

STUDENTS

Ralph Dawson	Moderator of the BSAY
	(Yale College '71)
William Farley	Chairman of the SSC
	(Yale College '72)
Gilbert Rochon	Coordinator of the UFPD
	(Philosophy graduate student)
Kurt Schmoke	Class Secretary
	(Yale College '71)

GOVERNMENT OFFICIALS

James Ahern	New Haven Chief of Police
John Dempsey	Governor of Connecticut
Bartholomew Guida	Mayor of New Haven
Harold Mulvey	Judge in the Black Panther trial
William Ruckelshaus	U.S. assistant attorney general; member of the presidential "strike force" on civil disorders

OTHERS

Frances Carter	Black Panther defendant
David Dellinger	Member of the Chicago Seven
	(Yale College '36)
Tom Dostou	Head of the NHPDC
Emory Douglas	Minister of Culture of the Black Panther party
Anne Froines	Wife of John Froines and member of the NHPDC
John Froines	Member of the Chicago Seven
	(M.S., Yale '64, Ph.D., Yale '67)
Charles Garry	Lawyer for Bobby Seale
Jean Genet	French playwright
Tom Hayden	Member of the Chicago Seven and co-founder of SDS
David Hilliard	Chief of Staff of the Black Panther party
Abbie Hoffman	Member of the Chicago Seven and Yippie leader
Elbert ("Big Man") Howard	Managing Editor of the *Black Panther* newspaper
Ericka Huggins	Head of the Black Panther party in New Haven until her arrest on May 22, 1969
Warren Kimbro	Black Panther defendant
William Kunstler	Lawyer for the Chicago Seven
	(Yale College '41)
Lonnie McLucas	Black Panther defendant
Doug Miranda	Head of the Black Panther party in New Haven after the summer of 1969
Alex Rackley	Alleged victim of murder by Black Panthers
Jerry Rubin	Member of the Chicago Seven and Yippie leader
George Sams	Black Panther defendant
Artie Seale	Wife of Bobby Seale
Bobby Seale	Chairman of the Black Panther party

180

Bibliographical Note

The significant available documents for this study include: seven published and two unpublished books; numerous articles and newspaper reports; published and unpublished letters; leaflets, announcements, minutes, notes and memoranda. Some important documents are not yet available. Brewster's office files, including his notes and correspondence, are in the Yale Archives. The by-laws of the university state that these must remain secret for twenty-five years, but Brewster has said that he would not have released this material under any circumstances. The contents of these files might clear up some important questions which remain unanswered even after a candid interview with Brewster. The office files of Reuben Holden, the Secretary of Yale until 1971, are also in the archives and unavailable for twenty-five years; it is unlikely that Holden's files include important new information. The minutes of Yale College faculty meetings are normally open only to those eligible to attend the meetings; however, the secretary of the faculty, Professor Edgar Boell, made available his preliminary drafts of the minutes for the meetings of April 23 and May 21, 1970.

Six of the nine source books do not deal with the May Day period in more than one chapter, although seven of the authors were direct witnesses of the events they describe. Robert Brustein's account is marred by his strong personal reaction to the situation, and the second chapter of Police Chief James F. Ahern's book on American law enforcement gives a somewhat exaggerated account of the police preparations. Alan Adelson's book on SDS, Donald Freed's book on the trial, and Gail Sheehy's book on the Panther party in New Haven are vague, impressionistic, and prejudiced. Nora Sayre's book, *Sixties Going On Seventies*, has a lucid, reliable chapter on the May Day events and interviews with Yale people held two years later.

Only one of the three books concerned entirely with May Day has been published. In his *Letter to the Alumni*, John Hersey used the framework of the May Day story as a platform for his personal political message. The book is based on minimal research and is for the most part confined to an account of the role of Pierson College, where Hersey was the master; written immediately after the strike, it was completed within a period of about four months. One unpublished book, obtainable in the Yale Archives, records the personal reminiscences of an undergraduate. The ninth book—the report to the Scranton Commission on Civil Disorders—also was not published. It is the only one of the nine books which makes a serious effort to research the subject, but it does little more than bring together newspaper reports and was written too hastily.

The articles written by witnesses usually suffer from bias and confusion, and those written by outsiders suffer from tendentiousness or ignorance. The reporting of the Yale student radio station (WYBC), the *Yale Alumni Magazine*, local newspapers, and the *Yale Daily News* was good. Most other newspapers did a mediocre job.

Additional sources include three movies, which are available in Yale's Audio-Visual Center. One of the movies is radical propaganda and another is a conservative pacifier designed for alumni by alumni. The third, *Bright College Days*, depicts much of the humorous side of May Day and effectively captures some aspects of the mood, but it is a series of vignettes rather than a balanced account of what happened. It was well received at Yale, in a nostalgic way, when it was released a year after May Day.

The core of the research for this book, and the most vital aspect of it, consisted of the formal interviews listed below and of innumerable informal interviews. Some of those interviewed did not wish their comments to be recorded, and a few wrote down their reminiscences in notes or letters. Occasionally, some refused to answer specific questions, but there were usually others willing to reply to those same questions. Quotations and information excerpted from the interviews were frequently revised by the interviewees about a year after the interviews took place; at that time, generally, statements and reminiscences were neutralized—rightists and leftists had moved toward the center as time passed. Participants also have contradicted the views that they expressed during the crisis. Hindsight has led many people to the conclusion that the most creditable position during the May Day events was the political center—opposing violence, taking a casual interest in the strike demands, and refusing to condemn anyone. Few people took this position in spring of 1970.

INTERVIEWS

James Ahern*	Jan. 6, 1973	Taft
Chris Argyris*	Feb. 15, 1972	Taft
Elizabeth Auchincloss*	May 6, 1971	Manville**
Houston Baker*	Sept. 3, 1975	Taft
Richard Band*	Feb. 9, 1972	Taft
Charles Beasley*	May 1, 1971	Taft
Charles Belson*	May 4, 1971	Manville
Louis Black*	Sept. 25, 1973	Taft
Edgar Boell	April 20, 1973	Taft
Kingman Brewster Jr.	May 18, 1971	Winn
Robert Brewster	April 3, 1971	Solomon
Peter Brooks*	Dec. 14, 1972	Taft
Roy Bryce-LaPorte*	March 12, 1971	Taft, Winn
Beekman Cannon	Dec. 15, 1972	Taft
Edward Capiello	Dec. 7, 1972	Cunningham
Henry Chauncey Jr.	April 5, 1971	Solomon, Taft
Elias Clark	Oct. 12, 1972	Taft
William Sloane Coffin	April 6, 1971	Manville, Taft
Joshua Cohen	April 3, 1971	Manville, Taft
Robert Cottrol	March 7, 1971	Manville, Taft
Ralph Dawson	April 19, 1973	Taft
Hester Eisenstein	March 20, 1971	Krieger
Kai Erikson	Dec. 4, 1972	Cunningham
Jonathan Fanton	April 18, 1971	Taft
William Farley	April 26, 1971	Taft, Winn
Alfred Fitt	April 9, 1971	Solomon, Taft
Abraham Goldstein*	April 12, 1971	Taft, Winn
W. Francell Gray*	May 10, 1971	Manville
Martin Griffin*	April 21, 1971	Solomon, Taft
Douglas Hallett*	May 3, 1971	Manville
George Harvey	April 3, 1971	Solomon
Gregory Hicks*	Dec. 8, 1972	Taft
William Horowitz	April 23, 1971	Winn
Gary Johnson	March 3, 1971	Manville, Taft
Donald Kagan	April 27, 1971	Manville, Taft
Michael Kegan	Sept. 24, 1973	Taft
Kenneth Keniston	April 7, 1971	Solomon
Thomas Kent*	May 25, 1972	Taft
Alvin Kernan	April 9, 1971	Winn
Albert Lauber*	May 2, 1971	Manville
Richard Lee	Sept. 24, 1973	Taft
R.W.B. Lewis*	April 26, 1971	Manville

183

Albert Machioni	Feb. 27, 1971	Manville
Georges May	April 8, 1971	Taft, Winn
Samuel Menafee*	May 9, 1971	Manville
Kenneth Mills	Feb. 24, 1972	Taft
James Morris	March 8, 1971	Manville, Taft
James Ogilvy	May 6, 1971	Solomon, Taft
Adam Parry	March 4, 1971	Taft
George Pierson*	Feb. 18, 1972	Taft
Jeffrey Pressman*	Dec. 13, 1972	Taft
Paul Rahe	March 1, 1971	Manville, Taft
Kenneth Robinson	Dec. 4, 1972	Taft
Gilbert Rochon	Sept. 25, 1973	Taft
William Rose	April 12, 1971	Manville
C.N. Rostow*	Feb. 18, 1972	Taft
Richard Sewall	April 19, 1971	Winn
Kurt Schmoke	March 31, 1971	Manville, Taft
Samuel Slie	April 20, 1971	Krieger
Alexander Spinrad	April 3, 1971	Manville, Taft
William Stackhouse*	May 4, 1971	Manville
Walter Stephans*	May 11, 1971	Manville
Gerard Swordes	Sept. 24, 1973	Taft
Charles Tharp	Nov. 16, 1974	Taft
Elizabeth Thomas	April 21, 1971	Manville
David Thorburn	March 15, 1971	Taft, Winn
Robert Triffin	April 20, 1971	Taft
J.P. Trinkaus	April 22, 1971	Taft
David Warren	April 30, 1971	Taft
John Wilkinson	April 26, 1971	Manville
C. Vann Woodward	April 9, 1971	Taft
Edward Yanowitz*	May 13, 1971	Manville
Richard Zackon*	May 1, 1971	Taft
J. Phillip Zaeder	April 15, 1971	Krieger

*Interview in note or letter form.

**The interviewers, other than the author, are Thomas Cunningham, Joel Krieger, P. Brook Manville, Neal Solomon, and David Winn.

Notes

ABBREVIATIONS

NHJC	The *New Haven Journal Courier*
NHR	The *New Haven Register*
NYT	The *New York Times*
SN	*Strike Newspaper*
WYBC	Yale Broadcasting Company
YAM	*Yale Alumni Magazine,* May 1970 (The main part of the *Yale Alumni Magazine* article on the May Day events was written by Ren Frutkin. Frutkin's preliminary notes and transcripts of tape recordings prepared for his article have also been cited.)
YDN	*Yale Daily News*
YLSM	"The Proceedings in the Black Panther Case," Yale Law School Memorandum, April 29, 1970.

Unless otherwise noted, all dates are in the year 1970 and copies of all un-published material are in the author's possession; much of the unpublished material is also available in the Yale Archives. Formal interviews are identified by the interviewee's last name; full information on the interviews may be found at the end of the bibliographical note.

NOTES

1 *Introduction*

2   On New Haven's black population and urban renewal: Lee interview; Andrew Kopkind, "Bringing It All Back Home," *Hard Times,* May 11-18, p. 1; Gail Sheehy, "The Consequences of Panthermania," *New York Magazine,* Nov. 23, pp. 46-47.

2 *The Rackley Case*

5   On the discovery of Rackley's corpse: Edward Jay Epstein, "The Panthers and the Police: A Pattern of Genocide?" *New Yorker,* Feb. 13, 1971, p. 51; *Newsweek,* March 30, p, 22; *NYT,* May 23, 1969, p. 24; *NHR,* May 22, 1969, pp. 1-2.

5-6   On the identification of the corpse: YLSM, pp. 4-5, 9; Gail Sheehy, "The Consequences of Panthermania," *New York Magazine,* Nov. 23, p. 55.

6   On the police alert: Sheehy, "The Consequences of Panthermania," p. 55; James F. Ahern, *Police in Trouble: Our Frightening Crisis in Law Enforcement* (New York: Hawthorn Books, 1972), pp. 32-33. On the break-ins and the search: *NHR,* May 22, 1969, p. 1; *NYT,* May 23, 1969, p. 24; YLSM, p. 5; Sheehy, "The Consequences of Panthermania," p. 55.

On the ballistics experts' findings: *NYT,* Dec. 30, 1969, p. 30.

On the stationhouse detention: Sheehy, "The Consequences of Panthermania," p. 55; *Panther Trial News,* Aug. 24 (Yale Archives); YLSM, pp. 6, 18-19; Gwirtsman/Foster, "Notes on the Bobby Seale-Panther trial" (leaflet).

On McLucas: Sheehy, "The Consequences of Panthermania," p. 55.

6-7   On Rackley's abduction, "trial," and murder: *NYT,* May 23, 1969, p. 24; *NYT,* Aug. 20, 1969, p. 15.

7   On the ninth arrest, re-arrests, and warrants: YLSM, pp. 7, 10.

On the arrests in Denver and Salt Lake City: YLSM, p. 9; Sheehy, "The Consequences of Panthermania," p. 56.

For McLucas's statements and his transferral to Connecticut: Sheehy, "The Consequences of Panthermania," p. 56; Epstein, "The Panthers and the Police," p. 54; YLSM, p. 9.

On Sams's flight and arrest: YLSM, pp. 6-8; Sheehy, "The Consequences of Panthermania," pp. 56, 66; Epstein, "The Panthers and the Police," p. 54; *Newsweek,* March 30, p. 22; *NYT,* Aug. 22, 1969, p. 33; *NYT,* March 22, p. 57.

On Sams's journey to New York and New Haven, and the Panthers' explanation: *Panther Trial News,* Aug. 9; Sheehy, "The Consequences of Panthermania," pp. 49-50; *NYT,* March 22, p. 57; YLSM, p. 6.

8   On Sams's background and ideological deviation: *Panther Trial News,* Aug. 9; *NYT,* March 22, p. 57; *Newsweek,* Aug. 17, p. 33; Sheehy, "The Consequences of Panthermania," pp. 49-50; Epstein, "The Panthers and the Police," pp. 53-54.

On Panther ideology in 1969 and 1970: *People's News Service,* April 5, p. 16; *U.S. News and World Report,* Sept. 21, pp. 82-83; *The Nation,* Aug. 11, 1969, pp. 102-3; Rochon interview.

On Seale's arrest: *NYT,* Aug. 20, 1969, p. 15; *NYT,* Aug. 22, 1969, p. 33; YLSM, pp. 6, 12.

8-9   For Ahern's reaction to the request for Seale's indictment: Ahern, *Police in Trouble,* p. 34.

9   On the denial of bail to Seale and his indictment: *NYT,* Aug. 22, 1969, p. 33; *NYT,* Aug. 28, 1969, p. 25; Donald Freed, *Agony in New Haven: The Trial of Bobby Seale, Ericka Huggins, and the Black Panther Party* (New York: Simon and Schuster, 1973), p. 309.

On Seale's trial in Chicago: *The "Trial" of Bobby Seale* (New York: Priam Books, 1970).

For Garry's interpretation of the murder: *Newsweek,* March 30, p. 22; *Time,* May 11, p. 29; Epstein, "The Panthers and the Police," p. 52; *NYT,* Jan. 17, pp. 1, 27; *NYT,* Mar. 22, p. 57; *YDN,* Mar. 12, p. 1.

Notes

For the Panthers' version of the murder: *Black Panther*, April 25, p. 13; *NYT*, March 22, p. 57.

9-10   For the charges against the defendants: YLSM, pp. 8-12.

10   On the guilty pleas of Sams and another defendant: *NYT*, Dec. 2, 1969, p. 59.

On Kimbro's guilty plea: *NYT*, Jan. 17, pp. 1, 23; *NYT*, March 22, p. 57; Epstein, "The Panthers and the Police," p. 54; Sheehy, "The Consequences of Panthermania," pp. 52, 57; *Panther Trial News*, July 27 (Yale Archives).

On the bail hearings and their outcome: YLSM, p. 21; *NYT*, Dec. 30, 1969, p. 30; *NYT*, March 25, p. 33; *NHJC*, April 15, p. 4.

On Seale's extradition: *NYT*, Jan. 1, p. 16; *YDN*, March 30, p. 1.

10-11   On the New Haven Panther chapter until March 1970: *NYT*, March 22, p. 57; Gail Sheehy, "Black against Black: The Agony of Panthermania," *New York Magazine*, Nov. 16, pp. 45-50, passim; Epstein, "The Panthers and the Police," pp. 59-60; Andrew Kopkind, "Bringing It All Back Home," *Hard Times*, May 11-18, p. 3; Ron Rosenbaum, "Either/Or at Yale: May Day & the Panthers," *Village Voice*, May 7, p. 1; Slie interview; Rochon interview; Robinson interview; Wilkinson interview.

11   On the efforts to involve Yale students: Baker interview; Wilkinson interview; Robinson interview; Mills interview; Trinkaus interview; Zaeder interview; *YDN*, Dec. 17, 1969, p. 1; *YDN*, Dec. 18, 1969, p. 1; *People's News Service*, April 6; Kopkind, "Bringing It All Back Home," p. 3.

For the NHPDC's announcement: *YDN*, April 6, p. 1.

11-12   On Dostou's background: ibid.; Kegan interview; Pressman interview; Spinrad interview.

12   On the NHPDC: *NHJC*, April 8, p. 4; *YDN*, April 6, p. 1; Pressman interview; Kegan interview; Spinrad interview; Ogilvy interview; Kenneth Keniston, "New Haven Notebook: May Day Weekend at Yale," *New Leader*, June 22, p. 12.

For Dostou's complaints: *YDN*, April 6, p. 1.

For Ahern's admission: Ahern interview.

On the police raid: Kegan interview; Pressman interview.

13   On Yale's peaceful response to political agitation: Brooks Mather Kelley, "The Brewster Years: A Question of Survival," *New Journal*, Dec. 12, 1974, pp. 6-7; *Yale Graduate Professional*, April 24, 1969, pp. 1-2; *YDN*, Nov. 4-14, 1969, passim; *YDN*, Dec. 17, 1969, p. 1; *YDN*, Dec. 18, 1969, p. 1.

For Garry's statements: Epstein, "The Panthers and the Police," p. 45.

"a series of gunbattles . . .": *Time*, Dec. 12, 1969, p. 20.

"lethal undeclared war": ibid.

For magazine articles implying persecution of the Panthers: ibid.; Epstein, "The Panthers and the Police," pp. 45-51, passim; *New Yorker*,

Feb. 21, pp. 30-33; *Newsweek,* Feb. 23, pp. 26-30; *Newsweek,* March 30, pp. 22-23; L. F. Palmer Jr., "Out to Get the Panthers," *The Nation,* July 28, 1969, pp. 78-82; Robert A. Jones, "Panthers' White Conference," *The Nation,* Aug. 11, 1969, pp. 102-103; *The Nation,* Dec. 29, 1969, p. 717; Robert Cover, "A Year of Harassment," *The Nation,* Feb. 2, pp. 110-113; *The Nation,* March 2, p. 229; *America,* Dec. 27, 1969, p. 629.

On the involvement of public figures: Epstein, "The Panthers and the Police," pp. 45-51, passim; *NYT,* Jan. 15, p. 50.

For the defendants' extensive complaint: YLSM, pp. 25-26.

For the charges of brutality: SSC press release, April 29; leaflets; *Yale Graduate Professional,* April 23, p. 3.

13-14 For the response to the defendants' other allegations: Goldstein interview; YLSM, p. 26.

14 For the contention of biased choices of legal options: Farley interview. For the defendants' complaint about their grand jury: YLSM, pp. 16-18.

For the complaint about Seale's grand jury: *NYT,* April 24, p. 23; *NHR,* April 23, pp. 1-2; *NHR,* April 24, pp. 1-2; *NHJC,* April 24, p. 27.

14-15 For the Panthers' four complaints cited in the next paragraphs and the counter-arguments: YLSM, pp. 18-22; Gwirtsman/Foster, "Notes on the Bobby Seale-Panther trial."

15 On the events of April 10: *YDN,* April 13, p. 1; *NHR,* April 10, pp. 1-2.

15-16 On the courtroom incidents of April 14: *NHJC,* April 15, p. 4; *Black Panther,* April 25, pp. 5-6; *People's News Service,* April 26, p. 14; *YDN,* April 15, p. 1.

"to reach for . . .": *YDN,* April 15, p. 1.

For Genet's claim: *People's News Service,* April 26, p. 14.

16 On Hilliard's status: *YDN,* April 15, p. 1; *NHJC,* April 15, p. 4.

On the other sentences and the incidents outside the courthouse: *NHJC,* April 15, p. 4; *NHR,* April 14, pp. 1-2; *YDN,* April 15, p. 1.

3   The Making of an Entente

17 For Dostou's prediction: *YDN,* April 6, p. 1.

On the demonstration of April 10: *YDN,* April 13, p. 1.

17-18 For Wilkinson's statement: Wilkinson interview.

18 For Chauncey's claim: Chauncey interview.

For Brewster's statement: Brewster interview.

For Ogilvy's feelings and actions in early April: Ogilvy interview; Ogilvy's letter to Brewster, April 11.

On Brewster's failure to respond: Ogilvy interview.

Notes

19-20   On the Woolsey Hall rally: *YAM*, pp. 18-19; *YAM* transcript; *YDN*, April 14, p. 1; *NHJC*, April 14, p. 4.

20   On Genet: *YDN*, April 14, p. 1; *YAM*, p. 18.

21   On the rally's "violent and unsettling" tenor: *YAM*, p. 18.
On the formation of an ad hoc committee: Ogilvy interview.
On the tone and composition of the April 15 meeting: Morris interview; Spinrad interview; Mills interview; Cohen interview; *YDN*, April 16, p. 1.
On the opening of the meeting: *YDN*, April 16, p. 1.
On the presentation of suggestions: Cohen interview.

21-22   On the desire to make impossible demands: Spinrad interview.

22   On the desire to make practical demands: Johnson interview.
For the four extreme suggestions: *YDN*, April 16, p. 1.
"If you want your manhood . . .": John Hersey, *Letter to the Alumni* (New York: Alfred A. Knopf, 1970), p. 95.
For the most extreme suggestion: ibid.; *YDN*, April 16, p. 1; John Fischer, "Black Panthers and Their White Hero Worshippers," *Harper's,* Aug., p. 26; Francine du Plessix Gray, "The Panthers at Yale," *New York Review of Books,* June 4, p. 29.
On the chief reaction to the suicide proposal: Spinrad interview; Morris interview.
"They laughed nervously . . .": Morris interview.

22-23   For Mills's statement: Eisenstein interview; Mills interview.

23   For the students' statements: *YDN*, April 16, p. 1.
"I don't think . . .": ibid.
On Dostou's conference in the corridor: Morris interview.
For Dostou's statement about rifles: ibid.; Hersey, *Letter to the Alumni,* p. 95; Spinrad interview.

23-24   On the outcome of the meeting: *YDN*, April 16, p. 1; Ogilvy interview.

24   On the subsequent college meetings: Spinrad interview; *YDN*, April 17, p. 1.
On the moratorium's impact on April 16: *YDN*, April 17, p. 1; *NHJC*, April 17, p. 4.

25   For Big Man's announcement: *NHJC*, April 16, p. 5.
On the Panthers' visits to Dwight Hall: William H. Farley, "Amerika the Ugly Spurs Revolutionary Reaction," *YDN* special issue, April 22, 1975, p. 1.
22, 1975, p. 1; Cohen interview; Ogilvy interview; Spinrad interview; Mills interview; Eisenstein interview.
For Miranda's threats: Spinrad interview.
For Doustou's suggestion: Farley, "Amerika the Ugly," p. 1.

25-26   For Miranda's exchange with a group of black undergraduates: ibid., pp. 1, 7.

26   On the difficulty of persuading black students: Ogilvy interview.
On the blacks' view of the Moratorium Committee: Rochon interview.

On the BSAY: ibid.; Ren Frutkin's notes; Robinson interview; Dawson interview; *U.S. News and World Report,* May 11, p. 42.
On the black students' skepticism and uncertainty: Dawson interview; Robinson interview; Farley, "Amerika the Ugly," pp. 7, 10.
On the radicals' admission to Dwight Hall: Warren interview.
26-27 On Dwight Hall's role at Yale: ibid.
27 On the conservatives' exclusion from Dwight Hall: Tharp interview; Spinrad interview.
On Dwight Hall's relations with the Yale administration: Zaeder interview; Warren interview.
"so long as . . .": Warren interview.
On the administration's payment to Dwight Hall: ibid.
On the conservatives' feelings: Tharp interview; Spinrad interview.
For May's opening statement at the faculty meeting: May interview.
27-28 On the grading debate: Kagan interview; *YDN,* April 17, pp. 1, 4.
28 For Ogilvy's reaction: Ogilvy interview.
For the resolutions on the trial: Peter Brooks, "Panthers at Yale," *Partisan Review,* no. 3, p. 425.
For May's statements after the meeting: *YDN,* April 17, p. 1.
For May's later statement: May interview.
On the rarity of ad hoc faculty meetings: May interview.
29 On the administration's response: Wilkinson interview.
For Brewster's reaction to the contempt sentences: Brewster interview.
On the administration members: Chauncey interview; Gerard Swordes's notes (in Swordes's possession); minutes of the Yale College Council of Masters meeting, April 24 (in Swordes's possession).
On the decision to extend an official welcome: Chauncey interview.
29-30 For Kernan's thoughts: Kernan interview.
30 On Mulvey's denial of bail: *YDN,* April 20, p. 1.
On the expectations of violence: *YAM,* p. 18; Hersey, *Letter to the Alumni,* p. 95.
On Coffin's effort to define his response: Coffin interview; Fitt interview; Warren interview; Zaeder interview.
30-31 For Coffin's sermon: *YDN,* April 20, pp. 2-4.
31 On the denunciation of Coffin: *NYT,* April 27, p. 39.
32 For Brewster's approval of the sermon: Coffin interview.
"worth three full professors": informal interview with a Yale alumnus.
"any illusion that . . .": *YDN,* April 20, pp. 3-4.
32-33 For Coffin's later comments: Coffin interview.
33 On the previous meetings of liberal faculty members: Mills interview; Trinkaus interview; Brooks interview.
On the April 18 meeting: Brooks, "Panthers at Yale," p. 426; Baker interview.
33-34 On the meeting with Brewster: Mills interview; Triffin interview; Fitt interview.

Notes

34   On Godard's talk and Mills's statement: *YDN*, April 20, pp. 1, 3; Mills interview.
      On Mills's return to Battell Chapel with Godard: Mills interview.
      "raise the level . . .": *YDN*, April 20, p. 1.
      For the four new demands: leaflets.
      "Doug Miranda did . . .": Schmoke interview.

35-36 On the Battell Chapel teach-in: Mills interview; Cohen interview; Spinrad interview; leaflets; *NHJC*, April 20, p. 4; *YDN*, April 20, p. 1.

37   For Mills's assessment of Miranda's speech: Mills interview.
      For Mills's remark to a friend: Cohen interview.
      For Brewster's public statement: text of a statement by Brewster, April 19.

38   For Osborne's statement on the committee: *YDN*, April 21, p. 1.
      On the annoyance of Branford and the black faculty: Bryce-LaPorte interview; Mills interview.
      On the black faculty's meeting: Mills interview; Bryce-LaPorte interview; Baker interview; *YDN*, April 21, p. 1.

38-39 For the black faculty's letter: letter to Brewster from the black faculty, April 20.

39   For Osborne's claim: *YDN*, April 21, p. 1.
      For Fitt's recollection: Fitt interview.
      For Mills's explanation: Mills interview.

40   On the Panthers' view of Mills: ibid.; Eisenstein interview.
      On Mills's view of the Panthers and his differences from other black faculty members: Eisenstein interview; Mills interview.
      On Baker's reaction: Mills interview.
      On the black faculty's status: ibid.; Rose interview; Baker interview; Bryce-LaPorte interview; Eisenstein interview.

40-41 For Bryce-LaPorte's statement: Bryce-LaPorte interview.

41   On the black faculty's influence on the BSAY: Robinson interview; Baker interview.
      On the black faculty's actions: Baker interview; Bryce-LaPorte interview.

41-42 On Abernathy's press conference: *NYT*, April 21, p. 26; WYBC news report, April 20.

41   For Dellinger's announcement: WYBC news report, April 21.

42   On the colleges' decisions about May Day and the Moratorium Committee's demands: *YAM*, p. 20; *YDN*, April 21, p. 1; *YDN*, April 22, p. 1; WYBC news reports, April 20, 21.
      On the Council of Masters meetings: WYBC news reports, April 21, 22; *YDN*, April 21, p. 1; *YDN*, April 22, p. 1; Swordes interview; Gerard Swordes's notes (in Swordes's possession).
      On arrangements for the Ingalls Rink rally: *YDN*, April 21, p. 1; Ogilvy interview; Eisenstein interview; Chauncey interview; Mills interview.

42-43 On the BSAY meeting: Mills interview; WYBC news report, April 20.

191

43-44   On the Afro-America House meeting: Mills interview; Rochon interview.

· 43   On Panther-BSAY relations: Rochon interview; Robinson interview; Baker interview.

       On the UFPD: Dawson interview; Rochon interview.

44   For the conservatives' petition and announcements: Spinrad interview; *YDN*, April 21, p. 1; *YAM*, p. 20.

       On the conservatives' discouragement: Tharp interview; Menafee interview; Spinrad interview; Cottrol interview; *NHR*, April 23, p. 17.

44-45   On the convening of the Student Senate and the composition of the meeting: Brooks, "Panthers at Yale," p. 426; *YDN*, April 20, p. 1; WYBC news reports, April 20; Johnson interview; Rahe interview.

45   On the suspension of the agenda: *YDN*, April 21, p. 1; WYBC news report, April 20; Johnson interview.

       For the first motion: Johnson interview.

       On the confusion of the meeting: ibid.; Rahe interview.

       "the tense, angry face . . .": Brooks, "Panthers at Yale," p. 427.

45-46   On the suggestion to dissolve the Student Senate: ibid.; Rahe interview; Machioni interview; *YDN*, April 21, p. 1.

46   For the senate's resolution: *YDN*, April 21, p. 1; WYBC news report, April 20; *U.S. News and World Report*, May 11, p. 42.

       On the speech after the adjournment: Rahe interview.

       "At that point . . .": Machioni interview.

       On the "atmosphere of intimidation" and Triffin's fright: Rahe interview.

       On the decision to have an open meeting: Johnson interview.

4   *The Panther and the Bulldog*

49   On the demonstration outside the courthouse: *Bright College Days* (movie); WYBC news reports, April 20, 21.

49-50   On the disorders and arrests downtown: WYBC news report, April 21; *NYT*, April 22, p. 52; *NHR*, April 21, pp. 1-2; *NHJC*, April 22, p. 5; *YDN*, April 22, p. 1; *U.S. News and World Report*, May 11, p. 42.

49   On the presence of Student Senate hecklers: Johnson interview.

50   On the turmoil in local schools: *NHR*, April 22, p. 7; *NHR*, April 23, pp. 1-2; *NHR*, April 24, p. 56; *NHR*, April 28, p. 48; *NHR*, April 30, p. 43; *NHJC*, April 23, pp. 1, 19; *NHJC*, April 24, pp. 1, 27; *NHJC*, April 25, p. 2; *NHJC*, April 29, pp. 1, 13; *NHJC*, April 30, pp. 1, 13; *NHJC*, April 27, pp. 1, 15.

50-51   On the legal proceedings of April 21: WYBC news report, April 21; *NYT*, April 22, p. 52; *NHR*, April 22, p. 2; *NHR*, April 29, p. 1; *NHJC*, April 22, p. 19; *YDN*, April 22, p. 1; *Black Panther*, April 25, p. 6.

50   On Seale's frequent appeals to the Constitution: John Fischer, "Black Panthers and Their White Hero Worshippers," *Harper's*, Aug., p. 26.

Notes

51   For Brewster's remark: tape recording of Brewster's press conference, April 30.

51-52 For Fitt's comments: Fitt interview.

52-53 On the Berkeley press conference: *YDN,* April 22, pp. 1, 5-6; WYBC news reports, April 21.

52   On Yale's promise of money and the blacks' resentment: Baker interview; Mills interview; *YAM,* March, p. 19; Kenneth Keniston, "New Haven Notebook: May Day Weekend at Yale," *New Leader,* June 22, p. 11; Nora Sayre, *Sixties Going on Seventies* (London: Constable, 1974), p. 163.

53   On the Osborne Committee's dissolution: Coffin interview; *YDN,* April 22, p. 1.

53-54 On the convention in New York: *NYT,* April 22, p. 47; WYBC news report, April 21; text of Brewster's address to the Bureau of Advertising of the American Newspaper Publishers Association, April 21.

Genesis of a Strike

55   On the opening of the Ingalls Rink rally: *YDN,* April 22, p. 1; Keniston, "New Haven Notebook," p. 11.

55-56 On the rally's agenda: Rochon interview.

56   For Rochon's opening remarks: ibid.
For Coffin's speech: *NYT,* April 22, p. 52; *YAM,* p. 21; *YAM* transcript.

56-57 For Rochon's response and its significance: Rochon interview; Mills interview; Dawson interview; Farley interview.

57   For the quotations from the four speakers after Coffin: *YAM* transcript.

57-58 On the speaker for Women's Liberation: ibid.; Robert Brustein, *Revolution as Theatre: Notes on the New Radical Style* (New York: Liveright, 1971), p. 55.

58   For Garry's speech: *YAM* transcript.

58ff.   Quotations from Hilliard at the Ingalls Rink rally, unless otherwise noted, are from Brustein, *Revolution as Theatre,* pp. 56-62, and the *YAM* transcript.

59   On Hilliard's previous experiences with crowds: Tom Hayden, "The Trial," *Ramparts,* July, p. 47.

59ff.   For Mills's comments on the Ingalls Rink meeting: Mills interview.

61   On the response to Hilliard's attempt at a reconciliation: *NHJC,* April 22, p. 19; Brustein, *Revolution as Theatre,* p. 60.

62   On the treatment of the white-shirted man: Mills interview; Eisenstein interview.

63   "Kick *all* these . . .": John Hersey, *Letter to the Alumni* (New York: Alfred A. Knopf, 1970), p. 101
For Mills's attempt to salvage the rally: ibid.; Mills interview; Brustein, *Revolution as Theatre,* p. 62.

64   For the intruder's remarks and his exchange with Keniston: *YAM* transcript; Brustein, *Revolution as Theatre,* pp. 62-64.

64-65   For Brustein's attack and the experience of the beaten man: Brustein, *Revolution as Theatre,* pp. 64, 137-43, passim.

65   "It isn't easy . . .": ibid., pp. 64-65.

       On the crowd's response to Mills: ibid., p. 65; *NHR,* April 22, pp. 1, 27; *NHJC,* April 22, p. 19.

       On the final speaker: WYBC news report, April 21; *YAM* transcript.

       "so wiped out by that meeting . . .": Mills interview.

       "to get out of school work": Rostow interview.

66   "a fascination with history and politics": Stephans interview.

       "boredom": Zackon interview.

       "fear": Beasley interview.

66-67   On the BSAY's "mobile unit": Rochon interview.

67   On threats during the college referenda: Spinrad interview; Band interview.

       On the presence of faculty members: Eisenstein interview; Ogilvy interview.

       On the personal threats against opponents of the strike: Tharp interview; Spinrad interview; Brustein, *Revolution as Theatre,* p. 78.

       On the moderates' realization that "the blacks meant business": Lauber interview.

       On the first Berkeley meeting: ibid.; Tharp interview.

67-68   On the second Berkeley meeting: Lauber interview; Rahe interview; Belson interview; Johnson interview; WYBC news report, April 22.

68ff.   The college referenda statistics, unless otherwise noted, are from *SN,* April 23, p. 4; this is the best source, but it sometimes conflicts with WYBC news reports, April 21, 22, 23; *YDN,* April 22, p. 1, covers this subject only vaguely.

68-69   On the politics of Branford: *Yale Graduate Professional,* April 24, 1969, pp. 1-2; Mills interview; Rose interview; Eisenstein interview; Trinkaus interview; leaflets.

68   For Trinkaus's statement and his political position: Trinkaus interview. For Trinkaus's declaration about the Paris uprising: Douglas Hallett, "Remaking the World is a Myth," *YDN* special issue, April 22, 1975, p. 11; all other quotations in the paragraphs on Branford are based on the author's personal observations and informal interviews.

69-70   On the Jonathan Edwards strike meeting: Cannon interview; Morris interview; Rostow interview.

70   On the Saybrook referenda: Griffin interview; Yanowitz interview.

Day of Equipoise

71   For Chauncey's statement: *YDN,* April 23, p. 1.

       On the BSAY's policy of interrupting classes: Rochon interview.

       On attendance at Organic Chemistry and Morgan's course: WYBC news reports, April 22.

72 On activities in the drama and graduate schools: ibid., April 22, 23; *NHJC,* April 25, p. 34; *SN,* April 23, p. 2; Brustein, *Revolution as Theatre,* pp. 66-70; leaflets (Yale Archives); press release issued by the Yale drama school, April 22.
On the April 22 meetings at Dwight Hall: *SN,* April 23, pp. 1-2; *NHR,* April 23, p. 17; *NHJC,* April 23, p. 1; *YDN,* April 23, p. 1; the SSC's list of its members.
For the BSAY's recommendations: manifesto of the BSAY, April 22; Robinson interview.
On the BSAY's aloofness: Rochon interview.
On the SSC's unsuccessful efforts: Ogilvy interview.

73 For Miranda's statement: *SN,* April 23, p. 2.
For the black community's statement: press release issued by the Black Coalition of New Haven, Heritage Hall Corporation, April 22 (Yale Archives).
On the black community's opinion of white radicals: Slie interview; Tharp interview; Bryce-LaPorte interview; Ren Frutkin's notes on a teach-in, April 29.

73-74 For the SSC's five demands: *SN,* April 23, pp. 1, 4.

74 On the plans for the demands: ibid., p. 1; WYBC news reports, April 23.
On the fate of the demands: WYBC news reports, April 23, 24; *NHR,* April 26, p. 1; *NHJC,* April 27, p. 1; *SN,* April 24, pp. 1, 4; *SN,* April 26, pp. 1, 4.
On the SSC's and the students' misunderstanding: Ogilvy interview; Rochon interview.
On WYBC's support of the strike: *NHJC,* April 22, p. 1.
For the *Yale Daily News*'s opposition to a strike: *YDN,* April 16, p. 2; *YDN,* April 21, p. 2.

74-75 For the *Strike Newspaper*'s stated purpose: *SN,* April 23, p. 1.

75 On the support given to the *Strike Newspaper*: Clark interview; Gerard Swordes's notes (in Swordes's possession); *YDN,* May 4, p. 1.
On the arrangements for Kennedy's speech: *YDN,* April 23, p. 1; WYBC news report, April 22; Coffin interview; Schmoke interview.
On Schmoke's actions: Schmoke interview; WYBC news report, April 22.
On the objections of conservatives: Tharp interview; Menafee interview.

76 On the students' speeches: *YDN,* April 23, p. 1; *NHJC,* April 23, p. 1; leaflet; *Yale Graduate Professional,* April 23, p. 1; WYBC news reports, April 22.
On the emotions of Kennedy and his audience: *Yale Graduate Professional,* April 23, pp. 1, insert A; Johnson interview.
On Kennedy's gesture to Dawson: Robinson interview.
For Kennedy's remarks: WYBC news reports, April 22; *YDN,* April 23, p. 1; *NHJC,* April 22, pp. 1, 15; *Yale Graduate Professional,* April 23, pp. 1, insert A.
For Kennedy's original speech: text of Edward Kennedy's address to the Yale Political Union, April 22.

For Coffin's speech at Battell Chapel: leaflet; WYBC news reports, April 22, 23; *NHJC*, April 23, p. 1; *NHR*, April 23, p. 1; *YDN*, April 23, p. 1.

76-77 For Brewster's statement to Coffin: Coffin interview.
77 For Coffin's remarks: ibid.
On the Beinecke Plaza rally: WYBC news report, April 22.
On the erratic nature of Yale audiences: Sayre, *Sixties Going On Seventies*, p. 163.
On the courtroom proceedings of April 22: WYBC news reports, April 22; *NHR*, April 22, p. 1; *NHJC*, April 23, p. 4; *NYT*, April 23, pp. 1, 28.

77-78 For Garry's statements in a local café: Johnson interview.
78 On New Haven's multi-alarm fires: *NHR*, April 22, p. 1; *NHR*, April 23, pp. 1, 2; *NHR*, April 24, pp. 1, 2; *NHR*, May 3, pp. 1, 2; *NHJC*, April 23, p. 1; *NHJC*, April 24, p. 1; *NHJC*, April 27, p. 4; *NHJC*, April 29, p. 1; WYBC news reports, April 22, 23, 24, 27, 29, May 2.
On the college fires: WYBC news reports, April 21, 22; *YDN*, April 22, p. 5.
On Brewster's hope: Rostow interview; WYBC news report, April 21.
For Brewster's response to the reporters: WYBC news reports, April 22.

5   *The Faculty's Verdict*

79-80 For Brewster's explanation: Brewster interview.
80 For May's comments: *YDN*, April 23, p. 1.
On the meeting of the Faculty Steering Committee: May interview; Thorburn interview.
81 On the membership of the second group: Trinkaus interview.
On the April 22 meeting at Trinkaus's house: Thorburn interview; Mills interview; Brooks interview; Trinkaus interview.
On the actions of Trinkaus's group on April 23: Peter Brooks, "Panthers at Yale," *Partisan Review*, no. 3, p. 431; Kenneth Keniston, "New Haven Notebook: May Day Weekend at Yale," *New Leader*, June 22, p. 11; Brooks interview; Trinkaus interview; Keniston interview; Eisenstein interview.
"We thought that . . .": Eisenstein interview.
For Mills's statements at Trinkaus's house: Thorburn interview; Brooks interview.

81-82 On the possible effect of Mills's statements: Thorburn interview.
82 For Keniston's feelings: Keniston interview.
For Mills's explanation: Mills interview.
On the black faculty's concerns and feelings: Bryce-LaPorte interview; Baker interview.
For Brewster's characterization: Brewster interview.

82-83 On the students' marches and demonstrations: WYBC news report, April 23; *NHJC*, April 24, pp. 1, 12; *NHR*, April 24, p. 56; *YDN*, April 24, p. 1; Ren Frutkin's notes.

Notes

83 For Turner's speeches and the interruption: *YDN,* April 24, p. 1; Ren Frutkin's notes; see also WYBC news reports, April 23.

    For Miranda's analogy: *YDN,* April 24, p. 1.

84 On the record attendance: May interview.

84ff. Unless otherwise noted, all information on the faculty meeting is from an early draft of the minutes of the Yale College faculty meeting, April 23 (in Edgar Boell's possession).

84 On the blacks present at the meeting: Dawson interview; Bryce-LaPorte interview; Baker interview.

    On May's policy toward people who were ineligible to attend: May interview.

    On the black faculty's motive for sitting together: Mills interview; Bryce-LaPorte interview.

    On Bryce-LaPorte's method of obtaining the floor: Keniston, "New Haven Notebook," p. 11; May interview.

84-85 For Brewster's assessment: Brewster interview.

85 On the black faculty's jauntiness and anticipated "theatricalities": Mills interview.

    For Mills's whisper and its meaning: ibid.

    For Bryce-LaPorte's opening statement: Bryce-LaPorte interview.

85-86 For the black faculty's proposals: resolution of the Yale black faculty, April 23 (in William Farley's possession).

86 For Bryce-LaPorte's comments on the proposals: Bryce-LaPorte interview.

    On the vote to "adjourn" the meeting: May interview.

    On the influence of the demonstrations: *YDN,* April 24, p. 1; Kernan interview; Pierson interview; Eisenstein interview; Robert Brustein, *Revolution as Theatre: Notes on the New Radical Style* (New York: Liveright, 1971), pp. 73, 138.

86-87 "Everybody just sat . . .": Schmoke interview.

87 For Schmoke's speech: ibid.; Kagan interview.

    On Schmoke's action after leaving the meeting: Ren Frutkin's notes; Schmoke interview.

    "When he finished . . .": Kagan interview.

    For May's claim: *YDN,* April 24, p. 1.

    For Brewster's prepared speech: text of Brewster's remarks at the Yale College faculty meeting, April 23.

88-89 For Brewster's clarification of "the [skepticism] statement": Brewster interview.

89 On the prevailing mood: Keniston interview.

    On the conservative resolution: Thorburn interview.

    For Mills's statement to Brooks: ibid.; Brooks interview; Baker interview.

90 For Kernan's explanation: Kernan interview.

    On the novice faculty members at the meeting: May interview.

    For Brewster's response: Brewster interview.

    On the conservatives' surprise at Brewster's attitude: Brooks interview;

Pierson interview.

For Parry's feelings: Parry interview.

91   For Bryce-LaPorte's explanation: Bryce-LaPorte interview.

For the political science professor's speech: Rose interview.

"charging down the aisle . . .": interview with a faculty member who prefers to remain anonymous.

For Segal's speech: Rose interview; Thorburn interview.

93   For Thorburn's statement and the liberals' concerns: Thorburn interview.

For Parry's feelings: Parry interview.

For Mills's response to the liberals' complaints: Brustein, *Revolution as Theatre,* p. 75.

93-94   For Thorburn's recollection: Thorburn interview.

94   For Mills's expectations: Mills interview.

For Dawson's suspicion: Dawson interview.

For Mills's public exhortation to continue the strike: *SN,* April 25, p. 1; WYBC news report, April 24.

On the rarity of a president putting the question: Francine du Plessix Gray, "The Panthers at Yale," *New York Review of Books,* June 4, p. 30.

For the response of several liberals to Mills's warning: Thorburn interview; Brooks interview.

94-95   For Pierson's statement: Pierson interview; Woodward interview.

95   For Brewster's explanation: Brewster interview.

For Brewster's subsequent declaration: Thorburn interview.

95-96   For Thorburn's comments: ibid.

96   On the rejection of Keniston's amendment: Brooks interview; *NHJC,* April 24, p. 27.

On the discussion after the vote: Thorburn interview; Baker interview.

For Bickel's feelings after leaving the meeting: Alexander M. Bickel, "The Tolerance of Violence on the Campus," *New Republic,* June 13, p. 16; Alexander M. Bickel, *The Morality of Consent* (New Haven: Yale University Press, 1975), pp. 136-137.

For the feelings of other professors: Gray, "The Panthers at Yale," p. 30; Brooks, "Panthers at Yale," p. 430; Brooks Mather Kelley, "The Brewster Years: A Question of Survival," *New Journal,* Dec. 12, 1974, p. 8; Bickel, "The Tolerance of Violence on the Campus," p. 16; *YDN,* April 27, p. 1.

On Trinkaus's reading of the resolution: Edward Samuels, "Dear Mom and Dad: An Account of May Day at Yale," p. 22 (Yale Archives).

For Mills's assertion: Gray, "The Panthers at Yale," p. 34.

97   On Brewster's appointment with Guida: Chauncey interview; Brewster interview; Fitt interview; Ahern interview; Lee interview; *NHR,* April 24, p. 56; tape recording of Brewster's press conference, April 30.

For Guida's statement to Ahern: Ahern interview.

"a medieval patrician . . .": ibid.

Notes

For Ahern's statement to Chauncey: Brewster interview; Ahern interview.

On Brewster's rephrasing of the faculty resolution: Baker interview.

97-98 On Brewster's drafting of a directive: May interview; Bryce-LaPorte interview; Baker interview.

98 For Brewster's directive: Brewster's directive to the Yale University faculties, April 23.

For the courtroom proceedings of April 23: *NYT,* April 24, p. 23; *NHR,* April 23, pp. 1-2; *NHR,* April 24, pp. 1-2; NHJC, April 24, pp. 1, 27; *Black Panther,* May 2, p. 7; WYBC news reports, April 23, 24.

6   *The Groundwork for May Day*

99 On the general attitude toward May Day: minutes of the Council of Masters meeting, April 24 (in Gerard Swordes's possession).

On the students' departure: Kenneth Keniston, "New Haven Notebook: May Day Weekend at Yale," *New Leader,* June 22, p. 13; Ron Rosenbaum, "Either/Or at Yale: Mayday & the Panthers," *Village Voice,* May 7, p. 48; *NHJC,* April 29, p. 4; *NHJC,* May 1, p. 1; WYBC news report, April 28.

On the Panthers' unclear policy: WYBC news reports, April 24; *YAM* transcript of a press conference, April 24; *People's News Service,* April 26; *Black Panther,* April 25, passim; ibid., May 2, p. 17; minutes of an SSC meeting, April 27.

On the black community's decision: Dawson interview; Paul Starr, "Black Panthers and White Radicals," *Commonweal,* June 12, p. 295; Gail Sheehy, "The Consequences of Panthermania," *New York Magazine,* Nov. 23, p. 58.

100 On the students' offer of rooms: *NHJC,* April 27, p. 15; *SN,* April 24, p. 1.

On class attendance: *SN,* April 24, p. 1; WYBC news report, April 23.

100-101 For Alinsky's speech: WYBC news report, April 23; *SN,* April 26, pp. 1, 4; *YDN,* April 27, pp. 1, 6.

101-102 On the arrangements for the teach-out, and its results: press release issued by the teach-out organizers, April 29; documents (Yale Archives); leaflet; *SN,* April 23, p. 3; *SN,* April 26, p. 3; *NHJC-NHR,* April 25, p. 34; *NHJC,* April 27, pp. 1, 15; *NHR,* April 29, pp. 1-2; *YAM,* p. 24; *YDN,* April 27, pp. 1, 6; *NYT,* April 25, p. 35; WYBC news reports, April 22, 23, 28.

102 For MacDonald's response to Brewster's "skepticism": *NHJC-NHR,* April 25, p. 1; *YDN,* April 27, p. 3.

For Brewster's letter: Brewster's letter to Herbert MacDonald, April 25.

On MacDonald's continued annoyance: *YDN,* April 27, p. 3.

103 For Marcus's statements: press release issued by Edward Marcus, April 27; Edward Marcus's letter to Brewster, April 27.

For Farley's letter: Farley's letter to *NYT* Editorial Board, April 24; for other students' letters to newspapers, see documents (Yale Archives). For Coffin's description of his more direct action: Coffin interview.

104   On Hersey's decision and the *New York Times*'s reaction: ibid.; Johnson interview; Cannon interview; Slie interview.

For Guida's announcement: *NHR,* April 24, p. 1.

On Brewster's frustrations: Lee interview; minutes of the Council of Masters meeting, April 24 (in Gerard Swordes's possession).

On Chauncey's meeting with administrators: Swordes interview; Swordes's notes (in Swordes's possession).

On Chauncey's meeting with students: WYBC news report, April 24; *SN,* April 25, p. 1.

For Brewster's statement: Brewster's statement on university plans for May Day, April 27.

For Brewster's and Chauncey's emphasis: *YDN,* April 28, p. 1; tape recording of Brewster's press conference, April 30.

On the silent vigil: *YDN,* April 27, p. 1; WYBC news report, April 23.

On Coffin's earlier involvement: *SN,* April 24, p. 2.

104-105 For Coffin's disclaimer: press release issued by Coffin, April 24.

105   For Coffin's sermon: *NYT,* April 27, p. 39.

For the interviews of two law professors: *YDN,* April 27, pp. 1, 3.

On the colleges' political activities: Baker interview; Bryce-LaPorte interview; Mills interview; *YAM,* p. 28; *SN,* April 28, p. 2; Ren Frutkin's notes; Hester Eisenstein's notes; teach-ins are also reported in *YDN, SN,* and WYBC news reports, April 22-May 2, passim.

105-106 On Farley's meetings before Saturday: minutes of an SSC meeting, April 25.

106   On the SSC's uncertainty: ibid.

On the militancy of the Panthers and the NHPDC: ibid., April 27; supra, p. 99.

For the SSC's decision: minutes of an SSC meeting, April 27.

On the SSC's subcommittee: *SN,* April 26, p. 1.

On the appointment of subcommittees: minutes of an SSC meeting, April 25.

For the revised demands: ibid., April 26; *SN,* April 27, pp. 1, 4; *SN,* April 28, pp. 1, 4.

107   For the support from the employees union: press release issued by the Yale employees union; WYBC news report, April 28; *YDN,* April 28, pp. 1, 3.

On the moderates' reaction: *NHJC,* April 29, p. 4; *SN,* April 29, p. 1; Argyris interview.

On the SSC's hopes and attempts: William Farley's notes (in Farley's possession); Ogilvy's proposal to the SSC, April 28; Ogilvy interview; minutes of an SSC meeting, April 25; ibid., April 26; WYBC news report, April 28.

On the SSC's final effort: minutes of an SSC meeting, April 27.

Notes

Advent and Prophecy

107   On the fire and robberies: *NHR,* April 27, pp. 1-2; *NHR,* April 30, p. 43; *SN,* April 27, p. 1; *NYT,* April 28, p. 44; *YDN,* April 27, p. 1; *YDN,* April 28, p. 1; *NHJC,* April 27, p. 1; WYBC news reports, April 27; Nora Sayre, *Sixties Going on Seventies* (London: Constable, 1974), p. 160.

107-108 For the graduate school dean's announcement: *YDN,* April 28, pp. 1, 3.

108   On the Graduate School Collective: ibid.; *Yale Graduate Professional,* April 29, pp. 1, 5; *SN,* April 28, p. 3.
       On the law school: *NYT,* April 28, p. 1; *YDN,* April 28, p. 1; WYBC news reports, April 27.
       On the divinity school's actions: *SN,* April 27, p. 3; *YDN,* April 29, p. 3; Yale Divinity School Central Steering Committee Report to the *Strike Newspaper,* no date (Yale Archives).
       On Boyd's involvement: Ren Frutkin's notes.
       On the elopement of Yale's Episcopal chaplain: Kegan interview.
       On the Monitoring Committee's formation: *SN,* April 28, p. 1; *YDN,* April 28, p. 1; press release issued by the Monitoring Committee, April 30.
       On the Monitoring Committee's visit to the NHPDC: Keniston, "New Haven Notebook," pp. 12-13; Peter Brooks, "Panthers at Yale," *Partisan Review,* no. 3, pp. 432-433; Coffin interview.
       On the organization of student marshals: *NHR,* April 28, p. 1; *NYT,* May 1, p. 4; Eisenstein interview; Coffin interview.

109   On the Monitoring Committee's work: Eisenstein's notes on a meeting of the Monitoring Committee, April 28; Brooks, "Panthers at Yale," p. 432-433.
       On the Council of Masters: Swordes interview; Trinkaus interview; Cannon interview; Brewster interview; Swordes's notes (in Swordes's possession); minutes of the Council of Masters meeting, April 24 (in Swordes's possession).
       For Brewster's decision: Brewster's statement on university plans for May Day, April 27.

109-110 For the statements of Farley and another student: Gerard Swordes's notes (in Swordes's possession).
       For Trinkhaus's observation about Chauncey: Trinkaus interview.

110   On Chauncey's effect on several masters: ibid.
       For Chauncey's explanation: Chauncey interview; Chauncey's explanation is supported by documents in the office files of Reuben Holden, which were examined by James Nuzzo.
       On Brewster's right: minutes of the Council of Masters meeting, April 24 (in Gerard Swordes's possession).
       For other discussions with students: Gerard Swordes's notes (in Swordes's possession).
       On the *Strike Newspaper's* arguments: ibid.; Swordes interview; Clark interview.

For the masters' offer and agreement: Clark interview; *YDN,* May 4, p. 1.

On the donations of $500 more: *Mayday Report,* a description of the May Day events issued by the "Operation Watchdog Information Center," June 11, p. 4; Gerard Swordes's notes (in Swordes's possession).

On the diversion of $2,800: *Mayday Report,* June 11, p. 4; *YDN,* May 1, p. 1.

110-111 On the contributions from other sources: Baker interview; *NHR-NHJC,* April 25, p. 34; *NHR,* April 28, pp. 1-2; *YDN,* April 28, p. 1; *NYT,* April 29, p. 28; Gerard Swordes's notes (in Swordes's possession); leaflet (Yale Archives).

111 On the emergency procedures: leaflets; Rostow interview; Johnson interview.

On the medical preparations and "comfort stations": Sayre, *Sixties Going On Seventies,* p. 160; document (Yale Archives); *YAM,* p. 29; *SN,* April 30, p. 3; Fanton interview; minutes of the Council of Masters meeting, April 24 (in Gerard Swordes's possession); Swordes's notes on a Council of Masters meeting, April 29 (in Swordes's possession); minutes of an SSC meeting, April 28; WYBC news reports, April 29.

112 On Schmoke's policy: Schmoke interview.

On Farley's policy: Farley interview.

On the blacks' policy: Baker interview; Robinson interview; Rochon interview; Dawson interview; Sayre, *Sixties Going On Seventies,* pp. 164-165; Rosenbaum, "Either/Or at Yale," p. 48; William H. Farley, "Amerika the Ugly Spurs Revolutionary Reaction," *YDN* special issue, April 22, 1975, p. 7.

For Mills's speech: *SN,* April 25, pp. 1, 4; WYBC news report, April 24; Dawson interview.

On the detailed set of demands: Rochon interview; Baker interview.

113 On the efforts and urgings of Yale blacks: press release issued by the UFPD, no date; Dawson interview; Mills interview; Baker interview; Bryce-LaPorte interview; WYBC news reports, April 22, 27, 28; Hester Eisenstein's notes on a teach-in, April 26.

On the attitude of New Haven blacks: *NHJC,* April 23, p. 19; Baker interview.

On the public remarks: Dawson interview.

On the physical clashes and ill feeling about Kimbro: Bryce-LaPorte interview.

On the feelings of community leaders: ibid.; Baker interview.

On the high school disruptions: *NHR,* April 22, p. 7; *NHR,* April 23, pp. 1-2; *NHR,* April 24, p. 50; *NHR,* April 28, p. 48; *NHR,* April 30, p. 43; *NHJC,* April 23, pp. 1, 19; *NHJC,* April 24, pp. 1, 27; *NHR-NHJC,* April 25, p. 2; *NHJC,* April 29, pp. 1, 13; *NHJC,* April 30, pp. 1, 13; *NHJC,* May 1, p. 5.

113-114 "did not have . . .": Cottrol interview.

Notes

114   For Schmoke's observation: Schmoke interview. Schmoke's views on
the BSAY's closer interaction with the community are supported by:
Baker interview; *NHR-NHJC*, April 25, p. 34.
On the BSAY's refusal to be pushed: Rochon interview; Dawson
interview; Wilkinson interview; Robinson interview; WYBC news
report, April 22; Farley, "Amerika the Ugly," p. 7.
On the emotional meeting: Robinson interview; Baker interview.
On the BSAY's unsuccessful effort to cooperate: Dawson interview.
On the outlook of Yale blacks: Brewster interview; Robinson interview.
On the beating of a white undergraduate: *NYT*, April 22, p. 52.
On the blacks' relations with the rest of Yale: Baker interview;
Robinson interview.
On the conservatives' feelings: Tharp interview; transcript of the
"Yale Today Panel," June 15.
On the BSAY's strike aims: Robinson interview; Rochon interview.

114-115 On the April 28 demonstration: Dawson interview; *YAM* transcript;
SN, April 28, p. 3; *YDN*, April 29, pp. 1, 3.

115   On the April 27 rally: *YAM* transcript; *YDN*, April 28, p. 1; *SN*,
April 28, p. 3; WYBC news reports, April 27, 28.
On Progressive Labor's view of blacks: Alan Adelson, *SDS: A Profile*
(New York: Charles Scribner's Sons, 1972), pp. 22-23; leaflet; Francine
du Plessix Gray, "The Panthers at Yale," *New York Review of Books*,
June 4, p. 33.

115-116 On the SSC meeting: minutes of an SSC meeting, April 28; Ogilvy's
proposal to the SSC, April 28; Farley interview; Ogilvy interview;
Rosenbaum, "Either/Or at Yale," p. 48; WYBC news report, April 28.

116-117 On the petition in support of Brewster: *NHJC*, April 29, p. 4.

117   For Dempsey's statement: *NHR*, April 29, p. 1; this statement is also
mentioned in *NHJC*, April 30, p. 4.
For Dodd's statement: *NHJC*, April 30, p. 1; see also *YDN*, April,
30, p. 1.
For Sevareid's newscast: WYBC news report, April 28.
For other attacks on Brewster: *NHR-NHJC*, April 25, p. 2; *NHJC*,
April 29, p. 5; *NHR*, April 29, p. 1; WYBC news reports, April 30,
May 1.
For Agnew's speech: *NHJC*, April 29, p. 13. See also: *U.S. News and
World Report*, May 11, p. 42; WYBC news reports, April 28, 29.
For Coffin's quip: WYBC news report, April 30; see also *YAM*
transcript of a press conference, April 30.

118   On the ordering of food: *YAM*, pp. 28-29; WYBC news report,
April 29.
On the arrest of two people: WYBC news report, April 28; James F.
Ahern, *Police in Trouble: Our Frightening Crisis in Law Enforce-
ment* (New York: Hawthorn Books, 1972), p. 60; Sayre, *Sixties Going
On Seventies*, p. 160; press release issued by Ahern, April 28; Griffin
interview; *YDN*, April 29, pp. 1, 3; *NHJC*, April 29, p. 1; *NYT*, April
29, p. 1.

On the SSC's press conference: WYBC news reports, April 29; *SN,* April 30, p. 1; press release issued by the SSC, April 29.

118-119 On the SSC meeting: WYBC news report, April 29; minutes of an SSC meeting, April 29.

119 On Brewster's acceptance of a petition: WYBC news report, April 29; *YDN,* April 30, p. 1; *SN,* April 30, p. 4; *NYT,* April 30, p. 1; *NHJC,* April 30, p. 4; *NHR,* April 29, p. 1; Sayre, *Sixties Going On Seventies,* p. 165.

On the general support for Brewster: *NHR,* April 29, p. 2; *YDN,* April 30, pp. 1, 3; press release issued by Louis Pollak; WYBC news reports, April 29.

For Duffey's remarks: *SN,* April 29, p. 3.

119-120 For Baldwin's remarks: *SN,* April 29, p. 3.

120 On Baldwin's defeat by Giamo: *YDN,* May 6, pp. 1, 3; WYBC news reports, May 5.

"unjustified, irresponsible, and self-serving remarks . . .": Horowitz's letter to Agnew, April 29.

For hostile responses to Agnew; *NYT,* May 3, Section 4, p. 14; WYBC news report, April 29.

On Brewster's correspondence: memorandum to Reuben Holden from the president's office, May 8.

120-121 On the Panthers' press conference: press release issued by the Black Panthers, April 29; *NYT,* April 30, p. 38. See also: Rosenbaum, "Either/Or at Yale," p. 50; leaflet; *Black Panther,* May 2, p. 6.

121 For the reports of administration and student efforts: *NYT,* April 30, p. 39. See also: ibid., p. 38; WYBC news report, April 30; leaflet; press release issued by the Black Panther party, April 29; Brewster interview.

On the removal of records and works of art: *Newsweek,* May 4, p. 52; Georges May, "Dean Recalls Strike, Impending Invasion," *YDN* special issue, April 22, 1975, p. 6; WYBC news reports, April 29, May 5; *NYT,* April 30, p. 39.

For Chauncey's reply: *NYT,* April 30, p. 39; Chauncey interview.

For the Monitoring Committee's findings: *SN,* April 30, pp. 1, 4; leaflet; Keniston, "New Haven Notebook," p. 13; press release issued by the Monitoring Committee, April 30; *YAM* transcript of the Monitoring Committee's press conference, April 30; WYBC news report, April 29.

For the hints: Gerard Swordes's notes (in Swordes's possession); tape recording of Brewster's press conference, April 30; supra, p. 97.

On the Harvard Square riot: *YDN,* April 17, p. 4.

For Ahern's refusal: Eisenstein interview.

For Ahern's later claims: Ahern, *Police in Trouble,* pp. 33-58, passim.

For Guida's insistance: Chauncey interview; supra, p. 97.

121-122 On the police's policy toward violent demonstrators: Ahern, *Police in Trouble,* pp. 42-43; *NHR,* May 10, pp. 1-2a; *NHR,* May 11, p. 40.

Notes

122   On Ahern's efforts, arrangements, and plans: Ahern, *Police in Trouble,*
pp. 35-46, passim; Capiello interview; *NHR,* May 10, pp. 1-2a; *NHR,*
May 11, p. 40.
On Ahern's granting of a permit: Ren Frutkin's notes.
For Guida's request: *NHR,* April 24, p. 56; *NYT,* May 1, p. 40; *SN,*
May 2, pp. 1, 4.
For the Adjutant General's announcement: *NYT,* April 29, pp. 1, 28;
WYBC news report, April 28.
For Guida's statement: *NHR,* April 30, p. 2.
On Yale's disappointment: Sayre, *Sixties Going On Seventies,* p. 160;
YAM transcript of the Monitoring Committee's press conference,
April 30; *NHR,* April 24, p. 56.
For Ahern's inability to recall: *NYT,* May 1, p. 40.
"confident that the . . .": press release issued by Ahern, April 30.
For Ahern's meeting with officers: *NHR,* April 28, p. 1; *YDN,*
April 29, p. 1.
For Ahern's statement about prior deployment: *NHR,* May 11, p. 40.
For Ahern's background: Ahern interview; *NYT,* May 2, p. 14;
biographical summary.

123   On Ahern's refusal of an FBI job: Ahern interview.
On Ahern's willingness to cooperate with Coffin: Coffin interview.
For Ahern's portrayal of Guida: Ahern, *Police in Trouble,* pp. 48,
55-57.
On Guida's concern with many problems: Black interview.
On the disagreement between Ahern and the state police commissioner:
Ahern, *Police in Trouble,* pp. 35, 46-47.
On the meeting with Dempsey: ibid., pp. 48-49, 56-57; *NHJC,* April
30, p. 13; *NHR,* April 30, pp. 1-2.
For Ahern's claim and his alarm "about the quality of information...":
Ahern, *Police in Trouble,* pp. 49-50.

123-124 For Ahern's point and his plausible suggestion: ibid., pp. 55-56.

124   For the public announcements: WYBC news reports, April 30; *NHR,*
April 30, p. 1; *NHJC,* May 1, p. 1; *NYT,* May 1, p. 1; *SN,* May 2, p. 4;
Sayre, *Sixties Going On Seventies,* p. 160.
For Dempsey's order: Ahern, *Police in Trouble,* p. 57 ; Ahern inter-
view; Black interview.
For the Ingalls Rink meeting's agenda: WYBC news report, April 28;
leaflet.
On the opening of the meeting: *YDN,* April 30, p. 1; *NHJC,* April
30, p. 13; Rosenbaum, "Either/Or at Yale," p. 50.

124-125 For the speeches at the meeting: *YDN,* April 30, pp. 1, 3; *SN,* April
30, p. 1; WYBC news reports, April 29.

125   On the fortification of the Panthers' household: Rosenbaum, "Either/
Or at Yale," p. 1.
For the moderate students' view of the trial issue: Sayre, *Sixties
Going On Seventies,* p. 162; Gray, "The Panthers at Yale," p. 32; *NHJC,*
April 27, p. 1.

126   On the exodus: *NHJC*, April 30, p. 13; *NHR*, April 30, p. 2; *SN*, April 30, p. 1; WYBC news report, April 29.
On the end of the meeting: *YDN*, April 30, p. 3; WYBC news report, April 29.
For Mills's thought and claim: Mills interview.
For Schmoke's comments: Schmoke interview.

May Day Eve

126   For the petitions supporting Brewster: press release issued by the Yale medical school, April 29; documents (Yale Archives); WYBC news report, April 30; *NHJC*, April 29, p. 4; *NHJC*, May 1, p. 1; *NHR*, April 29, p. 2.

126-127 On Brewster's press conference: *YAM*, p. 29; tape recording of Brewster's press conference, April 30; *YDN*, May 1, p. 1; WYBC news reports, April 30.

127   On the rightness of Brewster's contention: supra, p. 125.
On the presentation of the demands: *YAM*, p. 30.
On the Panthers' press conference: *SN*, May 1, pp. 1, 8; tape recording of the Panthers' press conference, April 30; WYBC news report, April 30.
For Dempsey's authorization: *NYT*, May 1, pp. 1, 40; *NHJC*, May 1, pp. 1, 19.
On Nixon's speech: *YDN* special issue, April 22, 1975, p. 1.

127-128 For the fantastic stories: Sayre, *Sixties Going On Seventies*, p. 160; Brooks, "Panthers at Yale," p. 433; Gray, "The Panthers at Yale," p. 32; Rosenbaum, "Either/Or at Yale," p. 48; Douglas Hallett, "Remaking the World is a Myth," *YDN* special issue, April 22, 1975, p. 11; *NHR*, May 1, p. 2; *YAM*, p. 31.

128   For the fright of several other Yale people: Swordes interview; Slie interview; Cannon interview.
On the medical preparations: Sayre, *Sixties Going On Seventies*, p. 160; *NHR*, April 30, p. 7; *YDN*, April 29, p. 1; *YDN*, April 30, p. 1; minutes of an SSC meeting, April 28.
On Afro-America House and the BSAY's advice: Robinson interview.
On other people's precautions: *NHR*, April 29, p. 1; leaflet on the neighborhood patrols.
For the accusations of purchasing weapons: *NYT*, April 29, p. 28; *NHJC*, April 30, pp. 1, 13.
For the reports of mysterious gun robberies: supra, p. 107; *YDN*, April 29, p. 1.
On the firebombings and arson: *YDN*, May 1, p. 1; *NHJC*, May 1, pp. 1, 19; WYBC news reports, April 21, 22, 30.
On the homemade bombs found at Yale: Chauncey interview.

On the picnic in Massachusetts: Brewster interview.

"They had had that trashing . . .": ibid.

129   "I was quite well aware . . .": ibid.

129ff. On the Thursday night meeting: ibid.; Trinkaus interview; Andrew Kopkind, "Bringing It All Back Home," *Hard Times,* May 11-18, pp. 3-4; Robert Brustein, *Revolution as Theatre: Notes on the New Radical Style* (New York: Liveright, 1971), p. 81; *NYT,* May 2, p. 14.

129   On Coffin's inability to obtain information: *YAM* transcript of the Monitoring Committee's press conference, April 30; Brewster interview.

129-130 "We thought [Coffin] . . .": Brewster interview.

130   On the decision to meet with Brewster: Trinkaus interview.

For the alarming piece of information: Lee interview; Eisenstein interview; Keniston, "New Haven Notebook," p. 13.

On Keniston's call to Moynihan: Keniston, "New Haven Notebook," p. 13.

On the hopes that Brewster would intercede: Trinkaus interview.

For Brewster's description of his telephone conversation: Brewster interview.

131   On Vance's presence at the meeting: ibid.

On the radical group's impression of Brewster: Trinkaus interview.

For Brewster's interpretation of the meeting: Brewster interview.

For Nixon's confirmation of the invasion: WYBC news reports, April 30; *NHR,* May 1, pp. 1, 9.

On the arrest of eighteen people: *NHJC,* May 1, p. 2; *SN,* May 1, p. 1; WYBC news reports, April 30.

7 *The Opening of Yale*

133   On the forbidding of police sirens: James F. Ahern, *Police in Trouble: Our Frightening Crisis in Law Enforcement* (New York: Hawthorn Books, 1972), p. 61.

For the associate chaplain's scattered thoughts: Phillip Zaeder's notes (in Zaeder's possession).

On the fire truck on the Green: *NHJC,* May 1, p. 4; *NYT,* May 2, p. 14; Ahern, *Police in Trouble,* p. 60.

For the numbers checked in by 9:30: WYBC news reports, May 1.

134   For the attitude of some arrivals: Harvey interview; R. Brewster interview. See also: *NYT,* May 2, p. 14; Nora Sayre, *Sixties Going On Seventies* (London: Constable, 1974), p. 165.

"Man, if you keep serving . . .": WYBC news report, May 1.

For Schmoke's remark: Schmoke interview.

On the exaltation at Trinkaus's house: Griffin interview; Eisenstein interview; Trinkaus interview; Mills interview.

134-135 On the problems of the Chicago Seven: Mills interview.

135   For Mills's recollection: ibid.

On the community's press conference: WYBC news report, May 1;

tape recording of the community's press conference.

On the neighborhood patrols: *NYT,* May 2, p. 14; *NHR,* April 27, pp. 1-2; *NHR,* April 29, p. 1; Lee interview; *YAM* transcript of the Monitoring Committee's press conference, April 30; see also *People's News Service,* April 5, 12, 26, passim.

On the outcome of the neighborhood solidarity: Pierson interview; Slie interview; Gail Sheehy, "The Consequences of Panthermania," *New York Magazine,* Nov. 23, p. 60; Paul Starr, "Black Panthers and White Radicals," *Commonweal,* June 12, p. 295; Sayre, *Sixties Going On Seventies,* pp. 161, 165; Robert Brustein, *Revolution as Theatre: Notes on the New Radical Style* (New York: Liveright, 1971), p.82.

135-136 On the Chicago Seven's press conference, May 1: WYBC news report, May 1; tape recording of the Chicago Seven's press conference, May 1; *YAM* transcript of the Chicago Seven's press conference, May 1; *SN,* May 4, p. 3.

136   For the remark of a Yale radical: Eisenstein interview.

On the guilt feelings of many whites: ibid.; Mills interview; *Time,* May 11, p. 29; Tom Hayden, "The Trial," *Ramparts,* July, p. 47.

"very militant folks . . .": Warren interview.

136-137 On the Woolsey Hall meeting: Ren Frutkin's notes.

137   For Rubin's speech: *SN,* May 2, p. 3; Sayre, *Sixties Going On Seventies,* p. 166; *YAM* transcript of Rubin's speech, May 1.

137-138 For Coffin's recollection: Coffin interview.

138   On medieval millenarianism as a prototype: Norman Cohn, *The Pursuit of the Millenium: Revolutionary Millenarians and Mystical Anarchists of the Middle Ages* (London: Temple Smith, 1970).

On the small fracas: Cannon interview.

On the use of food contributions: WYBC news report, April 29; Griffin interview; *Mayday Report,* June 11, p. 4; *YDN,* May 1, p. 1.

"that fine old": supra, p. 117.

For Brewster's participation in a civil rights march: Slie interview.

On the assembly of 3,000 on the Green: WYBC news report, May 1.

On the restaurants near the Green: ibid.

On the visibility of policemen: ibid.

On the binoculars and a pair of movie cameras: ibid.; *YDN,* May 4, p. 1; *SN,* May 2, p. 3; *NHR,* May 3, p. 2; Fitt interview.

On the presence of Dean: Brewster interview.

On the reports about police agents: leaflet; *NHR,* April 28, p. 1; Ahern, *Police in Trouble,* pp. 62-63.

139   On the cancellation of buses: WYBC news reports, April 30, May 1; Brewster interview.

On the influx of motorcyclists: WYBC news report, May 1; Ahern, *Police in Trouble,* p. 62.

On the arrival of 600 journalists: Ahern, *Police in Trouble,* p. 70.

On the return of 200 sugarcane cutters: *NYT,* May 1, p. 40; *Newsweek,* May 11, p. 32.

On the marshals: Kenneth Keniston, "New Haven Notebook: May Day Weekend at Yale," *New Leader,* June 22, p. 13; leaflet; *YDN,* April 29, p. 1; Eisenstein interview; WYBC news report, May 1.

On Froines's fears about the yellow headbands: Eisenstein interview. "people seemed relatively . . .": Warren interview.

139-140 On the Panthers' secret instigations: Ahern, *Police in Trouble,* pp. 63-64; Dawson interview.

140 On the SDS diversion: leaflet; WYBC news reports, May 1; Alan Adelson, *SDS: A Profile* (New York: Charles Scribner's Sons, 1972), pp. 23-24.

On WYBC's license: Ren Frutkin's notes.

For Brooks's description: Peter Brooks, "Panthers at Yale," *Partisan Review,* no. 3, p. 436.

140ff. The rally speeches, unless otherwise noted, are from: *YAM* transcripts; WYBC news reports, May 1.

141 For the Women's Liberation leaflet: leaflet.

For Mills's speech: Mills interview; Anthony R. Dolan, "New Haven: The Missing Context," *National Review,* May 19, p. 502; Sayre, *Sixties Going On Seventies,* p. 164.

142 On the close of the demonstration: Sayre, *Sixties Going On Seventies,* p. 165; *SN,* May 4, p. 4.

"a new kind of political process": WYBC news reports, May 1.

For Schmoke's view of the afternoon: Schmoke interview.

143 On the arrangements in Alumni House: Swordes interview; Chauncey interview; Black interview; *Chronicle of Higher Education,* May 11, p. 1.

On the National Guard units: *NHR-NHJC,* May 2, p. 5; *NHR,* May 3, p. 18a; *NHR,* May 13, pp. 1-2; *NYT,* April 29, p. 28; *SN,* May 2, pp. 1, 4; Ren Frutkin's notes; Keniston, "New Haven Notebook," p. 14; Steven Kellogg, "Guardsmen Sided with Students," *YDN* special issue, April 22, 1975, p. 12; Coffin interview.

143-144 On the attempts to have the guard units moved: Coffin interview; *NYT,* May 2, p. 14.

144 For Keniston's description of Hersey's success: Keniston, "New Haven Notebook," p. 14.

For Chauncey's statement on the National Guard: Chauncey interview; this is supported by Brewster interview.

On the withdrawing of the guard: *SN,* May 2, p. 4.

144-145 On the interruption of Rubin's speech: ibid., p. 1; Keniston, "New Haven Notebook," p. 14; Starr, "Black Panthers and White Radicals," p. 295; Sayre, *Sixties Going On Seventies,* p. 167; WYBC news reports, May 2.

145 On Brewster's movements earlier in the evening: Fanton interview.

For the student reporter's description: WYBC news report, May 1.

For Hoffman's speech: *SN,* May 3, pp. 2, 4; *YDN* special issue, April 22, 1975, p. 5.

On the aftermath of Hoffman's speech: WYBC news reports, May 1; Adelson, *SDS*, pp. 25-26; *SN*, May 2, pp. 1, 4.

145-146 For Wilkinson's recollections: Wilkinson interview.

146 For the report of Brewster's aide: Fanton interview.

On Chauncey's telephone calls: Chauncey interview.

On the Ingalls Rink bomb: WYBC news reports, May 1, 2; *NHR-NHJC*, May 2, p. 1; *NHR*, May 10, p. 1; Ahern, *Police in Trouble*, pp. 65-66. The police interpretation is contradicted in: Sayre, *Sixties Going On Seventies*, p. 167; Eisenstein interview.

146-147 On the march across the Green: WYBC news reports, May 1, 2; *YAM*, p. 32; *SN*, May 2, pp. 1, 4.

147 On the guard reinforcements: *SN*, May 2, p. 4; *NHR-NHJC*, May 2, p. 15.

On the Silliman meeting: Mills interview; *SN*, May 3, p. 3.

On the interaction between police, journalists, and demonstrators: Ron Rosenbaum, "Either/Or at Yale: Mayday & the Panthers," *Village Voice*, May 7, p. 52; *YDN*, May 4, p. 1; *SN*, May 2, p. 4.

For the associate chaplain's recollections: Zaeder interview.

On the efforts of the SSC, NHPDC, and Panthers: *SN*, May 2, pp. 1, 4; Rosenbaum, "Either/Or at Yale," p. 52.

147-148 On the efforts of Coffin and Mills: Mills interview; Coffin interview; Adelson, *SDS*, p. 27; Keniston, "New Haven Notebook," p. 15.

148 For Coffin's description of Mills's effectiveness: Coffin interview.

On the presence of guardsmen outside the Old Campus: *SN*, May 2, p.4. "lost his cool . . .": Chauncey interview; this is supported by Brewster interview.

On the consequences of opening Phelps Gate: *SN*, May 2, p. 4.

For Miranda's efforts: Keniston, "New Haven Notebook," p. 15; Coffin interview; Brooks, "Panthers at Yale," p. 437.

For Ginsberg's chanting: *SN*, May 2, p. 4; Rosenbaum, "Either/Or at Yale," p. 52.

149 "I went back . . .": Eisenstein interview.

"I picked up . . .": Chauncey interview.

On the final burst of excitement: WYBC news reports, May 2; *NYT*, May 3, p. 40.

For the reports of broken windows: Ahern, *Police in Trouble*, p. 65; Ahern's summary (Yale Archives); *SN*, May 2, p. 4.

For the reports of arrests: *NHR-NHJC*, May 2, p. 1; *NHR*, May 1, p. 1; *SN*, May 2, p. 4; WYBC news reports, May 1.

On the Yale-New Haven Hospital: *SN*, May 2, p. 4; *NHR*, April 30, pp. 1, 7.

150 For the National Guard's orders: WYBC news report, May 2.

"They no longer . . .": Keniston, "New Haven Notebook," p. 16.

"I was depressed . . .": Mills interview.

For Mills's disgust: ibid.

"virtually anything they said . . .": Warren interview.

Notes

150-151 On Yippie tactics: Mills interview.

151   On the police and the Black Panther sound truck: Ren Frutkin's notes; WYBC news reports, May 2.

On the last-resort policemen: Kent interview.

On the meeting in Branford: Brooks, "Panthers at Yale," pp. 437-438; Keniston, "New Haven Notebook," p. 16; WYBC news report, May 2. For Keniston's encounter with "a girl from Cornell": Keniston, "New Haven Notebook," p. 16.

On the Saturday morning workshops: leaflets; Ren Frutkin's notes; Brooks, "Panthers at Yale," p. 437; WYBC news report, May 2.

151-152 On the bomb warning: WYBC news report, May 2; Chauncey interview.

152   On the press conference: *SN*, May 3, p. 1; *SN*, May 4, p. 4.

"confrontations for the . . .": leaflet.

On the Panthers' resentment: Hayden, "The Trial," pp. 47-48.

On the few dangerous incidents: WYBC news reports, May 2, 3; Ahern, *Police in Trouble*, pp. 66-68.

On the peace symbols and marijuana: *YDN* special issue, April 22, 1975, p. 6; *NHR*, May 3, pp. 2, 18a; *SN*, May 4, pp. 3-4.

For Miranda's speech: *SN*, May 3, p. 3; *SN*, May 4, p. 4; Brustein, *Revolution as Theatre*, p. 82; Dolan, "New Haven: The Missing Context," p. 502; WYBC news report, May 2; Ren Frutkin's notes.

For the Gay Liberation speech: WYBC news report, May 2.

152-153 For Rubin's speech: Dolan, "New Haven: The Missing Context," p. 502; WYBC news reports, May 2; Warren interview; *SN*, May 3, p. 3.

153   For Mills's speech: *YAM* transcript; Keniston, "New Haven Notebook," p. 16.

For Artie Seale's tape of Bobby: *YAM* transcript; WYBC news reports, May 2; *SN*, May 4, p. 4.

On Women's Liberation and Miranda: WYBC news report, May 2.

For Hayden's speech: ibid.; *YAM* transcript; *SN*, May 3, p. 3.

On the Dwight Hall meeting: *SN*, May 3, p. 1; *YAM*, p. 32; Coffin interview.

154   For Mills's comments on Hayden: Mills interview; see also *NYT*, May 3, p. 40.

For one speaker's claim: Andrew Kopkind, "Bringing It All Back Home," *Hard Times*, May 11-18, p. 4; *NYT*, May 3, p. 40; *YDN*, May 4, p. 1; *NHR*, May 3, pp. 1, 4.

154-155 For Schmoke's interpretation: Schmoke interview.

155   On the strikes at other universities: *Chronicle of Higher Education*, May 11, p. 1; *NHJC*, May 1, p. 2; WYBC news reports, April 30, May 3.

On the incidents after the demonstration: WYBC news reports, May 2; *Chronicle of Higher Education*, May 11, pp. 1, 6; Coffin interview.

On the fire at 8:45: *Chronicle of Higher Education*, May 11, p. 6; Ren Frutkin's notes; *NHR*, May 3, pp. 1-2; *SN*, May 3, p. 1; WYBC news reports, May 2, 3; Ahern, *Police in Trouble*, p. 69.

155-156 On the attempts to control the crowd: Ahern, *Police in Trouble*, p. 69; WYBC news reports, May 2, 3; Sheehy, "The Consequences of Panthermania," p. 60; *Chronicle of Higher Education*, May 11, p. 6; *SN*, May 3, p. 1; *NHJC*, May 4, p. 25; *YDN*, May 4, p. 1.

156-157 On the interaction between the police and remaining demonstrators: *Chronicle of Higher Education*, p. 6; *SN*, May 3, pp. 1, 4; *NHR*, May 3, pp. 1-2; WYBC tape recording of a reporter's observations, May 2; Sheehy, "The Consequences of Panthermania," p. 60; Ahern, *Police in Trouble*, p. 69; Wilkinson interview; Horowitz interview; WYBC news reports, May 2, 3.

156   "to avoid giving . . .": Ahern, *Police in Trouble*, p. 69.
"If they want war . . .": *SN*, May 3, p. 4.
On the notification of officials: *NHR*, May 3, p. 1.

157   On the opening of intersections and Ahern's summary: *SN*, May 3, p. 4; WYBC news report, May 3.
On the damage to Yale: *NYT*, May 4, p. 43; *YDN*, May 4, p. 1; Sewall interview; Trinkaus interview.
For the arrest reports: *NHR*, May 3, p. 1; *NHJC*, May 4, p. 1; press release issued by Ahern, May 2.
On the arrest of one Yale student: WYBC news report, May 3; Keniston, "New Haven Notebook," p. 17.

8 *The Closing Down*

159   On the remaining police and guardsmen: *NHJC*, May 4, p. 1; *NYT*, May 4, p. 1; WYBC news report, May 3.

159-160 For Coffin's sermon: *NYT*, May 4, p. 43; *YDN*, May 4, p. 1; Coffin interview.

160   For Rudin's comments: *NYT*, May 4, p. 43; Thorburn interview.
On Rudin's reputation: Pierson interview.

160-161 For Schmoke's view of Rudin's speech: Schmoke interview.

161   On the congregation's reaction: *YAM*, p. 34; Thorburn interview.
For Brewster's comments: Brewster's opening statement at a press conference, May 3.
"How A Marathon . . .": *Chicago Sun-Times*, May 7, p. 6.
"Confrontation, But The Mood . . .": *Hartford Times*, May 3, p. 3A.
"Yale Proves Dissent . . .": *Life*, May 15, p. 38; for other favorable publicity, see *Newsweek*, May 11, pp. 31-32; for the New Haven black community's reaction, see the New Haven *Chronicle*, May, p. 1.
On Guida's press conference: *NHJC*, May 5, p. 4.

161-162 For Buckley's disapproval of Brewster: *NHJC*, May 1, p. 19; (Philadelphia) *Sunday Bulletin*, May 3, p. 5; for other unfavorable publicity, see Stewart Alsop, "Yale and the Deadly Danger," *Newsweek*, May 18, p. 124.

162   On Martin's survey: *YDN*, March 9, p. 1; Coffin interview.
For Nixon's reserved approval: *NHR*, May 12, p. 1.

Notes

For Trinkaus's feelings: *Mayday Report,* June 11, p. 2.
"an indication of moral bankruptcy . . .": Rahe interview.
"It is my confirmed belief . . .": Hallett interview.
For Coffin's disappointment: WYBC news report, May 5.
"brought the blacks . . .": Gray interview.
"Friends were made . . .": Auchincloss interview. rview.
"I don't think society . . .": Brewster interview.

163   For Brewster's "preliminary" response: Brewster's memorandum to the SSC, May 3.

163-164 For the SSC's response: leaflet issued by the SSC, May 3; see also *SN,* May 4, p. 3.

164   On the blacks' dismay and their interaction with Brewster: *YDN,* May 5, p. 1; *YDN,* May 11, p. 1; *NHR,* May 8, pp. 1-2; *SN,* May 5, p. 3; Rochon interview; Baker interview; press release issued by "The Seven Neighborhoods of New Haven," no date.
"Much that has been achieved . . .": Brewster's statement, May 3.

165   For May's statement: May's memorandum to the faculty and students of Yale College, May 3.
On the black faculty's request: Wilkinson interview; Dawson interview.

165-166 For Brewster's concession and his decision: Brewster interview.

166   On the sounding out of faculty members: May interview; Wilkinson interview.
On the Faculty Steering Committee session: Wilkinson interview; Thorburn interview.
"I opposed the grade reform . . .": Thorburn interview.

166-167 For May's attitude: May interview.

167   On Brewster's call to May and May's statement to a colleague: Thorburn interview.
On the trustees' communication with Brewster: tape recording of Brewster's press conference, April 30; Horowitz interview.
For Brewster's later explanation: Brewster interview.
On the cost of May Day: *YAM,* p. 34.
On the board's vote of confidence: *NYT,* May 11, p. 27.
On Sunday evening's political arrangements: WYBC news reports, May 3; Ren Frutkin's notes; *SN,* May 4, p. 1; *YDN,* May 4, p. 4.

168   On activities in the graduate and professional schools: WYBC news reports, May 4, 6; press release of the Graduate and Professional Student Senate, May 5 (Yale Archives); press release issued by the Yale sociology department (including the faculty and graduate students), May 5; resolution of the Yale medical students, May 6 (Yale Archives); *YDN,* May 5, p. 1; *YAM,* p. 34.
For the *Yale Daily News*'s editorial: *YDN,* May 6, p. 2.
For Hayden's assertion: Tom Hayden, "The Trial," *Ramparts,* July, pp. 49-50; see also Jean Genet, *Ramparts,* June, pp. 30-31.
also Jean Genet, *Ramparts,* June, pp. 30-31.
On the visits by Yale speakers to other campuses: Mills interview; Farley interview.

213

On the national strike conference: *YDN*, May 14, p. 1; *NHR*, May 12, p. 1.

For Brewster's proposal of a national drive: Brewster's statement, May 7.

168-169 On Brewster's trip to Washington: ibid.; *YDN*, May 7, p. 1; *YDN*, May 8, p. 1; *YDN*, May 11, p. 1; *YDN*, May 14, p. 1.

169 For Brewster's announcement in Washington: *YAM*, p. 34.

On the fate of the Princeton Plan: May interview; Pierson interview; Boell interview; Edgar Boell's notes (in Boell's possession).

On Miranda's condemnation and the BSAY's response: Robinson interview.

On the May 23 conference: Farley interview.

On the breaking up of the SSC: Ogilvy interview; *SN*, May 3-18, passim.

On the end of the NHPDC: Pressman interview; Kegan interview; *SN*, May 13, p. 1.

170 On discontinuation of the *Strike Newspaper: SN*, May 18, p. 1.

On the hopes and proposals of the Liberation School: ibid., p. 3; the Liberation School organizers' letter to Yale faculty members, May 21; the Liberation School's summer program.

For Wilkinson's report: Wilkinson interview.

On the departure of black students: Baker interview.

For Brewster's answer: Brewster interview.

On Yale's quiet rejection of the spirit of the demands: Nora Sayre, *Sixties Going On Seventies* (London: Constable, 1974), pp. 168-183; this is also based on numerous informal interviews.

9 Conclusion

171 For research discrediting the Panthers' claims of persecution: Edward Jay Epstein, "The Panthers and the Police: A Pattern of Genocide?" *New Yorker*, Feb. 13, 1971, pp. 45-77.

172 On the attitude of Yale people long after May Day: Nora Sayre, *Sixties Going On Seventies* (London: Constable, 1974), pp. 168-183; this is also based on numerous informal interviews.

On Brewster's efforts to accommodate conservatives: Brewster interview.

For Brewster's remarks to a group of Old Blues: *NHR*, June 18, 1972, p. 14a.

174 On Mills's involvement in the national strike: Mills interview; *YDN*, May 14, p. 1.

175 "stripped of their . . .": Norman Cohn, *The Pursuit of the Millenium: Revolutionary Millenarians and Mystical Anarchists of the Middle Ages* (London: Temple Smith, 1970), p. 286.

Index

Index

its policy and tactics, 26, 42-4, 52, 66-7, 71, 72, 73, 74, 112-15, 128, 169, 174; and the Panthers, 26, 43, 112, 113-15, 169; and Bryce-LaPorte, 41; its April 20 meeting, 42-4; and the black community, 52, 73, 112-15, 164; and the SSC, 72-4; given money, 110; submits demands to Brewster, 112, 164; sponsors a national conference, 169. *See also* black students

Buckley, William: 161-2

Calvin Hill Day Care Center: 163, 170

Calhoun College: 128

Cambodia invasion: *see* Vietnam war

Carmichael, Stokely: 8

Carter, Frances: 6, 10

Center Church on the Green (*see* photo): 156; press conference, 135-6, 138

Chappaquiddick incident: 75, 75n, 137

Chauncey, Henry Jr.: on the trial, 18; his role at Yale, 18, 29; his strategy, 29, 110, 121; lends Ingalls Rink to radicals, 42; denies auditorium space to conservatives, 44; on the strike, 71; at City Hall, 97; and Ahern, 97, 110, 129, 131, 143, 144, 149; prepares for May Day, 104, 105-6, 109-10, 143; his actions on May Day, 144, 146, 148; thanked by Brewster, 161

Chicago demonstrations: 9, 141

Chicago Seven: their trial, 9, 9n, 50, 57, 136-7, 141, 142; decide to visit New Haven, 41, 136; sympathize with Seale, 124-5, 136, 141-2; meet with Brewster, 129-31, 133; at the Paris peace negotiations, 131; their actions on May Day, 134-5, 135-6, 138, 144; their politics, 135, 136, 150-1; meet on May 2, 150-1.

City Hall: 3; April 23 meeting, 97; attacked, 140, 146-7. *See also* New Haven government

civil rights movement: considered old-fashioned, 32, 138

Coalition of Concerned Women: 72

Coffin, William Sloane (*see* photos): his meetings in early April, 30; his April 19 sermon, 30-3; his nonviolent march, 30, 32-3, 36, 56, 76-7, 123; on the trial, 30-2, 33, 56, 77, 159; criticized, 31-3, 56-7, 102, 108, 147-8, 160; and Brewster, 32, 76-7, 129; his background, character, and politics, 32-3, 56-7, 172-3; alters his strategy, 33, 37, 76-7, 104-5, 172; and the Osborne Committee, 38, 56; at the April 21 rally, 56-7, 77; diverts a mob, 75, 77; calls Reston, 103-4; April 26 sermon, 104-5; and the Monitoring Committee, 108-9, 129; on Agnew, 117; meets with Brewster, 129, 131; on the May Day experience, 142, 159, 162; moves the guard, 143-4; his May 3 sermon, 159-60; calls Schmoke, 160

Columbia University strike: 36, 103, 103n, 128

Connecticut National Guard: *see* National Guard

Connecticut politicians: criticize Brewster, 103, 116-17, 130, 131; defend Brewster and Yale, 119-20

Connecticut state police: 122-4, 127, 159

conservatives: and Brewster, 18-19, 90, 114, 169, 172; discriminated against, 27, 44; criticize Coffin, 32; circulate leaflets and a petition, 44; feel overwhelmed, 44, 67, 70, 71, 173; and the Student Senate, 45; appear unfashionable, 68, 173; oppose the strike demands, 74; in the Political Union, 75; in the faculty, 81-2, 85, 87, 89-90, 92; feared, 128, 135, 139, 146, 152; and the May Day demonstration, 142; appeased by Brewster, 165, 172; oppose the "Princeton Plan," 169

Conspiracy Eight: *see* Chicago Seven

Cornell University strike: 79-80, 80n, 87, 103, 113, 151

Council of Masters: prepares for May Day, 42, 109-10; and the *Strike* 50-2, 59-60, 77-8, 102, 103

217

Index

Index

Smith, Carol: 127

social democrats: threatened, 67, 71; their policy, 71, 113

Social Science Center: criticized, 36, 73, 163; defended, 163; stalled, 170

Southern Connecticut College: 151-2

Spock, Benjamin: 31

Sprague Hall (*see* photo): 79, 83, 96

SSC: 99-100, 112, 174; its membership, 18, 72; formed, 72; its demands, 72-4, 106, 107, 115-16, 124, 125-6, 127, 161, 163-4; and black students, 72, 74, 112; and Miranda, 73, 105-6; its April 24-6 meetings, 74, 105-6; and the *Strike Newspaper,* 74-5; prepares for May Day, 104, 105-6, 108, 109, 143; and the April 29 rally, 107, 115, 118-19, 124-6; its April 28 meeting, 115-16; its April 29 press conference, 118; its April 29 meeting, 118-19; and the grading changes, 118-19, 126; and Mills, 126, 174; discourages rioting, 147; thanked by Brewster, 161; disbanded, 169

Stanford University: 93-4

Strike Newspaper: 74-5, 110, 170

Student-Faculty Monitoring Committee: organized, 108; its effectiveness, 108-9, 151; its findings, 121, 129, 130

student movement: its characteristics and history, 1-2, 3, 13, 21, 32, 119, 126, 128, 138, 141, 162, 171-2, 173-5; discussed by Hayakawa, 53-4; discussed by Brewster, 54, 127; and the Panthers, 59; discussed by the *New York Times,* 102; and SDS, 115; discussed by Mills, 150

Student Senate: 44-7

"Task Force Bravo": *see* National Guard

terrorism: examples of, 78, 107, 114, 128, 145-6, 149, 155-6, 157

Thailand: *see* Vietnam war

Third World Liberation Front: 43, 72

Thorburn, David: opposes the faculty resolution, 93-4, 95-6; on

Brewster, 95-6, 166; on the grading changes, 166

Thurmond, Strom: 41

trial: location, 1; defense tactics, 8, 15; charges and pleas, 9-10, 15; bail hearings, 10, 15, 77; pretrial complaints, 13-15, 98; contempt citations, 15-16; special regulations, 16, 17; Hilliard and Douglas denied bail, 30; April 20 proceedings, 50-1; April 22 proceedings, 77; April 23 proceedings, 98; Seale and Huggins freed, 170

Triffin, Robert: meets with Brewster, 33-4, 39; at the Student Senate meeting, 46; at a strike referendum, 67-8

Trinidad: 140

Trinkaus, J. P. (*see* photo): meets with Panthers, 33; his April 18 meeting, 33; his background, politics, and character, 68-9, 172-3; calls a faculty caucus, 81-2; reads the faculty resolution, 96; and the Council of Masters, 109-10; meets with Brewster, 129-31; his actions on May Day, 134; on the May Day experience, 162; helps the Liberation School, 170

Trumbull College: 78

Turner, John: 82-3

UFPD: arranges the April 21 rally, 42; its April 20 meeting, 43-4; its membership, 43, 53, 56; its April 21 press conference, 52-3; its demands, 52-3, 112, 164; its aloofness from white radicals, 72, 112-13; its weakness, 163, 164

United States army: and Yale, 29, 129; alerted for May Day, 123-4, 127, 133; called off, 157

United States Congress: 168-9

University of Connecticut: 114

Vance, Cyrus: his role in the May Day events, 29, 128-9; meets with Brewster 129, 131; his actions on May Day, 145, 146

Vietnam war: and the student move-

223

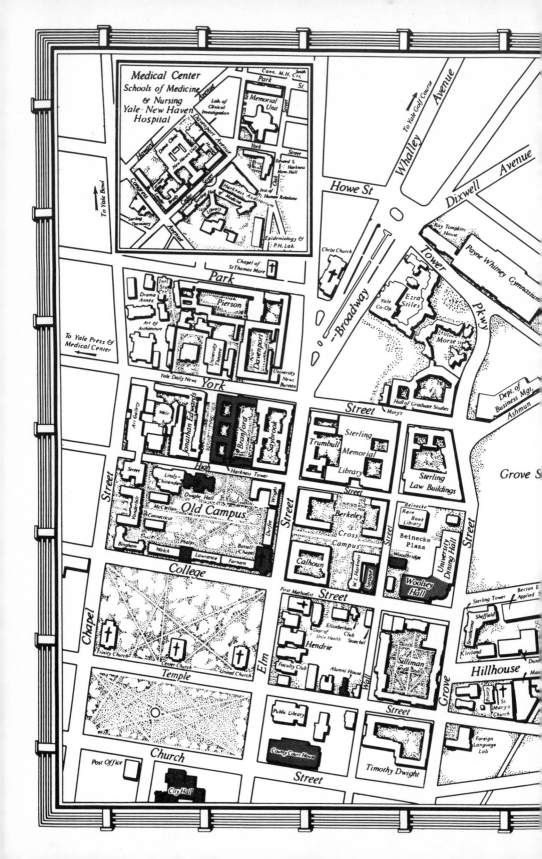